SANDRA GUSTAFSON

C H E A P
SLEEPS IN PRAGUE VIENNA BUDAPEST

**A Traveler's Guide to the
Best–Kept Secrets**

SANDRA A. GUSTAFSON

CHRONICLE BOOKS
SAN FRANCISCO

Printed in the United States of America.

ISBN 0-8118-2150-1
ISSN 1522-0915

Cover photograph: Dave Jacobs/Index Stock Imagery
Cover design: Yeong Sun-Park
Interior design: Words & Deeds
Maps: Ellen McElhinny

Distributed in Canada by
Raincoast Books,
8680 Cambie Street,
Vancouver, B.C. V6P 6M9

10 9 8 7 6 5 4 3 2 1

Chronicle Books
85 Second Street
San Francisco, CA 94105

www.chroniclebooks.com

To Sandy Busby,
a good friend and a
stylish Cheap Sleeper

Contents

To the Reader

A journey is a person in itself; no two are alike.
—John Steinbeck

Few cities in Europe guarantee a larger helping of majestic beauty than the combination found in Prague, Vienna, and Budapest. Though Austria belongs to the West and always has in terms of its culture and ideology, it has also always served as a bridge to the East, and there are many threads of similarity that join these three distinctive cities: an Imperial past; Baroque, Gothic, and Jugendstil architecture; and a love of hearty food, good beer, fine wines, rich pastries smothered in whipped cream, and beautiful women. In the aftermath of Communism, Budapest and Prague are now racing toward the future and hoping to emerge as powerful cities of the twenty-first century. Self-sufficient Vienna is content to thrive on its glorious past. Prague is currently a massive work in progress, and the creative energy that has so magnificently revitalized Prague in the last decade is showing no signs of letup. While the same breathtaking renovation projects are still awaiting funding and approval in Budapest, the new free economy and lifting of socialistic barriers is sending the city on a straight track into the new millennium. Many problems that once plagued visitors in the past are now gone: ordinary people in Prague and Budapest are no longer afraid to talk to or be seen with foreigners, and hardball customs officials who once engaged in extensive luggage searches and confiscation of Western goods, including music and printed materials, now make every effort to please the millions of visitors who descend on their cities each year with hard currency to spend.

There are some problems, however, to iron out in both Prague and Budapest, and one of the most urgent is the lack of acceptable, affordable hotel space in the city centers. The accommodations out in the suburbs are too remote for most visitors, and more often, they are not up to Western standards. The overcrowding has led to overbooking. However, you shouldn't need to worry about this too much. With the wealth of information given in *Cheap Sleeps,* plus the wide variety of listings reviewed, the savvy Cheap Sleeper in Prague and Budapest—as well as Vienna—should have no problems locating many gems and booking whatever accommodation most suits his or her needs and pocketbook.

Each listing in *Cheap Sleeps* has been included because I feel it has something special to offer, but the type of accommodation you desire depends on you. Do you want to stay in a hotel with a refined atmosphere, or one that is cozy and comfortable, with a soothing feeling of home? Some Cheap Sleeps are admittedly slightly worn or as old-fashioned as the button hook, and a few are sleek and modern with room faxes and modems for your computers. Most of the listings are very central, but I provide some that are farther out, offering peeks into neighborhoods where people like you and I might live and work, send our children to school, eat lunch, and shop. Many radiate charm and offer heartfelt friendly service. The prices of the hotels range from almost philanthropic to Big Splurges. And in Prague and Budapest, note that "customer service" is sometimes not all it could be. Cheap Sleepers may run into a certain level of rudeness and attitude problems here and there—which is the result of the strains of a free economy on historically socialistic societies. Management always tries, but there may be some run-ins with the Larry, Moe, and Curley Joe School of Hotel Management.

When I visit a potential Cheap Sleep, cleanliness is first on my list, followed by location, pleasant room surroundings, and the overall feeling of the hotel. Management attitude comes into play, as does the attitude of everyone else—from the front desk person to the cleaning staff. I check closets, open and close windows, bounce on the beds, and search under them for dust. I look for mold in the bathroom, thin wafers of soap, see-through towels, and toilet tissue that could double as sandpaper. I go to the breakfast room, climb the back stairs, and ask to see rooms in all the different price categories offered. If the hotel meets my criteria, I consider it. If I find too many things wrong, no matter how popular it is or how well-received it has been in the past . . . it falls into the pile of rejections.

In addition to giving the value-conscious Cheap Sleeper the inside track to the best hotel prices in Prague, Vienna, and Budapest, I include a section on Cheap Chic shopping and the best shopping techniques to follow in each city. If you are a dedicated shophound like I am, you are going to want to include some browsing and buying on your trip, and Cheap Chic (see page 173) will point you in the right direction.

Cheap Sleeps in Prague, Vienna, and Budapest is not a listing of the cheapest beds to be found in these cities. Economizers whose only concern is paying bottom-of-the-barrel prices should look elsewhere for their information. My goal is to offer fail-safe advice about accommodations that offer good value for money and to help readers maximize their hotel buying power without sacrificing comfort, cleanliness, and convenience in the process. I am responsible for all of the recommendations in this book—as I am for all those in the *Cheap Eats* and *Cheap Sleeps* series. You can measure your taste against mine and make your own decisions. To keep the standards of each book at their highest level, I personally visit every entry, plus literally hundreds that do not make the cut. To keep it objective, I arrive uninvited and unannounced and pay my own way, which allows me to receive and report on the same level of quality and service you can expect. I tell the truth—the good, the bad, and the scams—whether it benefits the hotel or not. I write these books for *you*, not for the benefit of any of the hotels or shops that appear in them.

However, when you do stay at a hotel that was recommended in this book, it is often helpful to tell the manager or staff where you read about it; hotels appreciate this information.

After many years and millions of miles of traveling, I have found there are three essentials for a good trip: a passport, enough money, and a sense of humor. Try not to take anything too seriously, and don't judge a city or a country by one person with whom you have had a problem. Travel lightly. Travel expectantly. Travel with an open mind. I hope that your trip to any or all of these cities gives you half the fun and adventure I had preparing this book for you, and I hope, by using this book, you will leave with many happy memories that will beckon you back for more. If I have been able to do this for you, I will have done my job well. I wish you a safe and rewarding journey: *Štastno Cestu! Gute Fahrt!* and *Jó Utázast!*

Tips for Cheap Sleeps in Prague, Vienna, and Budapest

Home is any four walls that enclose the right person.
—Helen Rowlands

1. Travel in the off-season, and if you can stand it, reserve a room with the bathroom down the hall.

2. Ask for a discounted rate no matter when you plan to go, and find out if there is a discount for paying in cash rather than by credit card.

3. The farther you stay from the city center, the less you will pay. Before you do this, consider the cost and time wasted commuting back and forth, and decide what the focus of your visit is going to be. If it is purely sightseeing—museum hopping with some shopping and eating out—maybe paying a little more to stay closer to your sphere of action, thus eliminating time, energy, and money spent commuting, makes better Cheap Sleeping sense.

4. Prague, Vienna, and Budapest are experiencing renewed popularity, and as a result, they have severe shortages of acceptable, reasonably priced, centrally located accommodations. Unless you like wasting vacation time standing in line at hotel booking offices and being forced to take pot luck on your room and its price, never leave home without confirmed reservations.

5. Always get your reservation in writing and take it with you to present upon check-in. It also does not hurt to reconfirm a few days before your arrival. Hotels in these cities are notorious for overbooking, and you don't want to be one of the hapless visitors left out in the cold because you have not reconfirmed or because, upon arrival, you are not able to prove that you do have a confirmed booking.

6. Notify the hotel if you expect to arrive after 6 P.M. Whether or not you have a deposit, the hotel can technically resell your room to someone else if you are not there by 6 P.M.

7. Ignorance is no excuse for an unpleasant room or high hotel costs. Always check out the room before you check in. Be sure it is what you want and can afford, then confirm the rate and understand the

cost of any extras, especially telephone calls (which can be paralyzing to a budget).

8. Single rooms are usually cramped and often on the back of the hotel. If you want something better, ask for a double room for single occupancy.

9. Not all doubles are created equally. Those facing the back with one large bed and a shower will cost less than a twin-bedded double facing front with a bathtub.

10. Breakfast is a moneymaker for the hotel and a budget gouger for you. Most hotels make at least a 100-percent profit on the meal—so getting it deducted can take some shrewd negotiating on your part. You may not be successful, but it never hurts to try.

11. Renting an apartment in a residence hotel or from an individual or agency can be a convenient and cost-cutting way to trim your hotel costs, especially for stays of a week or more. Not only will you get more space, but you can economize by cooking in. It also allows you to better experience your temporary neighborhood and the local day-to-day way of life.

12. Purchase trip insurance, especially if you rent an apartment, since they always ask for a percentage up front before arrival, and sometimes for the full balance. If for some reason you have last-minute changes, or can't go at all, getting a refund can be a draconian exercise in futility. Many agencies, and especially individuals, have only one refund policy: that is, they do not refund your money, period. To avoid this costly travel nightmare, please protect yourself with insurance. If you have to change dates, interrupt travel, or cancel altogether, you will be forever grateful for it. The Automobile Club of America has a list of carriers. Otherwise, contact Access America, Inc., 800-284-8300; Carefree Travel Insurance, 800-323-3149; Travel Guard International, 800-782-5151; or your travel agent.

13. Never use the hotel as your banker. Change money at a bank or go to an ATM.

14. Take with you a Xeroxed copy of your passport, airline tickets, hotel confirmations, and two or three extra, color, passport-size photos, and leave a list of your credit card numbers with a trusted person at home. Heaven forbid that any of these important items are lost or stolen, but if it does happen, you will be glad you have taken these simple steps, which will speed up the replacement procedures dramatically.

15. When walking around any foreign city, stay alert. Be aware of your immediate surroundings, and don't take chances you would not take at home. Pickpockets are everywhere, and they often

strike when you least expect it. Carry your valuables in a hidden
money belt, or better yet, leave them locked up in the hotel safe.
Women should carry their purses crosswise in front of their bod-
ies, away from the traffic side of the sidewalk.

16. Central European electrical circuits are wired for 220 volts. You
will need a transformer *and* an adapter plug for appliances you
bring that operate on 110 volts. Items such as hair dryers and
curling irons may have switches that convert the appliance from
one voltage to another. This only eliminates the need for a transformer, *not* for the adapter plug. If you are bringing a computer, be
sure you have a transformer with enough power, otherwise you
could end up damaging your equipment.

17. Pack a rubber door stopper. It is one of the cheapest forms of
security you can buy, and it works.

General Information

When to Go

The world is a great book, of which they who never stir from home only read a page.

—St. Augustine

Wouldn't it be wonderful to hop on a plane on the spur of the moment and head for Prague, Vienna, or Budapest? Unfortunately we're rarely that free. Most of us have demanding schedules and tight budgets, and we do considerable advance planning before packing our bags and flying off on a dream vacation. When deciding on a time to go, consider whether you can go in the low seasons, when you will find better availability and lower prices for hotel rooms, as well as lower costs for airline tickets. The best times to visit any of these cities are in the spring or autumn (often called "shoulder" seasons), when most of the other tourists are at home, the students are in class, and everything is generally easier to come by, including hotel and dinner reservations, a seat on the bus, and good-natured salespeople.

High season is during the summer, for two weeks at Christmas, and for the week of Easter. During winter, prices will be at their lowest, but the weather will be cold and wet, with darkness falling around 5 P.M. Of the three cities, Vienna is often the coldest.

Reservations

In order to be assured of a room at a price you can afford, advance reservations are essential. All three of these central European cities are hotel bottlenecks with severe room shortages that encourage overbooking policies, especially in the modest-to-moderate price category. Even on the slowest day in the low season, confirmed reservations will save you hours looking for a room and having to take whatever you can find, whether you know anything about the place or not. In Prague and Budapest, especially in the train stations, travelers are bombarded by persevering locals who offer rooms for rent in their homes. This can be a very dicey way to find lodgings. Many of these places are out in the sticks . . . or beyond, requiring hours of commute by a combination of foot, bus, tram, trolley, and the underground to get to the center of town. Even more important in my opinion is the safety of such situations. There's no way for you to know who you are dealing with, so why put yourself in a position that could become unpleasant and perhaps dangerous? If you are interested in staying in private homes, I suggest going through a recognized company that specializes in these stays. For more on this aspect of Cheap Sleeping, please see the "Other Options" sections of each city.

The easiest way to reserve is to let your travel agent do all the work. However, with *Cheap Sleeps* in hand, you can do it yourself. And frankly, with the ease and speed of the telephone, faxes, and email, it is not only easy to do but better because you are able to ask questions and get immediate answers about every aspect of your hotel stay—from discounted rates to the position of your room—without the delay of going through a middle person. In addition, the hotel may pass along to you their savings of the travel agent's commission. After reserving, you can usually guarantee your booking with a major credit card. In only a few cases in the cheapest Cheap Sleeps will you be asked to send an international money order.

No matter how you decide to make your reservation, the following points should be covered:

1. Dates of stay, time of arrival, and number of persons in the party.

2. Size and type of room (double or twin beds, extra bed and the type—fold-out chair-bed or a proper bed—adjoining rooms, suite, and so on).

3. Facilities needed: private toilet, stall shower and/or bathtub with hand-held or fixed shower nozzle, hall facilities if acceptable, and if you need accommodations suitable for a disabled person.

4. Location of room: view, on the street, on the courtyard, or in the back of the hotel.

5. Rates. *Always* try to negotiate a discounted rate.

6. Deposit required and method of payment.

7. Refund policy should you have to cancel. This is vital when renting an apartment.

8. Request a written confirmation by fax and take it with you when you check into the hotel.

Email and the Internet

The escalating use and fascination with cyberspace has not swept central Europe the way it has in the States, but it is only a question of time until it does. Whenever applicable, the hotel's email and/or Internet address have been given. During my visits to these cities, many Cheap Sleeps hotels told me they were going to jump onto the worldwide electronic bandwagon in the near future, so stay tuned for many changes in this area.

Fax

How did we live before fax machines? All but the smallest budget Cheap Sleeps hotels in Prague, Vienna, and Budapest have a fax machine because it is definitely the preferred way of securing a confirmed booking.

Remember, the telephone systems in both Prague and Budapest are undergoing the rigors of privatization, and this means that most numbers are changing—not only once but several times. It is a frustrating situation, and no one knows when it will stabilize. All of the telephone and fax numbers in this book have been checked and double-checked and were correct as of press time.

Telephone

To direct-dial any number in Prague from abroad, dial 011-42-2 + the number in Prague. To direct-dial any number in Budapest from abroad, dial 011-36-1 + the number in Budapest. To dial a number in Vienna from abroad, dial 011-43-1 + the number in Vienna. See the city sections for more specific telephone information on each city.

If you are making reservations over the telephone, time your call to reach the hotel during their business hours to avoid talking to a night clerk who has no authority to negotiate the various aspects of your stay. Before calling, write down all your requests and questions. The hotel will ask you to send them a fax confirming your telephone reservation. In your fax, cite the details of the conversation, including the date and time of your call, the rates agreed upon, and the name of the person with whom you spoke. In return it is very important for you to ask the hotel to send you a confirmation fax of your reservation as well.

Letter

With email, the fax, and the telephone at our disposal, why anyone would write for hotel reservations is a mystery to me—and to most hoteliers as well. Many have pointed out to me a stack of months-old letters from prospective guests requesting price information or reservations. Most of the hotels in *Cheap Sleeps* are small and have a limited staff, and they do not have time to answer letters. In addition, the postal service in Prague and Budapest is notoriously terrible. Delays of weeks, months, and even years can elapse before some mail reaches its destination. When you consider the cost of a telephone call or a fax against the entire cost of your trip, it amounts to a miniscule percentage, and the extra expense is certainly worth it in terms of speed and convenience.

Money Matters

When preparing for your trip, lay out all of your clothes and plan your budget. Then put half the clothes back in the closet and double your budget, and the trip will be a success.
—*One of the ten commandments of successful travelers*

Nothing on your trip has the potential for causing more frustration and confusion than money, even when you have enough of it. If you are on a limited budget, still try to have a little cushion that will enable you to enjoy a Viennese coffee and pastry, treat yourself to an afternoon at a spa in Budapest, or enjoy a special meal in Prague. Life is too short not to have the happy memories that come from simply enjoying where you are at the moment, without having to worry about squeezing every single penny.

Carrying large amounts of cash, even in a money belt, is risky business. Instead, try to prepay as much of your trip ahead of time as possible, charge big items on your credit card, carry some traveler's checks to convert as you go, and master the art of withdrawing money from ATMs abroad. Also, remember to carry a few personal checks. If you suddenly run out of money, you can use them to get cash advances, provided the credit cards you have allow this. Always arrive with enough local currency in your pocket to get you from the airport or train station to your hotel, and to buy a meal. True, you may pay a premium for this convenience, but if you only change $100 to $200 ahead, you will never miss the few cents extra it will cost. If you do exchange dollars for foreign currency before you leave home, you could be issued old bills. Because these bills are out of circulation, many businesses refuse to take them, but do not panic! Any bank in Prague, Vienna, or Budapest will exchange them evenly for the newer bills. For foreign currency exchange information and the nearest address of a Thomas Cook currency exchange office, contact Thomas Cook Currency Service, 630 Fifth Avenue, New York, NY 10101; tel 800-287-7362. Office hours in New York are Monday to Friday, 8:30 A.M. to 9 P.M.

Automatic Teller Machines (ATMs)

Finding an ATM in Prague, Vienna, or Budapest is not a problem, but sometimes your personal identification number (PIN) can be. If your PIN number is more or less than four digits, it won't work in these three cities. To avoid such a disaster, before you travel contact your bank or credit card issuer and take the necessary steps to change your PIN number, allowing plenty of time for all the paperwork to go through and, if necessary, receive a new card. Your issuer can also give you a list of ATM locations and the names of corresponding affiliated cash machine networks in these cities. You can expect some hefty fees for foreign ATM withdrawals and transactions, but you will be getting a wholesale conversion rate that is better than you would get at a bank or currency exchange office, so it will all even out. Naturally, you are limited to the amount you can withdraw by the type of account you have and your cash advance limit. You should also be aware that there are sometimes specific time limits imposed between withdrawals. To receive a directory of Cirrus ATMs, call 800-424-7787; for PLUS locations, call 800-843-7587. For information about Visa/Plus International, check the Internet at www.visa.com.

Credit Cards

Just about every hotel and shop on this planet accepts at least one credit card, and those in Prague, Vienna, and Budapest are no exception. I recommend using a credit card whenever possible. It is the safest way to pay because it eliminates the need for carrying large sums of cash, which, of course, you must first purchase by standing in line at a bank or currency exchange.

The credit card company gives you the rate of exchange on the day of processing, not at the time of purchase, and this can work to your advantage if the dollar is rising. A credit card purchase provides you with a written record of your spending, and you often get delayed billing of up to four or six weeks after you have returned home. If you pay in cash, the money is gone immediately, but with a credit card the money stays in your bank account, possibly drawing interest, until you need it to pay the final bill. If your card is tied in with an airline, you will be building up your frequent flyer miles on every transaction, and believe me this can add up fast. Emergency personal check cashing, access to ATM machines, and free travel insurance are only a few more benefits of using plastic instead of folding money. Check with your issuing bank to determine the list of benefits you have; you may be pleasantly surprised. Here are a few credit card tips:

1. Before using your credit card, ask the store or hotel if there is any discount if you pay in cash.

2. Keep a copy of all your credit card numbers with you and leave another copy at home. Keep them in a hidden, safe place—not lying around your hotel room.

3. Save your receipts to check against the statement when it arrives. Errors are frequent.

4. Before you leave on your trip, look on the back of your credit card for the toll-free customer service number to call in the States, and find out their corresponding toll-free number to use abroad. For further information, contact: American Express, 800-221-7282; Citicorp, 800-645-6556 in the United States, or collect world-wide 813-623-1709; Thomas Cook, 800-223-7373, or collect worldwide 609-987-7300.

5. Report the loss of your card immediately. Contact both the local police and the credit card company. When you get home, contact your insurance company to see if the loss is covered.

Currency Exchange

The worst exchange rates are at exchange offices, where the commission rate can climb to 10 percent. The next worst places to exchange money are at the airport, the train station, or in any hotel, shop, or restaurant. Someone is making money here and it is not you. Your best exchange rate will usually be at a bank. Traveler's checks used to be the only way to insure that a traveler would have the necessary funds to enjoy a trip. Now with ATMs and credit cards, traveler's checks have taken a back seat in money matters, but they are still very useful, and you should not leave home without them, since you will get the best rate for traveler's checks, not hard cash, when exchanging money. The hidden costs lie in whether you have to purchase the traveler's checks, and how much commission you pay to cash them. Holders of American Express platinum and gold cards can order their traveler's checks by phone, at banks, or at credit unions free of charge. Nonmembers and holders of American Express green cards pay a 1-percent purchase commission. American Automobile Association (AAA) members can purchase free American Express traveler's checks, but there is often a limit of $3,000. If you get free American Express traveler's checks, that is a good beginning because you can cash them commission-free at any American Express office. The rate may be slightly lower than at the bank, but since there is no commission, it will average out. The drawback here is that the lines are long and oh, so slow during the peak tourist seasons.

While American Express is the biggest in the travel check industry, there are others that are quickly catching up in services and may work better for you. Citicorp sells traveler's checks that give the holder access to a twenty-four-hour SOS hot line that provides travel-related services. For further information, call 800-645-6556. MasterCard International issues traveler's checks that are widely accepted. Call 800-223-7373 for information, or 800-423-3630 to buy them by phone using your MasterCard. Visa also sells traveler's checks at Bank of America locations or any bank with a Visa logo. For further information, call 800-227-6811.

NOTE: Exchanging money on the street is not only dumb and ill-advised but illegal. You will definitely get ripped off, and could easily be arrested in a sting operation. Do not do this, period.

Personal Checks

Yes, definitely take some personal checks with you. Other than sending in a credit card payment, you won't be able to use them to pay for anything on the trip, but you can use them to get cash advances from your credit cards at participating banks and at all American Express offices.

Wiring Money

When your money is history in Prague, Vienna, or Budapest long before you are, and you have exhausted your ATM and credit card options, you can increase your cash flow by calling home for money and having someone send you a moneygram. The transfer takes a few minutes, the sender pays the fees (which depend on the amount sent), and the money arrives swiftly. Here is the procedure to follow.

The cash-strapped Cheap Sleeper must contact the sender in the States, who in turn will send the money in either of two ways: by going to an office located in his or her city, or by giving a credit card number over the telephone. If you go with the telephone credit card method, there is a $500 limit. To send the money in person, the sender first calls 800-926-9400 (this number is staffed twenty-four hours a day, 365 days a year) to get the location of the nearest moneygram office, plus any other particulars for sending the money. To send up to $500 by calling in a credit card number, call 800-945-2244, Monday to Friday from 6 A.M. to 4:30 P.M. Mountain Standard Time. No matter which way the money is sent, there will be a sliding-scale fee based on the amount sent, and the voyager will be notified of the impending arrival of money and given a confirmation number and an address of where to pick up the funds. A photo ID must be presented upon receipt of the cash.

Tipping

The individual sections on Prague, Vienna, and Budapest detail tipping etiquette for each city. Remember that tipping is a personal choice. If you liked the service, reward it. If not, do not feel guilty about leaving nothing.

Safety and Security

General Tips

For special safety measures in each city, see the "Safety and Security" sections in Prague, Vienna, and Budapest. But no matter which city you are visiting, general safety rules apply. Smart travelers do not wander down dark streets at night, especially women alone, nor do they use public transportation that requires long walks down lonely streets to get to their destination. Wear a money belt or neck pouch inside your clothing, and carry in it only what essentials you need: passport, some money, and so on. Do not carry any valuables in your purse, wallet, or backpack. If you are wearing a backpack, thread a safety pin from the zipper on your backpack to pin it closed, and don't wear your fanny pack anyplace but in front of you. Keep a close eye on all possessions, and do not leave packages or suitcases unattended on any form of public transportation, when making a phone call, or getting into a taxi. Keep a close eye on your camera, and leave the flashy jewelry and Rolex watches at home. Lock up important papers, traveler's checks, extra money, and anything else of value in the hotel safe. Even if there is a charge for this, it is nothing when compared to the cost, inconvenience, and traumatic hassle of being robbed. Before you leave home, contact your insurance company to find out the limit covered for losses abroad. If you do not think it is adequate, consider a temporary rider to cover you while traveling.

Beware of pickpockets, especially on crowded public transportation and in tourist areas. Thieves in the underground stations lurk around the entry and exit doors. Others work in teams, with one person acting as the decoy to distract you as the other relieves you of your valuables before you are aware that something has happened.

Before you leave home, make two photocopies of every document that is necessary to the successful completion of your trip. These include airline and rail tickets, rental car vouchers, hotel confirmations and vouchers, a list of credit card numbers, your passport, and your driver's license. Leave one copy at home with someone you trust and bring the other one with you, to be kept locked up in the hotel safe. If things are lost or stolen, you have a record and replacing them will be easier. Also take several passport-size color photos, which come in handy if you have to replace a passport or purchase a weekly or monthly transportation pass.

The U.S. Department of State publishes a pamphlet called *A Safe Trip Abroad*. For a copy, write the Superintendent of Documents, U.S. Government Printing Office, Washington, D.C. 20402.

Hotel Safety Tips

1. If possible, avoid rooms on the ground floor that face the street.

2. Do not leave any valuables exposed in your room, even when you are sleeping.

3. When you leave your room, close and lock the windows and do not leave or hide valuables—lock them up in the hotel safe. Thieves know all the hiding places, as well as some you probably never thought of.

4. Valuables include more than money and jewelry. Don't forget about your camera, camcorder, computer, portable CD player, and fancy pen. Credit card receipts should not be left exposed.

5. If you are a victim of a theft, insist on filing a complete report with the local police as soon as possible. The more documentation you have, the better your chances will be for compensation from your insurance company.

6. Finally: If it is not critical to the trip, leave it at home.

What to Wear and Packing It Lightly

The best advice is often the shortest. In the case of what to wear, keep it simple and travel light. Porters are in very limited supply in rail and air terminals, and bellboys are nonexistent in almost all the hotels in the Cheap Sleeps category. This means you are going to have to do some lugging, even if your carrier has wheels. After trudging up the first few flights of stairs with heavy luggage, you'll agree that less is definitely best. Keep your wardrobe simple, color coordinate it, and remember, you probably are not going to be any one place long enough for anyone to notice that your wardrobe revolves around mixing and matching two pair of slacks, three shirts, a jacket, and a comfortable pair of walking shoes. Accessorize with scarves and some jewelry and call it a day. You will look great, and you'll definitely be traveling smarter.

You will find the locals dressed conservatively in all three cities. Jeans are universally accepted for sightseeing and casual dining, but they are not the best option if you are dining at a nice restaurant. Men don't need ties, and will feel comfortable in a turtleneck sweater in the winter and a nice shirt during warmer weather. Women will feel best in simple, well-tailored outfits, and you can never go wrong in black, no matter what the season. Short shorts, halter tops, baseball caps turned backward, jogging shoes worn for every occasion, and multiple cameras strapped to your chest spell "tourist," and you will be treated accordingly.

Air-conditioned hotel rooms are not standard issue in Prague, Vienna, or Budapest. In the summer, days can get uncomfortably hot, but the nights cool down, so pack a light sweater or jacket. It is cold in the winter, so don't forget to pack a hat along with a warm coat, gloves, and long underwear. No matter what time of year you are here, pack an extra pair of walking shoes, an umbrella, a plastic bag for damp or dirty laundry, blow-up hangers for drip-dry laundries, rubber go-aheads if you are staying in bathless accommodations, an extra pair of eyeglasses, and copies of all your prescriptions. Pack all of your toiletries in plastic bags placed in sealed waterproof bags. Those who have had airplane pressure blow the lid off their shampoo bottle or nail polish remover know what I am talking about.

Standards of Measure—Metric Conversions

1 centimeter is less than ½ inch
1 meter is about 1.1 yards
1 kilometer is ⅔ of a mile
1 kilogram is 2.2 pounds
1 liter is 1.06 quarts
1 gallon is 3.8 liters
To convert meters to feet, multiply the number of meters by 3.28
To convert feet to meters, multiply the number of feet by .305
To convert kilometers to miles, multiply the number of kilometers by 0.62
To convert miles to kilometers, multiply the number of miles by 1.61
To convert kilograms to pounds, multiply the number of kilograms by 2.2
To convert pounds to kilograms, multiply the number of pounds by 0.45
To convert liters to U.S. gallons, multiply the number of liters by 0.26
To convert U.S. gallons to liters, multiply the number of gallons by 3.79

Celsius	-18	-10	0	10	20	30	40
Fahrenheit		0	10	32	50	70	90	100

To convert Celsius to Fahrenheit, multiply the Celsius by 9 and divide by 5, then add 32.

To convert Fahrenheit to Celsius, subtract 32 from the Fahrenheit, multiply by 5, and divide by 9.

How to Use Cheap Sleeps in Prague, Vienna, and Budapest

Abbreviations

Every *Cheap Sleeps* listing states whether or not credit cards are accepted, and if so, which ones. The following abbreviations are used to denote which credit cards a hotel or shop will accept.

American Express	AE
Diners Club	DC
MasterCard	MC
Visa	V

Big Splurges

Big Splurges are those hotels that are higher priced, and they are included here because their location, amenities, service, and overall appeal will suit travelers with more demanding tastes and flexible budgets. Even though the prices are higher, the hotels all offer good value for money. Big Splurge hotels are marked in the text with a dollar sign ($), and they are indexed by city in the back of the book.

Accommodations: Checking In

Always arrive at your hotel with a written confirmation detailing the dates of your stay, type of room, and rates. After presenting your written confirmation, the next order of business is inspecting your room. If you are not satisfied, ask to see another. When you have approved your room, reconfirm the rate and whether or not you will be eating breakfast at the hotel. If you are not eating the hotel breakfast, be sure to determine how much will be deducted per day, per person from your total bill, and remember that once the decision has been made to eat in or go out, you will have to stick with it. This advance work prevents snafus at checkout time.

The hotel day begins and ends at noon. If you are arriving on an early morning flight, you can request that your room be ready upon arrival, but you can't count on it unless you book it for the night before and pay for it. If you think you will arrive after 6 P.M., be sure to notify the hotel or your room could be given to someone else, even if you have a deposit. If you wish to extend your stay, or cut it short, tell the desk at least twenty-four hours in advance. Sometimes if you stay even an hour or two beyond the checkout time, you can be charged the price of another night. If you leave early without giving the hotel sufficient notice and time to resell your room, you could be charged for your original length of stay.

Smoking/Nonsmoking Rooms

Every other person in central Europe seems to be puffing away on a cigarette. As a result, some hotel rooms smell like ashtrays. Of course, in the listings below I note which hotels have rooms dedicated solely for nonsmokers, but otherwise I recommend that you tell the hotel you want a room that has been aired out, which all too often means that the maid has opened the window and sprayed air freshener an hour before your arrival, but it is better than nothing. Fortunately, many of the hotel breakfast rooms are nonsmoking.

Paying the Bill

Most hotels in these three cities offer different rates throughout the year, always trying to get the most they can, even in the so-called low seasons. All of the prices in *Cheap Sleeps in Prague, Vienna, and Budapest* are for full rack rate and do not reflect discounts or deals. The listings tell you when and if lower off-season rates apply, or if special rates are granted to readers of this book. The rates can vary widely and depend not only on the time of year, the general economy, and the rate of inflation, but whether the hotel is fully booked, the length of your stay, and if you pay in cash or by credit card.

Hotel exchange rates are always stacked against the guest in favor of the hotel. If you are paying your bill in cash, convert you money at a bank before checkout time (see Currency Exchange under "Money Matters," page 19). Before paying either in cash or by credit card, take time to review your bill carefully, question anything you do not understand, and insist on a receipt marked *paid* before leaving.

Breakfast

Simply put, hotels make money hand over fist on breakfast, so if you can avoid paying for this overpriced meal, do so, but it is often not possible. In most of the hotels listed in *Cheap Sleeps in Prague, Vienna, and Budapest,* a breakfast of some sort is included and cannot be deducted, especially in high season. Very often it will be a serve-yourself buffet with the usual fruit juice, bread, and jam plus a variety of cheeses, meats, and sometimes hard-boiled eggs. If you eat well here, you can sometimes make do with a light midday snack, and concentrate your efforts on a nice dinner. If your hotel offers a breakfast buffet, *please* do not stuff your purse or carry bag with extra food to take out of the dining room to eat later in the day. This is the height of poor manners, and many hotels will charge you extra if they catch you.

English Spoken

After all, when you come right down to it, how many people speak the same language even when they speak the same language?
—Russell Hoban

Knowing the native tongue of the land you are visiting adds immeasurably to your overall enjoyment, but it isn't a requirement, and you should never think you cannot visit a country unless you know the language. All of the hotel and shopping listings in this book tell you whether or not English is spoken. While it is always nice to be able to greet the staff with a few words in their language, no one expects you to be conversant. See the individual glossaries in Prague, Vienna, and Budapest for a few phrases you will find most useful.

Fortunately, most of the hotels have someone on the front desk (at least during the day) who can speak English. The large department stores have English-speaking clerks, and in the smaller shops, you would be surprised at how far sign language and the few words you do know will go.

Facilities and Services

At the end of each hotel description is a brief summary of the facilities available at the hotel. Generally, the more facilities, the higher the price.

Nearest Tourist Attractions

The hotels in each city are listed alphabetically within specific city districts, and the list of tourist attractions at the end of each hotel description gives those sites within a comfortable walking distance.

Transportation

In each hotel listing, the nearest underground transportation stop is given. It is beyond the scope of *Cheap Sleeps in Prague, Vienna, and Budapest* to cover all the public transportation alternatives. Sometimes it makes better sense to use a bus or a tram, or a combination of the underground and a bus, to get where you want to be, so always inquire at your hotel's front desk as to what other transportation options you have.

If you plan on using taxis in either Prague or Budapest, please see their individual "Transportation" sections for important information on how *not* to be a target for taxi scams and ripoffs.

Maps

The maps in *Cheap Sleeps* are designed to aid the reader in locating the hotel listings, but bear in mind that they are artistic renderings and are not meant to replace detailed street maps. If you plan on being in any of the cities for any length of time, I suggest that you invest in a proper street map, such as a Hallwag map for Vienna, an ADAC city plan for Budapest, or a Prague City Map, all of which are available at most news kiosks.

All the accommodations are keyed to the maps with a number, which appears to the left of the hotel name in the listings in text as well as on the map itself.

Important Telephone Notice for Prague and Budapest

Currently, the telephone systems in both Czechoslovakia and Hungary are being privatized, and this means—much to the dismay of visitors, residents, and travel writers—that the telephone numbering systems in both Prague and Budapest have been and will be changing. Unfortunately, the phone numbers are being changed piecemeal over an extended period of time, and no one seems to know when the process will be complete. Equally upsetting is that the automated system for keeping track of the changes—and that tells you the new number when you dial the old number—is extremely limited and can't be relied upon by the visitor.

If you are calling from the United States and you dial a number that's no longer working, dial 00 and ask for international directory assistance. The operator will connect you with an English-speaking operator in the foreign city you are trying to reach. If you are calling from within either Prague or Budapest, ask your hotel desk clerk to assist you. He or she will be able to negotiate the phone system more efficiently and may have access to the most up-to-date information.

The phone numbers given with each *Cheap Sleeps* listing have been rechecked and were correct at press time, but you can almost be assured that some will have changed by your arrival. For their help in verifying telephone numbers, I would like to thank Philip Zvonicek at the Embassy of the Czech Republic in Washington, D.C., for his help with Prague and Tünde Varga for her help with Budapest.

PRAGUE

I can see a vast city whose fame reaches to the stars.
—Princess Libuše, renowned for her prophetic powers

For centuries people have been fascinated by Prague and have ranked her as one of the most beautiful and romantic cities in the world. Every historical epoch has left its mark on her appearance, and Europe as it once was still stands today in her streets and squares, where you can see the rich heritage of the past in Romanesque architecture, Gothic churches, Renaissance and Baroque palaces, and Classicist houses, all combining to form a glorious artistic whole. Prague's spirit shines as it reflects her six hundred years—having survived wars, revolutions, and occupations and having been mercifully spared the destruction of bombs.

In 1918, following World War I, the Czechoslovak Republic was pieced together out of the Austro-Hungarian empire. Twenty years later Hitler occupied it, precipitating World War II, after which the Communists took over. Finally, in 1989 the Velvet Revolution peacefully liberated the country from the stale grip of Communism. This was followed soon after by the Velvet Divorce, when Slovakia split away from Bohemia and Moravia. These last two countries are now joined to form the Czech Republic—with Prague as not only its head but its heart. Prague is a city that has known good times and bad, glory and tragedy, and is once again a place of great opportunity economically, educationally, artistically, and culturally.

In the decade since the collapse of Communism, the rise of new capitalism has been nothing short of spectacular. This I know from experience. I lived for two years in the early 1980s in Prague when the STB (the secret police) followed and photographed members of my family wherever we went, tried to implant a microphone chip in the neck of my dog, bugged our house and our car, and took regular reports about our activities from the household help. Consumer goods were virtually nonexistent, food was scarce, and creature comforts very few for the locals. One joke about the health care suggested that fly swatters were part of every hospital's emergency room equipment. The black market was alive and well, and a second currency consisting of cigarettes and scotch worked wonders whenever any service or favor was needed.

Today the countryside has not changed significantly from the old days, but Prague . . . that is another story. The city wears the face of freedom, and it is firmly grasping a bright future. Capitalism has caught on and is running rampant. The only constant is change—everything all at once and at breakneck speed. The city is alive with the buzz of construction crews working seven days a week restoring, rebuilding,

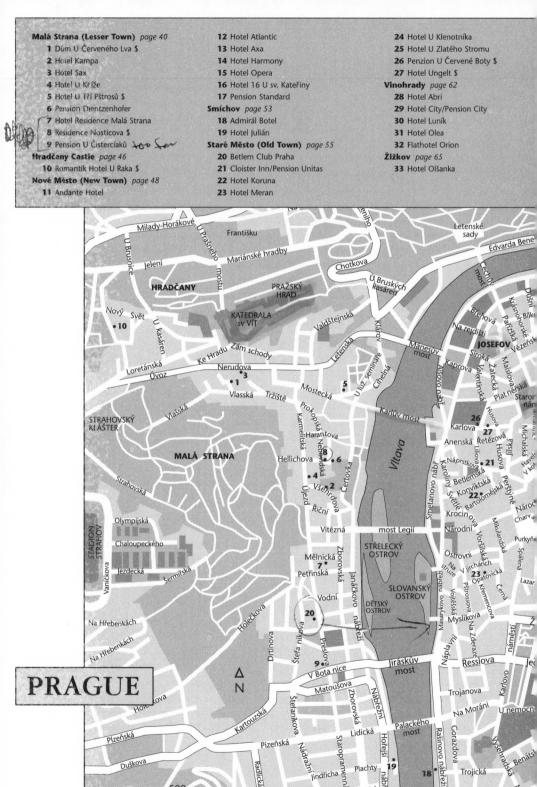

PRAGUE

500 m

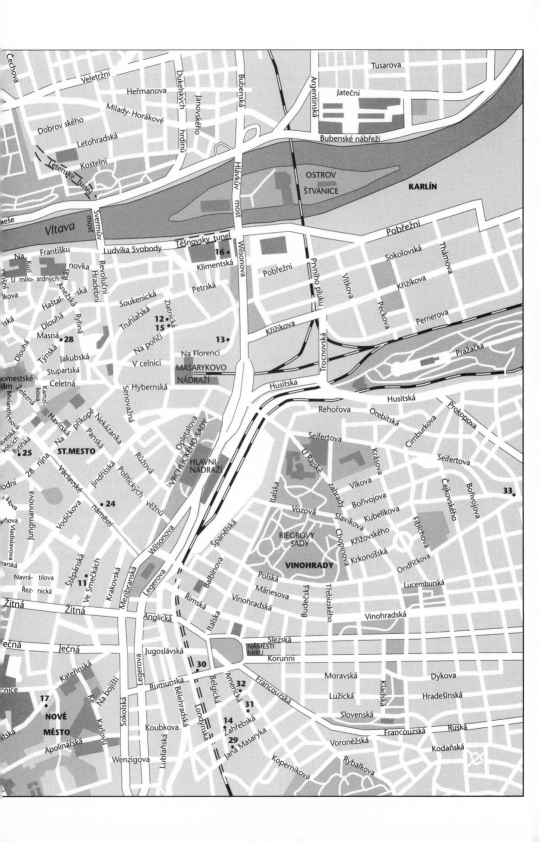

redoing the city. Even the secret police building across from the American Embassy has been redone in salmon pink with white trim. Shop windows are filled with Western goods, and locals are out in large numbers, not only looking, but buying. Big Macs sold under the Golden Arches are in every neighborhood, restaurants are springing up overnight, and imported foods, wines, cheeses, and delicate fruits and vegetables from France and Italy are routine supermarket buys.

Although the Velvet Revolution has changed the face of Prague, the hotel industry lags behind. Last year 1,750,000 visitors, 96,000 of them Americans, descended on the city, which has a population of 1,300,000. A 20 to 30 percent increase in visitors is expected each year for at least the next five years. In a city already notorious for room shortages, especially in the midprice range, this is a problem with a capital P, as demand will continue to far exceed supply. Even though whatever you want in a hotel room is here, the choice of acceptable hotel rooms is definitely limited, forcing people to consider accommodation options they would not accept in other major European capitals; people pay more and yet settle for less in terms of charm, amenities, and service. Not only this, but if you aren't careful, you could book a room in one of the Libyan-controlled hotels in Prague and thereby violate U.S. government economic sanctions—leading to substantial fines of up to $25,000 and a possible prison sentence of ten years! The hotels to avoid are the Prague Forum and the Panorama in the Corinthia Group; this Libyan-controlled company falls under the U.S. sanctions placed against the Libyan regime of Mu'ammar Gadhafi.

To get the hotel of your choice, and the best value for your money, Cheap Sleepers in Prague should make reservations as far in advance as possible, secure them with a deposit, get a written confirmation, and telephone a few days prior to arrival to reconfirm their booking. To help you determine the best hotel for you, *Cheap Sleeps in Prague* is divided into the sections of the city where the visitor is most likely to be. Room choices include such possibilities as a tent on the outskirts of the city, beautifully restored noble homes now run as hotels, rooms done in Art Nouveau or Art Deco, and a delightful pension along the Kampa Park in Malá Strana. Others, while clean and serviceable, have uninspired decor and limited amenities. If you are staying in a real Cheap Sleep, consider taking your own bar of soap and investing in some local light bulbs. Also, the attitudes of staff in a few hotels have not adapted to the values of a free economy. They do not know much about pleasing, and they certainly won't fall all over themselves to be of service to their guests. An advantage for many weary visitors is that the majority of hotels have some sort of restaurant that serves dinner, but gourmet expectations should be kept to the barest minimum.

General Information

When to Go

Spring is unquestionably the most beautiful time of year in Prague, when the fruit trees on Petřín Hill are in full color. From mid-May until the first week in June, the Prague Spring Festival is held. This three-week-long music festival begins with a performance of Smetana's symphonic poem "Má Vlast" (My Country) and includes performances by the country's top musicians. Advance tickets are available starting in November from the festival office (located on Hellichova 18, Prague 1; tel: 2451 0422). Late September and October are other desirable times to go, when the leaves are turning and the weather is still warm. In the summer the city is overrun with tourists, and the Czechs leave for their country cottages to escape the heat and humidity. During the winter months, the days are short, the thermometer dips, and the pollution from the coal-burning furnaces rises to unhealthy levels, but the tourists are few, hotel rates are at their lowest, and the city is almost magical under a light blanket of snow.

Holidays

The Czech Republic celebrates the following holidays each year when banks, most shops, and all government offices will be closed. Public transportation operates on a Sunday schedule.

January 1	New Year's Day
Easter Sunday and Monday	Dates vary
May 1	Labor Day
May 8	Liberation Day
July 5	Cyril and Methodius Day
July 6	Jan Hus Day
October 28	Independence Day
December 24, 25	Christmas Eve and Christmas Day
December 26	St. Stephen's Day

Money

The Česká koruna (abbreviated as Kč), or Czech crown, is the currency of the Czech Republic. Currently there are about 32Kč to one U.S. dollar, but that is always subject to change due to inflation and the economic and political situation. Major credit cards are widely accepted and ATMs are mushrooming. When paying by credit card, in addition to writing the numerical total on the face of the credit card slip, always spell out the amount you are paying, and draw a line through all the blank boxes on the slip. For example, write the words four thousand three hundred and ten Kč on the credit card slip in addition to 4,310Kč in the numerical box.

Never change money on the street. Use an ATM, a bank, or an official currency exchange office. Look for the silver line on one side of every bank note to make sure it is real.

Tipping

How much is too much and what is enough? In restaurants, rounding off the total bill is appreciated by waiters if the service was exceptional; otherwise nothing is called for. In a deluxe restaurant, leave a 10 percent tip. In hotels, the maids are poorly paid and so is anyone you found to carry your bags, so it is nice to reward their service with 30Kč per day for the maid and 20Kč per bag carried. At the hair salon, always give the shampoo girl a little something as well as the person who cuts and styles your hair and the manicurist. Washroom attendants demand two or three crowns, and have a saucer ready for you to put them in. Taxi drivers expect to have the price of the ride rounded up, but don't do it if they are rude to you. Tipping in hard currency is always welcome, and no one will ever turn down U.S. greenbacks. Many travelers to Prague take a bundle of one-dollar bills to use exclusively for this purpose.

Safety and Security

All of the general safety and security measures discussed in the "General Information" section apply to Prague, along with a few other safety suggestions visitors should keep in mind. Avoid the main train station (Hlavní nádraží) late at night, and don't wander around Václavské náměstí (Wenceslas Square) after dark—it's frequented mainly by hookers and those looking for one. Pickpockets and petty thieves account for most of the crimes against tourists, and naturally they position themselves in the most popular tourist areas: Wenceslas Square, Old Town Square, the Castle, and the Charles Bridge. Remember, the sale of a camcorder or Nikon camera would equal several months wages for the average Czech citizen.

Telephones

The sign in the hotel read: *O čekáváme změnu tel čísle*—"We expect a change of telephone numbers." What the sign did not say is that because Prague's woefully inadequate telephone system is now being privatized, not only is this hotel's telephone and fax number subject to change, but so is every other telephone and fax number in the city. Trying to determine when this change will be complete, and how the numbers will change, is an exercise in hair-raising futility. I know. I have tried, with the help of everyone from the Czech Embassy in Washington, D.C., to the telephone company in Prague. No one has an answer. As of press time, the telephone and fax numbers have been rechecked and are correct, but neither the publisher nor I can be held responsible if—due to the abysmal phone system and the seeming lack of foresight on the part of the telephone company—you are faced with telephone and fax problems in Prague. If that happens, please call the information operator in Prague at 120. Prague currently has over one million telephone subscribers, with 110,000 applications waiting on hold. Let's hope the telephone company gets its ducks in a row quickly!

Most public telephones now take phone cards, which are on sale in kiosks and post offices. Prudent Cheap Sleepers in Prague will purchase one (sold in increments from 50 to 500Kč). Hotel telephone surcharges can be as much as four times the regular rate, so it is much more economical to use a phone card in a public phone.

Useful Telephone Numbers and Addresses

Emergency and Medical Numbers

Alcoholics Anonymous	Na Poříčí 12, YMCA room 237, Prague 1; tel: 2487 2220
Ambulance	155
Crisis Center	Ke Karlova 11, Prague 2; tel: 297 900; open 24-hours daily
Fire	150
First Aid	155
Medical treatment, nonemergency	First Medical Clinic of Prague, Vyšehradská 35, Prague 2; tel: 292 286. Clinic is open 24-hours daily, but walk-in hours are Mon–Sat 7 A.M.–8 P.M.
Medical emergencies	Foreigners' Medical Clinic, Na Homolce Hospital, Prague 5; tel: 5292 2146 or 5292 2191
Pharmacies, open 24-hours	Belgická 27, Prague 2; tel: 258 189; metro: A, Náměstí míru Štefánikova 6, Prague 5; tel: 2451 1112; metro: B, Anděl
Police, Czech	158
Police, Prague City	156

Useful Numbers

Czech country code	42
To call Prague within Czech Republic	dial 02 + the local number
To call Prague from the U.S.	dial 011+ 42 + 2 + the local number
To call the U.S. from Prague	dial 001 + the area code + the local number
American Embassy	Tržiště 15, Prague 1; tel: 2451 0847
American Express	Václavské náměstí , 56, Prague 1; tel: 2421 9992, fax: 2422 7708

American Express	
currency exchange	Mosteka 12, Prague 1; tel: 5731 3636
Information, city	120
Lost Property	Karoliny Světlé 5, tel: 2423 5085
Post Office	Main office, Jindrišská 14, Prague 1; tel: postal information 2422 8856, 2422 9051; Telecom information: 232 0837. Regular mail and phone/fax services daily, 24-hours; there is a clearly marked window for English-speaking customers.
	Customs office (for packages requiring duty), Plzenská 39, Prague 5; tel: 2451 1754; open Mon–Tues, Thur–Fri 7 A.M.–3 P.M., Wed until 6 P.M.
Prague Information Service (free guides, cultural programs, sightseeing tours, and concerts)	Main office, Na příkopě 20, Prague 1; tel: 264 022 Railway station (Hlavní Nádraží) branch; open all year, summer hours are Mon–Fri 9 A.M.–7 P.M., Sat and Sun until 5 P.M.
Tourist Information	Čedok, Na příkopě 18, or Václavské náměstí 24, both in Prague 1; tel: 2419 7111. Open Mon–Fri 8:30 A.M.–5 P.M., Sat until 12:30 P.M. Čedok is now a regular travel agency dispensing tickets and tour packages with more enthusiasm than they give free information. Čedok in the U.S.: 10 East 40th Street, New York, NY 10016; tel: 212-689-9720

Transportation

The transportation system in Prague is reliable and easy to master. In the center of the city you can ride either the tram or the metro; buses have been banned to the suburbs due to the pollution they cause. While the metro may be faster, the tram provides much better scenery, especially if you take the No. 22, which runs from Národní třída downtown through Malá Strana to the Castle (Pražsky hrad stop) and finally to the Strahov Monastery. In the winter the tram seats are heated, a real bonus when it is below freezing outside. There are bus and tram connections at every metro station and all of the railway stations are connected to the metro. The metro runs from 5 A.M. to midnight, and night buses and trams run from midnight to 5 A.M. At rush hour trains come every two minutes; otherwise the wait is five to ten minutes. You can check the clock on each platform to see the time elapsed since the last train.

The best public transportation map, which shows all metro and tram lines, is in the free city guide available from the Prague Information Service (see page 36). The hotel and shop listings for Prague give the closest metro stop, but often a tram will be just as good. Inquire at your hotel for the best mode of travel to your desired destinations. Tickets are good for any form of transit; buy them individually or as a pass. Passes are sold for a variety of timespans, from a day to up to a year, at any metro station, at news kiosks marked Tabak or Trafika, and often at your hotel desk. Tickets should be validated as soon as you step onto a bus or tram and when you enter the paid area of the metro station. There are no gates or uniformed personnel to check your tickets, but there is a small army of plainclothes inspectors who might ask to see your ticket. If you don't have one, it will cost you a fine of around 200Kč. If you are stopped by someone, you should demand to see his or her photo ID, and get an official written receipt for your fine payment. If either are refused, you are being robbed.

If you think driving in Italy is crazy, just wait until you get to Prague, where the drivers seem hell-bent on destroying everything in their path, driving manners are appalling, and there is absolutely no regard for signs and lanes. To maintain sanity, and to protect your life, forget about joining the suicidal automobile derby in Prague. This also means that pedestrians do not have the right of way and must be extremely cautious: cross streets *only* where there are lights.

Taxis

My best advice about taxis is: *Avoid them unless all else fails.* If you do plan to use them, please read this section carefully.

Taxis in Prague are a sore point for cabdrivers and customers alike. Recently, more than 2,500 taxi drivers demanded that the mayor of Prague resign because, they said, he had hurt honest drivers by openly declaring that most cabbies were thieves, a statement that most Czechs agree with because it is true. Complaints are extensive about these drivers and include fast flipping, speed ticking meters that quadruple a normal fare, hardball tactics to extract fares, refusing to return luggage to a passenger who balked about an excessive charge, and installing electrified whoopie cushions to zap irate customers. The situation sunk to its lowest level when the Prague city council deregulated the system, leaving drivers free to charge whatever they liked with no possibility of being prosecuted. Fortunately, the hue and cry for reform was worldwide and included Milos Forman, a former U.S. ambassador to the Czech Republic, and last but not least Václav Havel, president of the Czech Republic. The city council was forced to reinstate fare structuring, and it required cab drivers to post their fares on car doors and stick to them.

But still, it remains a given that if you ride in a taxi, you will pay too much. Here are a few tips to help you keep the gouging to a minimum:

1. Hailing a taxi in the street or getting in one lined up near a hotel, tourist attraction, or outside the main railway station or Prague airport is an invitation to being overcharged. Ask the hotel or restaurant to call one for you and use one of the companies listed below.

2. Use only an authorized taxi, clearly marked with registration numbers and fares printed on the doors and a black-and-white checkered stripe along the side.

3. Insist that the driver turn on the meter, or agree on a fare to your destination.

4. Don't put anything in the trunk unless it is absolutely necessary.

5. At the end of the ride, the driver should provide you with a receipt that has the name and address of the taxi comany; the taxi registration number; the date, time, and place of pick up and drop off; rate per kilometer; distance; price; and the name and signature of the driver. As you can see this is a lot of work and drivers do not do it unless forced. Honest drivers will give you a receipt printed on the machine attached to the meter. Taxi mafiosos will write something on a scratch pad.

Bottom line: As one cabbie succinctly put it, "If someone is asked for 10,000Kč [$320] for a taxi fare anywhere in Prague *and pays it*, that person shouldn't be in a taxi, but in an ambulance going to a lunatic asylum."

Taxi Companies in Prague: AAA (tel: 1080, or 3399, or 312 2112); ProfiTaxi (tel: 1035, or 6104 5555, or 6104 5550).

Taxi Complaints (Good luck!): Prague City Hall, Department of Local Revenues, Mariánské náměstí 2, Old Town, Prague 1 (tel: 2448 1111). Or, the Taxi Guild (tel: 643 2476).

Discounts

Senior Citizens

Unfortunately, there isn't much in the way of discounts for senior citizens, but it never hurts to ask. The shadow of Communism continues to prevail in many ways in Prague, especially for those over fifty. People retire much earlier, receive a pension, live in subsidized housing, have free medical care, and are satisfied with much less than those of us in the consumer crazy West. Coupon clipping, early-bird and two-for-one dining deals, and most other tricks of discount living have simply not arrived as yet in Prague for those past the half-century mark.

Students

No student under twenty-six years old should travel without the International Student Identity Card (ISIC), which is available from university travel agents, some travel stores, or from the Council on International Educational Exchange (CIEE), 205 East 42nd Street, 16th floor, New York, NY 10017; tel: 212-661-1414, 800-438-2643, or 888-COUNCIL; fax: 212-822-2699; email: info@ciee.org. Office hours are Monday to Friday from 9:00 A.M. to 5 P.M. EST. This card is worth ten times its price (around $20) because it entitles the bearer to discounts on selected museums, transportation costs, student lodgings, and more— not only in Prague, but everywhere you go in Europe. It also provides you with medical, accident, and hospital insurance. Teachers can get some of the same discounts and all of the benefits by purchasing the International Teacher Identity Card (ITIC). For further information and application forms, contact CIEE.

Disabled Travelers

In Prague, all buildings constructed after 1994 must be suitable for handicapped access, but those undergoing restoration are not required to provide it, though many do anyway. Prague's cobblestoned streets and narrow alleyways are almost impossible to navigate in a wheelchair, and ramps are few. All hope is not lost, however, thanks to the Prague Wheelchair Association. They publish the guidebook *Accessible Prague* (Přístupná Praha), which has maps and lists hotels, toilets, restaurants, theaters, and concert halls that are accessible to those in a wheelchair. They also operate taxi and airport pickup services. If you need this service, it should be arranged as far in advance as possible. Contact them at Centre for Independent Living, Beneditská 6, Nové Město, Prague 1; tel: 232 5831, 232 5803; fax: 2481 6231; metro: Námestí republiky. It's open Monday to Thursday 10 A.M. to 5 P.M., Friday until 3 P.M.

Hotels in Prague
by Area

Prague is divided into ten districts, but for the casual visitor few hold much interest other than the central district, which is the heart of the city: Prague 1. The district is subdivided into the familiar areas of Malá Strana, Hradčany, Nové Město, Josefov, and Staré Město. Buildings in Prague have two sets of numbers. The street number is on the blue sign, and the red sign is the Prague registry number. All you need to worry about are the blue numbers . . . nevermind the red ones.

MALÁ STRANA (LESSER TOWN) ───────

The area on the west bank of the Vltava River between the Letná and Petřín Hills and up the slope of Hradčany is known as Malá Strana, or Lesser Town. After crossing the Charles Bridge and walking through the two Malá Strana bridge towers onto Mostecká, which has served as a main road of the quarter since the Middle Ages, visitors enter the second town of Prague, founded by Přemysl Otakar II in 1257. Dominating Malostranské náměstí is the massive presence of the Church of St. Nicholas, the most splendid ecclesiastical Baroque building in Prague. Its interior is no less impressive, with its ceiling fresco in the nave (1,500 square meters) ranking as one of the largest paintings in Europe. The atmosphere in Malá Strana, which has remained almost untouched to this day, has a marked individuality due to the quarter's picturesque streets and wealth of historical Baroque palaces, Renaissance architecture, and charming squares. The beauty and special charm of the area is also enhanced by numerous gardens laid out on terraced slopes, which today provide the opportunity for quiet, romantic walks. Interesting boutiques, unique hotels, and quaint restaurants add further allure to this picturesque part of Prague.

Kampa, a romantic island separated from Malá Strana by a branch of the Vltava called Čertovka (which means the Devil's Stream), is a quiet place for walks and a rest from the crowds crossing the Charles Bridge on the way to the Castle. It also offers a spectacular panorama of the famed bridge and the Old Town embankments all the way to the gilded railings of the roof of the National

Theater. The water of the Čertovka was originally used to power the old, picturesque wooden water-mill wheels you still see today, and the houses along the lower part of Čertovka are referred to as "Prague Venice." From the seventeenth century on, Kampa was a pottery center, and today you can still buy Kampa pottery in several of the artists shops that fill this pretty area.

HOTELS

OTHER OPTIONS

Note: A dollar sign ($) indicates a Big Splurge.

(1) DŮM U ČERVENÉHO LVA $
Nerudova 41, Prague 1
7 rooms, all with shower or bath and toilet

Dům U Červeného Lva, or the House at the Red Lion, is in the historical center of Prague on the Royal Route leading from Malá Strana to Prague Castle. The first records of the building date back to the fifteenth century. The basement section is from the Gothic period, the painted beam ceilings represent the Renaissance, and the entry door is from the time of Baroque reconstruction. The facade is attributed to Peter Brandl, a famous seventeenth-century painter of altar pictures, who was born in the house.

A stylish renovation project completed in 1995 created three double rooms and four suites, plus a bar and restaurant in the Gothic cellar. The rooms and suites are all oversized and have a nice collection of period furnishings and separate built-in entries. Those on the first two floors have painted beams. Room 1, an odd-shaped twin,

TELEPHONE
53 72 39, 53 81 92
FAX
53 81 93
INTERNET
www.interacta.cz/accol.htm
METRO
A, Malostranská
CREDIT CARDS
AE, DC, MC, V
RATES
Single 5,500–6,500Kč, double 6,000–7,300Kč, triple 8,700Kč, quad 9,600Kč; lower off-season rates
BREAKFAST
Buffet included

with a small mirrored entry and wooden floors, has a new bathroom with three shelves, heated towel racks, and an enclosed stall shower. Room 13 is as nicely furnished as all the others, but it seems to be cut up. The entrance is from a back outdoor stairway and the access to the bathroom, which is private to this room, is outside the room and down the hall. One of the best is No. 21, which has a beautiful ceiling. A setee and two chairs provide attractive seating. The white tiled bathroom has extra shelf space and good lighting. Room 31 is a two-room suite with a view to Petřín Hill from the second bedroom. The restaurant is open continuously from 7 A.M. to 11 P.M., and there is a bar for quick refreshments throughout the day.

ENGLISH SPOKEN Yes

FACILITIES AND SERVICES Bar, direct-dial phone, hair dryer, three floors (no elevator), minibar, parking for 250Kč per day, satellite TV, restaurant, room safe

NEAREST TOURIST ATTRACTIONS On main road leading to the Castle, can walk to everything in Malá Strana and across the Charles Bridge to Old Town

(2) HOTEL KAMPA
Všehrdova 16, Prague 1
85 rooms, all with shower or bath and toilet

TELEPHONE
5732 0508, 5732 0404

FAX
5732 0262

METRO
A, Malostranská

CREDIT CARDS
AE, MC, V (5% discount if pay in cash)

RATES
Single 2,300–3,300Kč, double 3,700Kč; extra bed 1,500Kč; lower off-season rates

BREAKFAST
Continental included

The Hotel Kampa was originally an armory, built in the Baroque style at the beginning of the seventeenth century. After extensive renovation in 1992, it was opened as an eighty-five-room hotel in a quiet section of Malá Strana near Kampa Park. A walk through this picturesque park alongside the Vltava River leads to the Charles Bridge and the beautifully restored streets of Malá Strana. Rooms are plain but adequate and very clean. Tiled bathrooms provide the basics, including a light over the mirror and a hook . . . two very elementary essentials missing in many Prague hotels. Best bets are the rooms overlooking the park. The vaulted dining room is enormous and is certainly a port in a storm if wandering far for a meal seems too much to do.

ENGLISH SPOKEN Yes

FACILITIES AND SERVICES Direct-dial phone, hair dryer available, lift, minibar, parking 150Kč per night, cable TV, restaurants, office safe

NEAREST TOURIST ATTRACTIONS Kampa Park, all of Malá Strana, Charles Bridge

(3) HOTEL SAX
Jánsky Vršek 328/3, Prague 1
22 rooms, all with shower or bath and toilet

TELEPHONE
53 84 22

FAX
53 84 98

METRO
A, Malostranská

CREDIT CARDS
AE, DC, MC, V

RATES
Single 3,500Kč, double 4,000Kč, suite 4,900Kč; lower off-season rates

BREAKFAST
Buffet included

This sleekly modern hotel is built around an open atrium with a bar and restaurant on the first floor and many rooms overlooking the inside courtyard. The management team is as young and as hip as the hotel attempts to be. The hotel has a certain appeal for those seeking a streamlined look, but frankly, the rooms do not live up to expectations. Those looking onto the atrium have windows that open on the walkways guests use, thus making any sort of security questionable along these stretches when the windows are open. The biggest and best accommodations are on the third floor and face the street. Most bathrooms have stall showers and medicine chests with sidebar lights. The restaurant is doing its part to be with-it by offering spiced tofu with rice as one of the non-Czech entrées.

ENGLISH SPOKEN Yes

FACILITIES AND SERVICES Bar, direct-dial phone, hair dryer, lift, minibar, four free parking places, restaurant, satellite TV, office safe

NEAREST TOURIST ATTRACTIONS Prague Castle, all of Malá Strana

(4) HOTEL U KŘÍŽE
Újezd 20, Prague 1
22 rooms, all with shower or bath and toilet

TELEPHONE
53 33 26, 53 33 98, 53 56 69

FAX
53 34 43

METRO
B, Andel

CREDIT CARDS
MC, V

RATES
Single 3,300Kč, double 3,500Kč, suite 3,500–4,200Kč; lower off-season rates

BREAKFAST
Continental included

The hotel opened in 1995, and for most Cheap Sleepers in Prague, it has a lot going for it. To start, Jana Sobotková, the reception manager, is both gracious and helpful to all her guests. The hotel itself is well done and attractive. The site was a ceramic factory, and during the reconstruction of the present hotel, workers found buried objects dating from the fifteenth and sixteenth centuries. Some of the more important pieces are displayed in a glass cabinet in the main part of the hotel.

The rooms, furnished in reproduction farm rustic, are exceptional by Prague standards. The crisp white sheets and duvets on the beds are made from antiallergic materials, and the room colors and fabrics are coordinated. The biggest double room is No. 2, with two windows, a wood-beamed ceiling, and a comfortable, burgandy red velvet upholstered chair. Room 17 is a favorite, even though it is on the street. The gray tiled bathroom has a stall shower, good towels, and shelf and hook space. The room has a small desk, two chairs, two luggage racks, and plenty of bright light from the window. Room 22 is on the top floor under a slanted roof that could be a problem for tall guests. Room 9 is a white two-level suite with a red velvet sofa and winding stairway leading to the bedroom, which has twin beds placed foot-to-foot. Another requested two-room suite is No. 1, with a fold-out sofa bed in addition to a double and a larger bathroom with a tub. A downstairs breakfast room with a big picture window lined with plants is a welcoming place to start the day. Those eager to add another unusual cuisine experience to their list can order roast filet of kangaroo in the restaurant dining room. Otherwise, the menu sticks to the usual Czech fare.

ENGLISH SPOKEN Yes

FACILITIES AND SERVICES Bar, direct-dial phone, hair dryer available, lift, minibar, parking 250Kč per night, cable TV, office safe

NEAREST TOURIST ATTRACTIONS Walking distance to most of Malá Strana and the Charles Bridge

(5) HOTEL U TŘÍ PŠTROSŮ $
Dražického náměstí 12, Prague 1
18 rooms and suites, all with shower or bath and toilet

TELEPHONE
5732 0565

FAX
5732 0611

METRO
A, Malostranská

CREDIT CARDS
AE, DC, MC, V

RATES
Single 5,100Kč, double 7,000Kč, suite 8,900–234 10,000Kč; extra bed 1,300Kč; $263 lower off-season rates

BREAKFAST
Continental included

U Tří Pštrosů, a jewel of Gothic architecture standing next to the famed Charles Bridge, was the first coffee-house in Prague (see *Cheap Eats in Prague, Vienna, and Budapest*), and it is now one of the most charming and historic hotels in the city. The original building was burned during the time of the Hussite upheaval and rebuilt by Jan Fuchs, a supplier of ostrich feathers, who had the front of his house decorated with ostriches. During the reign of Charles IV, a foreign delegation carrying three ostriches as a present for the emperor stayed here, and these three ostriches became the symbols and name of the house from then on. During this century the house has had several owners, including the state. Finally, in the 1980s it was returned to private ownership, and today visitors are welcomed in fourteen rooms and four apartments, the majority of which have their original Renaissance wood ceilings.

The rooms on the third and fourth floors have views so close it seems you can reach out and touch the magnificent Charles Bridge. While these are indeed desirable, they do get the noise from the throngs lingering, loitering, and walking across the bridge. All the rooms are furnished with Czech antiques, but some of the singles, No. 101 in particular, are tiny and have no views. Room 105, a two-room suite with a sitting room, bedroom, and small office entryway, has a green marble bathroom and a glass-enclosed tub and shower. Heavy painted beams and comfortable furniture complete the picture. The view from three windows tells you without question that this *is* Prague.

ENGLISH SPOKEN Yes

FACILITIES AND SERVICES Bar, direct-dial phone, no elevator (four floors), minibar, TV, restaurant, room safe in suites, office safe

NEAREST TOURIST ATTRACTIONS Virtually on the Charles Bridge, Malá Strana

(6) PENSION DIENTZENHOFER
Nosticova 2, Prague 1
7 rooms, all with shower and toilet

The sixteenth-century building is protected under the historical monuments act because it is the birthplace of one of the great Baroque architects, Kilian Ignaz Dientzenhofer, who built the sacristy and great dome of the Church of St. Nicholas, which dominates Malá Strana. The pension consists of one single room, three doubles, and three suites, and it is owned and run by Dr. Josef Kábele, his wife, and their daughter, who have built a well-deserved reputation as accommodating and caring hosts. The house overlooks the tranquil Kampa Park and the small Čertovka River running through it. It is a lovely setting anytime, especially in the spring and summer when the flowers and trees are in full bloom. In fact, it is so beautiful that the garden is in great demand for weddings and receptions. The rooms and suites are attractively done with simple, matching furnishings and fabrics. The family personally prepares a very special breakfast that includes not only the usual cereals, juices, and assorted breads but cheese, assorted cold meats, homemade cakes, and eggs if you want them. It is served in a homey dining room with tables positioned so that you can either read your paper and be alone or strike up a friendly conversation with other guests if you wish. This is one of the most sought-after pensions in Prague, thus it is never too early to make your reservations.

ENGLISH SPOKEN Yes, and French

TELEPHONE
53 16 72, 53 88 95

FAX
5732 0888

METRO
A, Malostranská, or Tram Nos. 12 or 22 to Hellichova

CREDIT CARDS
AE, DC, MC, V

RATES
Single 1,900–2,500Kč, double 2,500-3,300Kč, suite (1–4 people) 2,700–5,300Kč; lower corporate rates

BREAKFAST
Large breakfast included

FACILITIES AND SERVICES Bar, direct-dial phone, lift, parking 150Kč per day, radio, cable TV, office safe, all rooms equipped for handicapped, laundry service

NEAREST TOURIST ATTRACTIONS Kampa Park, Malá Strana, Charles Bridge

HRADČANY CASTLE

Like Malá Strana, Hradčany has preserved its medieval design and buildings as a noble quarter. Distinguished by the Prague Castle, the magnificent St. Vitus Cathedral, Strahov Monastary, Loreto Church, and Černin Palace, it is the best-preserved district in Prague. The most glorious time of the quarter was during the reign of Charles IV, when Prague became the largest and most important city in central Europe. The Prague Castle, which is over one thousand years old, is laid out around three interconnecting courtyards that open onto Hradčany Square, where the colorful changing of the palace guards takes place every day at noon. From the end of the ninth century until 1918, it was the official seat and place of coronation of Czech sovereigns, and since 1918, it has been the official office of the Presidents of the Czechoslovak (now the Czech Republic). No tour of Hradčany would be complete without a visit to the tiny street of fairytale houses known as Golden Lane (Zlatá ulička), which lines the wall of the Castle beyond the end of the Basilica of St. George. These miniature houses were built by members of the palace guard who worked at various trades when their armed services were not needed. The street is also famous as the place where Franz Kafka came when he visited his sister. Today the houses are occupied by tourist shops and boutiques (see "Cheap Chic in Prague," page 176).

HOTELS

(10) Romantik Hotel U Raka $	**47**

Note: A dollar sign ($) indicates a Big Splurge.

(10) ROMANTIK HOTEL U RAKA $
Černínská 10/93, Prague 1
6 rooms, all with shower or bath and toilet

For a Big Splurge you will remember, reserve a room at Romantik Hotel U Raka, one of the most unusual hotels you will experience anywhere, and certainly in Prague. Prague is a city that has had hostile takeovers and occupations, but it has not suffered the mass destruction of wartime bombings. Therefore, almost all of the buildings in the old sectors have long, interesting histories, and U Raka is no different. The oldest report of it comes from 1739 when it was purchased for 80 Rhine guilders to be used as a cowshed, and then in 1794 it was named U Raka (which means At the Sign of the Crayfish) and turned into living quarters. Several other wood-timbered houses were added until there were eight in all. Time took its toll on the wooden structures, and by 1987, when the present owner acquired them, they were falling down and could not be saved. After two years of reconstruction, faithful copies of the exteriors of the original buildings were completed and the interiors then turned into a picturesque, romantic hotel that pairs a comfortable Czech farmhouse with the tranquility of Japanese gardens. It is quite a combination, and the results are beautiful. Everywhere you look, there is something appealing to the eye. The owner is a professional photographer, his wife a well-known artist, and their daughter a sculptor, and their work is beautifully displayed throughout the hotel.

The rooms and public areas have been thought out to the last detail. They employ natural materials, the liberal use of beautiful plantings, and the calming effects of rippling water. Hallogen lights, cross beams, and green antiqued furniture are the constants in the rooms, but each also has something unique about it. Room 1, on two levels, has an interesting stone entryway and steep stairs leading to a mezzanine bedroom with half porthole windows. In No. 5, pine furnishings and old farm baskets are set off by a pitched stucco ceiling with small dormer windows and brick accents. A large white tiled bathroom with double sinks, nice toiletries, and a good mirror has an enclosed stall shower and a separate bathtub. In the morning, breakfast is served in the main building on Czech blue-and-white onion-patterned china. Another restaurant is open during the afternoon for light snacks. U Raka is away from the Prague tourist

TELEPHONE
2051 1100

FAX
2051 0511

EMAIL
uraka@login.cz

METRO
A, Malostranská, or Tram No. 22 (both a long walk)

CREDIT CARDS
AE, DC, MC, V

RATES
Single 5,200Kč, double 6,300Kč, suite 7000Kč; lower off-season rates

BREAKFAST
Buffet included

ballyhoo in the picturesque Novy Svět neighborhood behind the Prague Castle, which means guests here will have a fair walk from either the underground or the tram stop.

ENGLISH SPOKEN Yes

FACILITIES AND SERVICES Air-conditioning in five rooms, direct-dial phone, hair dryer, no elevator (but not necessary), minibar, free parking, restaurant for light snacks, TV, office safe

NEAREST TOURIST ATTRACTIONS Prague Castle

NOVÉ MĚSTO (NEW TOWN) ─────────

Nové Město (or New Town) was founded in 1348 by King Charles IV to create extra market space and to house the increasing number of craftspeople coming to Prague.The area is bigger than Malá Strana, Hradčany, and Staré Město combined, but it's far less important in terms of history and architecture. Today it is the business hub of the city, which is concentrated around Zlaty kříž—the "golden cross" formed by Václavské náměstí (Wenceslas Square), Na příkopy, and Narodní třída, and where you will find shops, cinemas, restaurants, and hotels. At the north end of Václavské náměstí is an underground metro station with links to all points of the "golden cross."

HOTELS

(11) ANDANTE HOTEL
Ve Smečkách 4, Prague 1
32 rooms, all with shower or bath and toilet

TELEPHONE AND FAX
2221 1616-8, 2221 0584-5, 9622 2060-1

EMAIL
andante@netforce.cz

INTERNET
www.andante.cz

The Andante Hotel comes wrapped in the aura of faceless modernism that is the modus operandi for many newer hotels, which are opening at a breakneck speed today in Prague. That is not to say it is not perfectly acceptable. It is that and more; it just doesn't ooze with character or reminders of the beautiful city of Prague. So, what can Cheap Sleepers expect? Thirty-two identically fitted rooms, each with a desk and wardrobe space, a comfortable bed with white duvet covers, and an elfin bathroom with one narrow shelf, a mirror, and an enclosed stall shower. There is a basement restaurant and bar with upholstered, mirrored booths where both lunch and dinner are served. The stripped down lobby offers black oversized leatherette sofas and a glass showcase of Czech crystal for sale—which would only come in handy if for some reason you could not fit in an hour or two of shopping near Wenceslas Square.

ENGLISH SPOKEN Yes

FACILITIES AND SERVICES Direct-dial phone, lift, minibar, restaurant, satellite TV, office safe, three offices with secretarial and interpretation services on request

NEAREST TOURIST ATTRACTIONS Wenceslas Square

METRO
A or C, Muzeum

CREDIT CARDS
AE, DC, MC, V

RATES
Rates are in German marks; single 171–186DM, double 208DM, triple 268DM, suite 275 DM; extra bed 45DM; children up to age 6 are free, age 7 to 12 are half price; lower off-season rates

BREAKFAST
Buffet included

(12) HOTEL ATLANTIC
Na Poříčí 9, Prague 1
60 rooms, all with shower and toilet

Those demanding Hollywood glamour better forget this one. Before the Velvet Revolution, visitors to Prague would have been glad to find it. But now, frozen in its socialist past with drab browns, ugly lamps, and glaring globe light fixtures on the ceiling, it serves as a reminder of how far Prague hotel accommodations have come in the past few years. In spite of this, it does have some value. It is a clean, middle-of-the-road choice for those who want to be close to the business hub of the city. It has a restaurant and even billiards, if by some rare chance you run out of things to do in Prague. I would avoid Room 111, which is large but on the back with a view of a pigeon post and a peeling building. No. 110 has a stall shower but no curtain, slightly better closet space, and a foam pad atop the mattress.

ENGLISH SPOKEN Yes

FACILITIES AND SERVICES Bar, billiards, direct-dial phone, hair dryer, lift, some minibars, three free parking places, restaurant, satellite TV, office safe

NEAREST TOURIST ATTRACTIONS Good shopping, can walk to Staré Mesto, Wenceslas Square

TELEPHONE
2481 1084

FAX
2481 2378

METRO
B, Náměstí Republiky

CREDIT CARDS
AE, DC, MC, V

RATES
Single 3,300–3,700Kč, double 4,200Kč, triple 5,200Kč; lower off-season rates

BREAKFAST
Buffet included

(13) HOTEL AXA
Na Poříčí 40, Prague 1
131 rooms, all with shower and toilet

TELEPHONE
2481 2580

FAX
2421 4489

EMAIL
axapraha@mbox.vol.cz

METRO
B, Náměstí Republiky

CREDIT CARDS
AE, DC, MC, V

RATES
Single 2,400–3,300Kč, double 3,500Kč; extra bed 670Kč; dog or cat 230Kč; health club 200Kč per day; pool 60Kč per hour; sauna 200Kč per hour; massages 5Kč per minute; lower off-season and group rates

BREAKFAST
Buffet included

The popular Axa wins the Cheap Sleeps award for sheer volume of facilities not found elsewhere in Prague hotels. A trip to the health club, a few laps in the twenty-five-meter pool heated to 26 degrees centigrade, and a relaxing massage is tough to beat for relaxing after a long day hiking the tourist trails. Don't worry about ruining your hair in the process—the hotel hairdresser can put you back together in no time. The hotel is almost completely redone, but for best success, be sure to specify that you want a newly renovated room, one of the two-bedroom suites, or if you want a view, one of the four rooms on the sixth floor, which look toward Prague Castle. Another reason for being on this floor is to avoid the worst of the trolley bell and street noises below.

ENGLISH SPOKEN Yes

FACILITIES AND SERVICES Bar, direct-dial phone, lift, some minibars, restaurant for lunch, satellite TV, office safe, health club with pool, sauna, solarium, and massages

NEAREST TOURIST ATTRACTIONS Old Town, Wenceslas Square

(14) HOTEL HARMONY
Na Poříčí 31, Prague 1
60 rooms, all with shower and toilet

TELEPHONE
232 0016

FAX
231 0009

METRO
B, Náměstí Republiky

CREDIT CARDS
AE, DC, MC, V

RATES
Single 2,600Kč, double 3,400–3,600Kč, suite 3,800Kč; lower off-season rates

BREAKFAST
Continental included

The "harmony" in the Hotel Harmony must be that its rather drab commercial location matches its sterile rooms, where frills are few. After a fast face-lift in the early nineties, it now offers clean, economical rooms done in modern blond furniture with hanging space either in armoires or open closets. All have a luggage area and five are fitted for handicapped guests. Bathrooms are simple and shower curtains in the minority. Rooms on the front suffer from noise from the trams running along Na poříčí.

ENGLISH SPOKEN Yes

FACILITIES AND SERVICES Direct-dial phone, hair dryer available, lift, minibar in suites, parking 450Kč per day, restaurant, cable TV, office safe

NEAREST TOURIST ATTRACTIONS One underground stop to Wenceslas Square and Old Town

(15) HOTEL OPERA
Těšnov 13, Prague 1
64 rooms, all with shower and toilet

The neo-Renaissance peppermint pink facade of the Hotel Opera proves once again that you can't judge a book by its cover. You would think the interior would reflect its ornate exterior, but evidently the two main reconstructions in the 1930s and finally in mid-1990 erased all vestiges of character from the rooms. Now they are basic yet dependably respectable, clean places to hang your hat during a stay in Prague. As hotels go in a city with the rapid redevelopment Prague is now experiencing, that can be taken as a compliment.

Mucha prints decorate the walls of Room 107, which is large enough to accommodate a pink velvet-covered daybed, a couple of armchairs, and a coffeetable. The new bathroom is exceptional: it has good light, a large mirror, and a deep tub with a hand-held shower above. On the same floor is No. 106, a corner room with a pair of armchairs facing the windows, a small louvered armoire with shelves, and a big bathroom. While the hotel is not in a tourist hot spot, the transportation on both the underground and trams is excellent. Another benefit is the efficient, uniform-clad management team, which operates from the reception desk across from a tiny lobby area. They state that their main aim is to offer a high quality of service, and they ask, "Dear guests of the Hotel Opera, please, consider this effort." Many have and are satisfied.

ENGLISH SPOKEN Yes

FACILITIES AND SERVICES Bar, conference room, direct-dial phone, hair dryer, lift, minibar, restaurant, satellite TV, office safe (100Kč per stay)

NEAREST TOURIST ATTRACTIONS Vltava River

TELEPHONE
231 56 09

FAX
231 14 77

METRO
C, Florenc, or Tram Nos. 3 or 8 (which stop at the door)

CREDIT CARDS
AE, DC, MC, V

RATES
Single 3,500Kč, double 3,850Kč, suite 6,200Kč; lower off-season rates

BREAKFAST
Buffet included

(16) HOTEL 16 U SV. KATEŘINY
Kateřinská 16, Prague 2
16 rooms, all with shower and toilet

A stay at the Hotel 16 U sv. Kateřiny (St. Catherine) puts Cheap Sleepers in Prague about a ten- or fifteen-minute walk away from Wenceslas Square. Closer to home is the Botanical Garden, a peaceful green oasis in midcity. The appealing hotel is built around a glass-enclosed atrium. On exhibit in the breakfast area, and in many of the rooms, is a collection of drawings done by the architect who designed the hotel, and in the small

TELEPHONE
29 53 29, 29 13 13

FAX
29 39 56

METRO
C, I. P. Pavlova, or B, Karlovo náměstí

CREDIT CARDS
MC, V

RATES
Single 2,200Kč, double
2,900Kč, junior suite 3,300–
3,900Kč; lower off-season rates

BREAKFAST
Continental included

lobby is an interesting showcase with some of the better objects for sale from the bazaar junk store next door. Don't laugh . . . sometimes there are real treasures to be found in these shops. Padded leatherette doors lead to clean, well-constructed bedrooms with built-ins that allow for more living space. Closets are good, and so are the bathrooms. Many of the rooms have a sitting area and separate bedroom with either a double bed or twins, and several bathrooms are fitted for the handicapped.

ENGLISH SPOKEN Yes

FACILITIES AND SERVICES Bar, direct-dial phone, hair dryer, no elevator (three floors), minibar, two street parking spaces, satellite TV, room and office safe

NEAREST TOURIST ATTRACTIONS Botanical garden, easy walk to Vltava River, two stops to Wenceslas Square

(17) PENSION STANDARD
Rašínovo nábřeží 38, Prague 2
11 rooms, all with shower and toilet

TELEPHONE
29 87 97, 29 76 13

FAX
29 87 97

EMAIL
standard@alphanet.cz

INTERNET
www.alphanet.cz/~standard

METRO
B, Karlovo náměstí, or Tram
Nos. 3 or 17

CREDIT CARDS
None

RATES
Single 2,000Kč, double
2,600Kč; suites: single
2,700Kč, double 3,150Kč,
triple 3,700Kč; extra bed
700Kč; children under age 7
are free; half board 160Kč per
person, full board 320Kč per
person; lower off-season rates

BREAKFAST
Buffet included

At the Pension Standard you can count on just what the name implies . . . clean, unexciting, standard rooms geared to Czech tourists in from the provinces. Its location on the banks of the Vltava River, between the National Theater and Vyšehrad, means that public transportation or a long walk is required to get to the heart of Prague's main sites. The restaurant, which offers either full- or half-board meals in addition to à la carte, may be a boon to those not willing to venture far for lunch or dinner. The rooms lack style, but they are at least clean, and all have a sofa bed in case you want to add an extra person for a minimal supplement. There are only two losers. Number 8, a double on the ground floor, has a depressing view of a back alley of a private home. Only the bathroom passes muster, in that it has an enclosed stall shower. In No. 9 the window is covered with bars and chicken wire and looks out onto the same gloomy alley. Other than these, the rest of the hotel's rooms won't invite too many complaints.

ENGLISH SPOKEN Yes

FACILITIES AND SERVICES Direct-dial phone, hair dryer available, lift, minibar in suites, parking 140Kč per day, restaurant, satellite TV

NEAREST TOURIST ATTRACTIONS Vltava River, but otherwise must use public transportation

SMÍCHOV

Smíchov is Prague's second-oldest suburb, and now it is a rather dull district of unattractive factories. In its heyday, there were some beautiful villas here, most notably Bertramka, which was owned by the composer and pianist František Xaver Dušek and his wife, Josefína, a well-known singer. The couple were friends of Mozart, who during his four trips to Prague stayed at Bertramka and composed some of his works here. In the fifties, the building was restored and turned into the W. A. Mozart and Dušek Museum.

HOTELS

(18) ADMIRÁL BOTEL
Hořejší nábřeží, Prague 5 (20 meters from Palackého bridge)
84 rooms, all with shower and toilet

If you are attracted by the romantic atmosphere of sleeping, eating, and enjoying yourself on a ship, even if that ship never sails from port, then perhaps a stay at a Prague botel is for you. These botels, which are floating hotels anchored on the Vltava River, came into being in the sixties when local officials needed to find an inexpensive way to alleviate the lack of acceptable hotel rooms. For many years the need was so great that some were booked a year in advance. The botels are not actual ships, as they were built especially for this purpose. Where ships have engines, botels have furnace rooms that use natural gas to heat the rooms, and their staffs are not required to have any type of maritime experience. Even though they cannot sail, they are still considered to be vessels because they float and guests enter on a bridged walkway. The life expectancy of a botel is about thirty-five years, and when they are gone, that will signal the end of this hotel alternative in Prague—since the city government is not going to allow new botels once the existing ones are declared obsolete.

There are five botels in Prague. The Admirál is not only the most centrally located but in the best condition. The ship shape, compact quarters are on two levels, with the best ones being those with a river view. They all have

TELEPHONE
5732 1302

FAX
54 96 16

METRO
B, Andel

CREDIT CARDS
AE, MC, V

RATES
Rates in U.S. dollars; single $75, double $85; lower off-season rates

BREAKFAST
Buffet included

two beds, decent storage, and either a sea-green or blue-and-red color scheme, and river-view rooms cost the same as those facing the shore. There is a restaurant and popular night club plus a summer terrace deck, which is one of the loveliest places in Prague to spend a warm afternoon.

ENGLISH SPOKEN Yes

FACILITIES AND SERVICES Bar, direct-dial phone, no elevator (but not necessary), free parking, restaurant, night club, office safe 50Kč per day

NEAREST TOURIST ATTRACTIONS Twenty- to thirty-minute walk to Malá Strana and Charles Bridge, good public transportation connections

(19) HOTEL JULIÁN
Elišky Peškové 11, Prague 5
31 rooms, all with shower or bath and toilet, one suite with a kitchen

TELEPHONE
5731 1150, 5731 1144-46

FAX
5731 1149, 5731 1147, 54 75 25

EMAIL
casjul@vol.cz

METRO
B, Andel

RATES
Single 2,500Kč, double 2,900Kč, suite (1–2 persons) 3,500Kč; extra bed 800Kč; lower off-season rates

BREAKFAST
Buffet included

Cheap Sleepers in Prague like the Hotel Julián for a variety of reasons. Although it is away from the mainstream tourist centers, it is well-connected via public transportation, and if you don't mind a bracing walk, it is about equidistant from Malá Strana and the National Theater. The Art Nouveau–style building underwent remodeling in 1993 and now has twenty-nine spotless rooms and two suites, one with a kitchen. The main areas of the hotel are very nice. I like the arched sitting rooms: one is casually done in wicker and the other is a library with a wall of books, fireplace, and comfortable chairs that invite lingering over the daily papers. In the breakfast room some rather unusual artwork complements the black furniture with gray-blue upholstery. To get to your room, either take the royal red velvet padded lift or sprint up the granite stairway with a wrought-iron and wood banister.

When you arrive, you will find bright pink sheets on your bed and a piece of candy on your pillow. The two suites are good picks for those who want more living space. No. 403 on the front of the hotel is a good bet, thanks to three skylight windows in the sitting room, a five-drawer dresser, and a wall of wardrobes. Accent pieces include an odd barber-type light and three live trees. If you need a kitchen, request No. 402, which can sleep up to six people. Don't worry if you do not have a suite, as the hotel rooms won't disappoint. They have the illusion of more space because most have an entry hall or a little sitting area with a chair. Even the backside views are nice, especially when the trees are in bloom. Try No. 206, a big, bright white expanse done in blue-grays. The four-drawer chest and excellent closet provide welcome unpacking space. Another top contender is No. 208; it has a bathroom outfitted for the handicapped that includes grab bars, a pull-down seat in the shower, and a lighted magnifying mirror. Those in Prague for business will appreciate this hotel: you can rent a PC-equipped office with Internet access, a printer, and a fax machine, and you can arrange for a conference for up to twenty-five people. Finally, there is parking for eight cars in an enclosed courtyard at the back of the hotel.

ENGLISH SPOKEN Yes

FACILITIES AND SERVICES Air-conditioning in some rooms, bar, conference room, direct-dial phone, hair dryer, lift, parking 200Kč per day, satellite TV, office safe, room safe 180Kč per day, PC rental 100Kč per hour, nonsmoking rooms, handicapped-accessible rooms

NEAREST TOURIST ATTRACTIONS Ten- or twenty-minute walk to Malá Strana or the National Theater

STARÉ MĚSTO (OLD TOWN) _____

The Old Town of Prague is one of the most interesting quarters in the city. Historical records regarding the city's oldest district, and its beautiful centerpiece Old Town Square (Staroměstské náměstí), go back to the thirteenth century and the reign of Wenceslas I. The focus of the lively square is the Astronomical Clock set in the facade of the Town Hall Tower. The clock dates from 1410, and around its edge are the names of all the saints for every day of the year. On the hour, every hour, crowds gather to watch the ritualistic dance of the figures next to the main clock and to receive solemn benediction from the twelve apostles as they file past the two door openings at the top. Even though the large Jewish Quarter and the adjoining streets of Old Town were subjected to insensitive changes in the nineteenth and twentieth centuries, when many of the ancient buildings were replaced with Art Nouveau styles, many of the historically valuable buildings have been rebuilt or restored to their former glory.

The majestic Charles Bridge (Karlův most), stretching over the Vltava River, is the oldest bridge in Prague, dating back to 1157, and ranks as the greatest tourist attraction in the city. It is part of the Royal Route, leading from the Old Town, through Malá Strana, and up to Hradčany and Prague Castle. The bridge is 516 meters long, 10 meters wide, rests on sixteen piers, and is built of sandstone blocks. Standing on the bridge is an open-air gallery of thirty sculptures and groups of statues.

HOTELS

OTHER OPTIONS

Apartment Rentals and Residence Hotels

Note: A dollar sign ($) indicates a Big Splurge.

(20) BETLEM CLUB PRAHA
Betlémské náměstí 9, Prague 1
22 rooms, all with shower or bath and toilet

TELEPHONE
2421 6872

FAX
2421 8054

METRO
B, Národní třída

CREDIT CARDS
None

RATES
Single 2,600Kč, double 3,400Kč, suite 3800Kč; lower off-season rates

BREAKFAST
Buffet included

What a location! Right across the street from the Bethlehem Chapel where Jan Hus, who was one of the greatest theological reformers, delivered his antipapal sermons, and as a result was burned at the stake in 1415. Today, the very plain structure is one of the must-sees for many Prague visitors. You would think a hotel so close to this landmark would somehow reflect something of the historical significance of its surroundings. Wrong. The Betlem Club Praha is as low on atmosphere as it is on space. The glass lift lets you see the interior of the hotel, but if it is taking you to rooms on the third floor, watch out. These pigeon roosts have low ceilings and tiny windows that match the tiny TVs, tiny leather stools, tiny closets, and of course, the tiny bathrooms. For enduring these lilliputian quarters, guests are rewarded with views of the Bethlehem Chapel. People have a love/hate relationship with Room 401. The access to it requires scaling a steep ladder into a miniature room with a creaking floor. Its redeeming feature is the view of the chapel across the street. What is to recommend here? Certainly No. 101, even though it is done in shining black laminated plastic and trimmed in brass with seating on two backless tufted red velvet stools. The room is large enough, closet space is okay, and in the bathroom you have a great trio: shower, tub, and shower curtain. To top it off there is a view.

ENGLISH SPOKEN Yes

FACILITIES AND SERVICES Direct-dial phone, hair dryer, lift, minibar, satellite TV, office safe

NEAREST TOURIST ATTRACTIONS Old Town, across the street from the Bethlehem Chapel

(21) CLOISTER INN/PENSION UNITAS
Bartolomějská 9, Prague 1
Cloister Inn: **25 rooms, all with private facilities**
Pension Unitas: **34 rooms, no private facilities**

Card-carrying Cheap Sleepers in Prague will have a tough time beating the value for money at either the Cloister Inn or the Pension Unitas, but first, some interesting historical details about the property's dramatic background are in order. The Cloister Inn sits on medieval convent grounds founded in the Middle Ages by the Jesuits. Since 1856 it has been occupied off and on by the Grey Sisters of St. Francis. On the cloister grounds is the Church of St. Bartholomew, which was where Beethoven performed the only concert he gave in Prague. After 1948, the cloister became an interrogation center and residental prison for the Czechoslovakian secret police (the STB, the equivalent of the KGB and CIA), who used the chapel for a shooting range. The most famous repeat "guest" was Václav Havel, who was interred here three times for a total of twenty-seven months. His last imprisonment was in August 1989, only two months before he led the Velvet Revolution, which drove the Communists out of Czechoslovakia. The buildings were returned to the Sisters soon after, and since then all the buildings have undergone restoration. In 1992 the Prince of Wales came to the Cloister Inn to see cell P6, where his friend Havel had been incarcerated.

Today, the Cloister Inn and Pension Unitas are run simultaneously, but they offer quite different accommodations. The rooms in both are simple, spotless, quiet, and nonsmoking. The Cloister Inn, aimed toward independent travelers, has twenty-five well-proportioned

TELEPHONE
23 24 833, 23 27 700

FAX
23 27 709

EMAIL
jvn@cloister-inn.cz

INTERNET
www.cloister-inn.cz

METRO
B, Národní třída

CREDIT CARDS
Cloister Inn: AE, MC, V
Pension Unitas: None, cash only

RATES
All rates are in U.S. dollars.
Cloister Inn: single $85, double $100, triple $115, children under age 6 are free
Pension Unitas: single $34, double $35, triple $50, quad $60, five people $70, six people $80, children under age 6 are free

BREAKFAST
Buffet included for both

accommodations, all with private bathrooms. Room 103 is an attractive choice with a sofa that makes into a bed; it also has a desk, two windows, plenty of shelf, drawer, and luggage space, and a white tiled bathroom with a stall shower. The Pension Unitas is geared toward student groups and anyone else on a budget. It has thirty-four neatly furnished rooms, all with separate male and female hall toilets and bathing facilities. In addition to its no-smoking policy, no liquor is allowed—but you can bring your dog, provided it has the proper vaccination certificate.

ENGLISH SPOKEN Yes

FACILITIES AND SERVICES *Cloister Inn:* Direct-dial phone, hair dryer available, lift, laundry service, luggage room, parking 200Kč per day, TV, room safe, secretarial services, dogs allowed with valid international vaccination certificate. *Pension Unitas:* Parking 200Kč per day, office safe, dogs allowed with valid international vaccination certificate, rooms are all nonsmoking and alcohol is forbidden

NEAREST TOURIST ATTRACTIONS Old Town, Jewish Quarter, Charles Bridge

(22) HOTEL KORUNA
Opatovická 16, Prague 1
22 rooms, all with shower or bath and toilet

TELEPHONE
2491 5174

FAX
29 24 92

METRO
B, Národní třída or Karlovo náměstí

CREDIT CARDS
MC, V

RATES
Single 1,650Kč, double 2,850 Kč, triple 3,600Kč, suite 5,000Kč; lower off-season rates

BREAKFAST
Buffet included

No, this is not my first choice, or even my second, but for a sturdy, old-fashioned Cheap Sleep close to Old Town, this bears considering. The dated rooms are testimony to pre–Velvet Revolution days when socialistic decorators favored brown, beige, and orange color schemes and chrome-trimmed black leather furniture. Yes, it does need redoing, but it is a clean, safe spot to sleep for a few nights if cost is your main concern. You can brush up on your Czech by watching the Czech-only channels on your room television, and hopefully you will sleep soundly and warmly on the simple mattress under a floral-covered duvet.

ENGLISH SPOKEN Yes

FACILITIES AND SERVICES Direct-dial phone, lift, TV, office safe

NEAREST TOURIST ATTRACTIONS Vltava River, Old Town

(23) HOTEL MERAN
Václavské náměstí 27, Prague 1
18 rooms, all with shower or bath and toilet

The Meran is a Cheap Sleep find smack in the middle of the most famous street in Prague, Václavské náměstí, better known as Wenceslas Square. This location suggests nonstop noise, but Václavské náměstí is restricted to most vehicular traffic, so motor noise and congestion is at a minimum. However, there is no getting around the waves of people who ply both sides of this famous avenue almost twenty-four hours a day. The Meran's next door neighbor is the venerable Evropa, Prague's famous Art Nouveau hotel, which unfortunately, as a result of severe deferred maintenance, offers seriously faded, tattered, and crumbling accommodations to the uninformed. However, if you love Art Nouveau, please wander through the common areas of the Evropa, which are filled with massive vases, period furnishings, graceful arches, mirrors, and scattered palms, all under a vast skylight.

When you first arrive at the Meran, don't be turned off by the plain white lobby, which consists of the reception desk and a drink machine. It is the rooms that count, and they are way above average, especially those on the fifth floor. Solo voyagers are assigned No. 501, a small single that consists of a bed, a table with three cubby holes and a drawer, a wardrobe in the entry, a newer bath with a stall shower and toiletries, and a rooftop view. Room 503 houses up to three and faces Václavské náměstí, but you are high enough to escape most street noise. No. 502, with a cocoa brown color theme, is a good double because it has two armchairs and plenty of light from the two windows, plus a floor lamp and bedside lights. The bathroom provides a tub and plenty of towels. The breakfast buffet is served in a pleasant streetside room with banquette seating.

ENGLISH SPOKEN Yes

FACILITIES AND SERVICES Direct-dial phone, hair dryer available, lift, office safe

NEAREST TOURIST ATTRACTIONS Right on Wenceslas Square, easy walking distance to Old Town, excellent public transportation

TELEPHONE
2423 8440

FAX
2423 0411

METRO
A or B, Můstek; A or C, Muzeum

CREDIT CARDS
AE, DC, MC, V

RATES
Single 2,700Kč, double 4,000Kč, triple 4,400Kč; lower off-season rates

BREAKFAST
Buffet included

(24) HOTEL U KLENOTNÍKA
Rytířská 3, Prague 1
10 rooms, all with shower and toilet

TELEPHONE
2421 1699

FAX
26 17 82

METRO
A or B, Můstek

CREDIT CARDS
AE, MC, V

RATES
Single 2,500–3,100Kč, 100Kč extra on state holidays; double 3,600Kč, triple 4,300Kč; lower off-season rates

BREAKFAST
Buffet included

It would be difficult to imagine a more central location for a visitor in Prague. Within an interesting five- or ten-minute walk from the front door of the U Klenotníka (At the Jeweller's) is Old Town and Wenceslas Squares. At the end of the street is the Stavovské divaldo (Theatre of the Estates), where Mozart's Don Giovanni was premiered in 1787. A short stroll from the back of the hotel leads to a street market and the Prague Stock Exchange on Na můstku. The hotel was an old burgher house, and the basement foundations date from the eleventh century. It has since been rebuilt several times and had many occupants. From 1900 to 1948, it was a famous jeweller's shop, thus the name of the present hotel. The rooms are very clean and acceptable for the price. They have white walls, inexpensive laminated furniture, and industrial-strength mottled brown carpets. Wardrobe and storage space tends to be limited. An attractive restaurant with a painted ceiling seems to be a local drawing card, especially during the noon hour. Displayed throughout the common areas of the hotel are paintings by a local artist. Depending on your taste and perspective, they are either avant-garde or downright wierd. It's your call.

ENGLISH SPOKEN Yes

FACILITIES AND SERVICES Air-conditioning in two rooms (no extra charge), bar, direct-dial phone, hair dryer, no elevator (three floors), minibar, restaurant, satellite TV, office safe 50Kč per day

NEAREST TOURIST ATTRACTIONS All of Old Town, Wenceslas Square, Charles Bridge

(25) HOTEL U ZLATÉHO STROMU
Karlova 6, Prague 1
23 rooms, all with shower or bath and toilet

TELEPHONE
2422 1385, 26 51 03

FAX
2422 1385

METRO
A, Staroměstská

CREDIT CARDS
AE, DC, MC, V

RATES
Single 3,800Kč, double 4,000Kč, suite 6,000Kč; extra bed 500Kč; lower off-season rates

From here you can walk to almost everything, and shoppers will be almost dizzy from the hundreds of boutiques that line this famous stretch of real estate leading from Malá Strana across the Charles Bridge to Old Town. Rustic beams and unfinished pine furniture are the significant characteristics of rooms at U Zlatého Stromu (At the Golden Tree). The black-and-white tiled bathrooms are modern and storage space is ample. Six of the rooms can be joined to form minisuites. Room 11, which is on the back side with a view to the courtyard and other rooms, can be made up as either a twin or a double. No. 12 is definitely a twin room, with the beds sitting toe-to-toe along one wall and the rest of the furniture resting against the opposite wall. Breakfast is served in the antique- and semi-antique-filled hotel dining room, which has booth seating.

ENGLISH SPOKEN Yes

FACILITIES AND SERVICES Bar, direct-dial phone, no elevator, minibar, restaurant, satellite TV, room safe

NEAREST TOURIST ATTRACTIONS Old Town, Wenceslas Square, Charles Bridge, Malá Strana

(26) PENZION U ČERVENÉ BOTY $
Karlova 5, Prague 1
4 suites, all with shower, bath, and toilet

There is only one word for the four-suite Penzion U Červené Boty: *fabulous*. First there is the location, right in the historical center of Prague's Old Town and steps away from the Charles Bridge, which leads to one of the most beautiful and picturesque parts of the city, Malá Strana. The building dates from the seventeenth century and was renovated in 1996 to form this truly wonderful accommodation, which discerning guests would be happy to find anywhere, but especially in Prague, where quick and easy modernism often replaces charm and character.

I would be happy to check in for a long stay in any of the four individually designed suites, all luxuriously furnished with assorted traditional Czech antiques and period pieces. Guests staying in Suite 2 have a stone-paved entryway with a beamed ceiling. On the left the large bedroom has an antique twin bed set with matching marble-topped side tables and cupboard. There is no view, but it really doesn't seem to matter. The bathroom . . . ah, yes, it is to die for—a big corner tub, a marble sink with shelf and drawer space, mirrors galore, and a heated towel rack. Next to the bedroom is the sitting room with three windows, a setee and matching chairs, a lovely painting of old Prague, an antique wall clock, a working desk, and a beautiful gray marble-topped sideboard. Your breakfast will be served to you here, or you can go downstairs and have it in the wine cellar. Suite 3 has the same bedroom layout and the same great bathroom as No. 2, but the sitting room has a slightly more contemporary feel thanks to the style of the sofa and

BREAKFAST
Continental included

TELEPHONE
9003 2800

FAX
9003 2802

METRO
A, Staroměstská

CREDIT CARDS
AE, MC, V

RATES
From 8,000Kč, depending on size of suite and number of guests; much lower rates for extended stays and during the off-season

BREAKFAST
Continental included

chairs. Suite 4 is the largest and is definitely Art Deco. The bathroom here is just as nice as all the others, only smaller, and the slanted roof makes the sitting room more intimate. This is a good suite to consider if you are traveling with children—they won't at all mind the adventure of climbing the stairs to the second bedroom with a skylight view of Prague rooftops.

ENGLISH SPOKEN Yes

FACILITIES AND SERVICES Direct-dial phones with optional fax hookups, hair dryer, laundry service, lift, minibar, office safe, radio, satellite TV, terry robes, wine cellar

NEAREST TOURIST ATTRACTIONS Old Town, Charles Bridge, Malá Strana

VINOHRADY _____

Vinohrady takes its name from the extensive vineyards that flourished here from the time of Charles IV. There is a large park here, but not much else to entice a tourist bent on living in the midst of Prague's must-do sightseeing.

HOTELS

OTHER OPTIONS

Apartment Rentals and Residence Hotels

(28) HOTEL ABRI

Jana Masaryka 36, Prague 2
26 rooms, all with shower and toilet

TELEPHONE
2423 3332, 2423 2451, 2423 7328, 2423 8067

FAX
2425 4240

METRO
A, Náměstí míru

CREDIT CARDS
AE, MC, V

The plain-Jane rooms couldn't possible offend anyone with their lookalike blond furniture and tiled baths. The luggage rack, flat work space, and decent closets are all standard issue here. Two rooms, Nos. 109 and 209, are equipped for the handicapped. Some guests like being able to have either lunch or dinner in the hotel dining room, which is open daily until 9:30 P.M. The neighborhood is quite central, but it's quiet and provides a look at what slightly more affluent Prague citizens have at their disposal. The management team stresses that their sole objective is to make their guests' visit to Prague as comfortable and as pleasant as possible. From what I observed, they have succeeded—and given the "what do we care" attitude of some of Prague's other hotel managers and reception crews, this is saying a great deal for the Abri.

ENGLISH SPOKEN Yes

FACILITIES AND SERVICES Direct-dial phone, hair dryer available, lift, free parking, restaurant, TV, office safe, two rooms handicapped accessible

NEAREST TOURIST ATTRACTIONS Vinohrady Park, a fifteen- to twenty-minute walk to Wenceslas Square

RATES
Rates are quoted in German marks, payment expected in Czech currency; single 160DM, double 187DM, triple 210DM; half pension 12–16DM per person, per meal; children under 3 are free (but no bed provided!), children age 3 to 12 are half of single room rate; lower off-season rates

BREAKFAST
Continental included

(29) HOTEL CITY/PENSION CITY
Belgická 10, at Záhřebská 16, Prague 2
19 rooms, 7 with shower and toilet, 12 with no private facilities

Hotel City/Pension City wears two hats at the same time. Hotel City is the upmarket side and is made up of seven rooms, all with private facilities. Die-hard Cheap Sleepers will forgo this side and live in Pension City. Big spenders will go for No. 23 at Hotel City. It is a bright orange corner room with two extra, red sofa beds and laminated furniture à la K-Mart. There is a big table, two chairs, a dresser, and a nonfunctioning kitchen. Four Cheap Sleepers could make do in Nos. 24A and 24B on the Pension City side, where the bathroom is shared between the two rooms. This is a step up from a similar situation I had to endure in the early 1980s in Bánská Bystrica—where the only partition separating my room from my neighbor (whom I did not know) and our shared bathroom was a plastic shower curtain.

ENGLISH SPOKEN Yes

FACILITIES AND SERVICES Direct-dial phone by special order (40Kč per day), lift, TV 60Kč per day, office safe

NEAREST TOURIST ATTRACTIONS One underground stop from Wenceslas Square

TELEPHONE
69 11 334

FAX
69 11 334, 69 10 977

METRO
A, Náměstí miru

CREDIT CARDS
AE, MC, V (5% discount if pay in cash)

RATES
Single 1,110–1,580Kč, double 1,480–2,180Kč, triple 1,730–2,447Kč, quad 1,910–2,625Kč; lower off-season rates

BREAKFAST
Buffet included

(30) HOTEL LUNÍK
Londynská 50, Prague 2
35 rooms, all with showers and toilets

Members of the same family have owned this hotel since 1924. Until 1967 it was known as Hotel Skřivan, but when the hotel was redone in 1992, it was changed

TELEPHONE
2425 3974

FAX
2425 3986

METRO
A, Náměstí míru

CREDIT CARDS
None

RATES
Single 1,800Kč, double 2,500Kč, triple 3000Kč; lower off-season rates

BREAKFAST
Continental included

to the Luník, after the granddaughter who now runs it. Framed prints of the hotel in its early days tell an interesting story, and so does the collection of dining room menus dating from 1926. Just look at those seemingly philanthropic meal prices and tell me inflation has not gone rampant! The rooms are small, but the bottom line is that they are clean and the price tags affordable. Rooms in the back are quiet and have better light. No. 301, overlooking the garden next door, has a small bathroom with a corner shower and a funny pull-down toilet. The room itself has twin beds, a chair, and a two-seat daybed, which can be made into a third bed. Next door is No. 302, a twin on the front. This room suffers from poor lighting and no work space. The single rooms are some of the best around, and so is the attractive terrace in front of the hotel, where guests are encouraged to gather for refreshments in the summer.

NOTE: Reservations are accepted no more than six weeks ahead of arrival.

ENGLISH SPOKEN Yes

FACILITIES AND SERVICES Bar, direct-dial phones, hair dryer available, lift, TV in bar only, office safe

NEAREST TOURIST ATTRACTIONS Vinohrady Park, ten- to fifteen-minute walk to Wenceslas Square

(31) HOTEL OLEA
Americká 16, Prague 2
7 rooms, all with shower or bath and toilet

TELEPHONE AND FAX
69 10 050

METRO
A, Náměstí míru

CREDIT CARDS
AE, DC, MC, V

RATES
Single 1,750Kč, double 2,420Kč, triple 2,730Kč, quad 3,320Kč

BREAKFAST
Continental included, at Cafe Pink Floyd next door

Forget charm, forget location, and think Cheap Sleeps with extra perks. At the Hotel Olea there are two styles of rooms. If you wind up in Nos. 1, 3, 5, or 7, you will have a sitting room with a corner kitchen area (no stove) and a double bedroom with an extra chair that doubles as a fold-out bed in a pinch. The hanging space is acceptable, and so is the work area if you need to spread out the contents of your briefcase. There is a separate toilet and stall shower off the entry hall. Those Cheap Sleepers landing in Nos. 2, 4, or 6 also have a sitting room and plenty of storage space, plus an extra bedroom and a small cooking area. Of these three rooms, I like No. 6 because you don't have to walk through one room to get to another, or to the bathroom, which is large enough for several aerobic enthusiasts to do their daily workouts. The hotel has no dining room, so in the morning guests go next door to Cafe Pink Floyd; in the summer guests are served in the adjacent garden.

ENGLISH SPOKEN Yes

FACILITIES AND SERVICES Direct-dial phone, lift, minibar, cable TV, office safe, automatic tea and coffee makers in the rooms, corner kitchen area (only No. 6 has stove)

NEAREST TOURIST ATTRACTIONS None, must use public transportation

ŽIŽKOV

Žižkov, which is east of the historic town center, has very little to offer a Prague tourist, unless you are interested in the National Memorial, the final resting place of the leading representatives of the Czech working class and of unknown soldiers from various Czech battlefields.

HOTELS
(33) Hotel Olšanka   **65**

(33) HOTEL OLŠANKA
Táboritská 23, Prague 3
240 rooms, all with shower or bath and toilet

For a monolithic monument to some of the worst Soviet-influenced architecture in Prague, you need look no further than this 240-room cement monstrosity, which is, amazingly, only four years old and located beyond the tourist fringes of the city. Not a very enthusiastic opening remark, is it? Quite frankly, unless you are one of those travelers for whom a fitness routine is more important than where you sleep, I don't recommend it. But for Cheap Sleeping health enthusiasts, this one is for you. Actually, the fitness part of the hotel is not at all bad. In fact, the pool is a quantum leap ahead of the public pool I swam in three times a week during the years I lived in Prague. Of course, I only paid the equivalent of 75¢, and that price included a trip to the steam room after my swim. At the Olšanka, you pay 60Kč per hour, which is less than $2, so it is still a bargain. The indoor tennis court is good, and so is the gym—where you can lift weights to work off all those Czech dumplings and pork stews you have been eating. Afterward, treat yourself to a facial or a trip to the hotel hairdresser.

The hotel is geared to groups who will put up with the cheesy rooms done in those charming Communist colors of orange, beige, and brown. They don't get

TELEPHONE
6709 2111, 6709 2202

FAX
27 33 86, 27 84 34

EMAIL
info@olsanka.cz

INTERNET
www.olsanka.cz

METRO
A, Flora

CREDIT CARDS
AE, MC, V

RATES
Single 2,300Kč, double 3,000Kč, luxury double 3,500Kč, suite 3,100–4,600Kč

assigned to the deluxe rooms, which are a step or two above. While the decor in the better rooms still leaves a lot to be desired, at least the carpets are clean and the bathrooms better. If you don't stay here, but still want to work out, get in some laps in the pool, or play a game of tennis, the fitness center is open to the public from 6 A.M. until 10 P.M. The commute is easy, since the Flora underground stop is close to the hotel.

ENGLISH SPOKEN Yes

FACILITIES AND SERVICES Bar, café and restaurant, direct-dial phone, elevator, parking 200Kč per day, satellite TV, office safe 50Kč per day, and fitness center: pool or aerobics 60Kč per hour, indoor tennis court 350–400Kč per hour, racket rental 50Kč, tennis balls for sale

NEAREST TOURIST ATTRACTIONS None, must use public transportation

Other Options

Accommodation Agencies

Prague has suffered for decades from a lack of adequate housing. This desperate situation has been exacerbated by the tourist explosion that began in the early 1990s after the Velvet Revolution. There simply are not enough hotel rooms at any price, in any category, to meet demand. Some local citizens, seeing an opportunity, have doubled up in their own bedrooms to somehow free a room or two in their own flat, which they then rent to tourists paying hard currency. It can be a win-win situation for the local and the visitor, since the visitor usually pays a very modest price for the priviledge of sharing a flat and facilities with a local. Some visitors have had great luck with this, but others tell horror stories of being ripped off big time by unscrupulous people eager to cash in on unknowing tourists.

Even though the hotel shortage has recently improved to a degree, there are still Czech citizens plying the railroad stations and popular tourist gathering spots selling sleeping space in their homes. If you are interested in this type of accommodation, I think the best approach is to make the arrangements through an accommodation agency. This way you have someone to turn to if something goes wrong. As a general rule of thumb, prices should start around $25 per person, per night, and should not exceed $50. Some of the agencies listed below also have short-term apartment rentals and operate full travel agencies. Below are some pointers to keep in mind if this is your kind of Cheap Sleep in Prague.

Cheap Sleeps Tips for Private Home Accommodations

1. Keep expectations to an absolute minimum.

2. Remember, you are a guest in someone's home, not in a hotel, so unless you are lucky, don't expect new towels or linen changes more than once a week.

3. Chances are great that you will not have a private bathroom; you will be sharing the only one in the home with the host family. Keep your bathing short, and always be neat.

4. Respect your host's privacy. Don't assume you have kitchen priviledges or can stretch out on the couch and read the paper or watch a sporting event on television.

5. Don't be frightened by the outside of the building. Many buildings in the outskirts of the city need repairs, but owners are reluctant to spend the money and red tape is legion. Wait until you see the room before you panic.

6. Pay as little as possible in advance. This way, if you can't stand the place, you are not out too much.

7. Many of the cheaper rooms are located on the edges of Prague and beyond. Try for something located in Prague 1, or close-in in Prague 2.

8. If you have a long commute, consider how far away the nearest transportation stop is, especially if you plan on coming home late at night.

Warning: Don't Let This Happen to You!

One company I contacted, Tom's Travel, is an example of how bad accommodation agencies in Prague can be. This company has little conception of what the normal visitor to Prague would find minimally acceptable in an apartment accommodation. As they showed me their offerings, I can honestly say that I was horrified at what I saw. The flats were positively hideous, done in a rainbow of psychedelic colors guaranteed to incite nightmares. Aside from the garish colors, the furnishings were atrocious, the kitchenware material for the trash can, and the bathrooms dreadful, to say the least. Nevermind that they were located in delapidated buildings either in unsavory neighborhoods or in places where the traffic noise rivaled a pit stop at the Indy 500. If I had to rely on this company for my Prague stay, I would not leave home in the first place. So beware: Always insist on seeing your accommodations before you pay in full, and don't assume or believe anything anyone tells you ahead of time.

AVE
Hlavní nádraží, Wilsonova 8, Prague 2 (main railway station)

AVE opened its doors in 1990, and now it has over one hundred employees operating out of eleven branches in the Czech Republic, making it one of the largest accommodation agencies in the country. With its main office at the Prague railway station and branches at the airport and in central Prague, it is a handy option for those who arrive at the last minute with no reservations. In addition to booking lodgings in private homes, hotels, and hostels, AVE can arrange for short-term apartment rentals; book sightseeing tours, excursions, and packages for independent driving tours; secure tickets for musical and cultural events; and organize special programs for school groups. Should you want to visit other cities in the country, AVE can make your advance reservations. Be patient, though, as service can be inefficient.

BRANCH LOCATIONS Airport Ruzyně, Prague 6; Prague Castle, Pohořelec 9 & 18, Prague 1; Old Town Square 1, Prague 1; Mostecká, Prague 1; Na Příkopě 18, Prague 1; and Americká 16, Prague 2

TELEPHONE
2461 7133, 5731 5191/2
FAX
5731 5192-3, 5731 2983/4
EMAIL
avetours@avetours.anet.cz
INTERNET
www.ave.anet.cz
METRO
C, Hlavní nadraží
HOURS
Main office, daily 9:30 A.M.–11 P.M.; airport and train station from 6 A.M.
CREDIT CARDS
AE, DC, MC, V
ENGLISH SPOKEN
Yes

CITY OF PRAGUE ACCOMMODATION SERVICE
Hašťalská 7, Prague 1

TELEPHONE 23 10 202
FAX 2481 0603
METRO A, Staroměstská
HOURS Daily 9 A.M.–7 P.M.
CREDIT CARDS None
ENGLISH SPOKEN Yes

Known for its good service, this agency can arrange for centrally located, short- or long-term apartment rentals, hotel accommodations, and reasonable car rentals.

TOP TOUR
Rybná 3, Prague 1

Jan Topiarz works hard. He was a pioneer in his field, opening Top Tour only fourteen days after the victory of the Velvet Revolution. He told me in the beginning he worked day and night to get started, and now he has to work nearly as hard to stay a step ahead of the competition. The long hours have paid off. Top Tour is one of the best agencies of its kind in Prague. Their motto is, "Everything is almost free . . . you don't need much

TELEPHONE
23 21 077, 23 14 069
FAX
2481 1400
EMAIL
topia@serverpha.czcom.cz
METRO
B, Náměstí Republiky

HOURS
Daily 9 A.M.–8 P.M. May–Oct; daily 10 A.M.–7 P.M. Nov–April
CREDIT CARDS
None, cash or traveler's checks
ENGLISH SPOKEN
Yes

money at Rybná 3." Though there's some poetic license in this statement, it's true that you will get good value for your money. The company specializes in self-contained, private apartments, as well as rooms in private homes, which are well located in the center of Prague. There are two categories of lodging available: first and second class. The first-class accommodations have private facilities; the second-class ones do not. In addition, Top Tour is a travel agency and can arrange for city sightseeing tours, full- and half-day trips, and other programs.

TRAVELER'S POTPOURRI
6724 West 83rd Street, #303, Overland Park, KS 66204-3955

TELEPHONE
913-341-6828; toll-free 800-273-7133
FAX
913-341-1248
EMAIL
travpor@kcnet.com
INTERNET
www.travelsmarter.com/exciting
CREDIT CARDS
None

Don and Marie Marsolek have a going concern with their Traveler's Potpourri, which specializes in family B&Bs and apartment rentals in Budapest, Prague, Slovenia, and a limited number in Slovakia. Operating out of a suburb of Kansas City, they act as the middle-persons between you and your host family in whatever city you are visiting. Once you contact Traveler's Potpourri and state your needs and wishes, they will get back to you with descriptions, and sometimes photos, of what is available to you under either Plan A or B. With Plan A, they mail you copies of profiles or letters that the host family has sent. Wherever possible, at least five options are offered. Traveler's Potpourri has a $30 fee for this service, and you may ask for further information at any time with no additional payment required. After you have selected your family or apartment, you make your own arrangements with the family. With Plan B, Traveler's Potpourri sends you the descriptions and also makes the reservations for you; they charge a $30 fee for each accommodation booked. They will provide testamonies from clients who have used their services with great success. Many of these clients say that their stay with a host family was a high point of their trip, since it provided the opportunity to learn more about the people and culture of the city and country they were visiting. Many also feel much more comfortable making these arrangements on this side of the Atlantic. Additionally, Traveler's Potpourri is a full-service travel agency and can arrange for your entire trip, from your flight to any and all accommodations, car rentals, and sightseeing tours.

Apartment Rentals and Residence Hotels

If you want to be more than a visitor during your stay in Prague, the best way to do this is to rent a short-term apartment. It not only gives you more space than a hotel and often for less money but it lets you become a real part of the neighborhood. When renting a flat, be sure you specify all of your needs, including types of beds, smallest amount of closet space you can live with, whether or not you need a lift, and so on. Be realistic, but do spend some time coming up with your bottom line of acceptance. *Always* ask for detailed photos in advance, especially if you are booking a private flat—and a map with the location marked on it—so you know you're not in the sticks.

Then, get a guaranteed rate and buy cancellation insurance. This is the number one thing to remember, since there are no refunds (ever) if your plans change and you cannot go, or if you have to leave the flat ahead of schedule. For companies to call, see "Tips for Cheap Sleeps in Prague, Vienna, and Budapest," page 12.

Lastly, find out exactly how you're going to take possession of the flat and who you are to contact if something goes wrong—because it will. You will either be asked to go to the agency address to pick up the key and pay the balance due, or else someone will meet you at the apartment to give you the key, collect payment, and show you the ropes. The second option is far preferable, as this also gives you a chance to review the flat before you finish paying for it.

(7) HOTEL RESIDENCE MALÁ STRANA
Mělnická 9, Prague 5
35 apartments, all with shower, toilet, and fitted kitchens

The Residence Malá Strana offers an option for those Prague visitors who need more space and enjoy the benefits of a small kitchen. The junior suites (one room) are designed for those on a short stay. They have twin beds, a fold-out sofa bed, and a small kitchen. The colors are coordinated and bathrooms have a half-tub and shower. Drawer space is lacking. Senior suites offer more space, another bedroom, and a larger kitchen area. Cheap Sleepers sixty and over can take an extra 20 percent off the daily hotel plan, making this Cheap Sleep a good one.

TELEPHONE
53 41 31

FAX
53 45 60

METRO
B, Andel (long walk)

CREDIT CARDS
AE, MC, V

RATES
Rates are in German marks, but payment can be in Czech currency. Junior suite: daily rate, one person 195DM, two persons 220DM, extra bed 25DM; weekly rates, one–two persons 1,100DM; monthly

rates 3,420DM. Senior suite: daily rate, one person 245DM, two persons 275DM, extra bed 25DM; weekly rate, two to four persons 1,355DM; monthly rates 4,200DM. Lower off-season rates and for longer stays, but these must be negotiated in advance. For daily hotel rates only: children up to 12 stay free in parent's room and 20% senior citizens discount from Jan–Mar, July–Aug, and Nov–Dec.

BREAKFAST
Buffet included in daily rate; 100Kč per person, per day for weekly and monthly rate

TELEPHONE
5731 2513

FAX
5731 2416

EMAIL
nostic@bohem-net.cz

METRO
A, Malostranská, or Tram Nos. 12 or 22 to Hellichova

CREDIT CARDS
AE, DC, MC, V

RATES
Rates are in U.S. dollars; Suite $150, Royal $230, Imperial $270; maid service $10; lower rates for longer stays

BREAKFAST
$8 per person, per day

ENGLISH SPOKEN Yes

FACILITIES AND SERVICES Bar, direct-dial phone, hair dryer, fitted kitchen, laundry service, lift, weekly maid and linen service, towels changed twice weekly, room safe 200Kč for stay

NEAREST TOURIST ATTRACTIONS Short, direct tram ride to heart of Malá Strana, otherwise about a twenty-minute walk

(8) RESIDENCE NOSTICOVA $
Nosticova 1, Prague 1
10 apartments, all with shower or bath and toilet, fitted kitchens

Residence Nosticova is a perfect choice for a very special stay in Prague. The seventeenth-century building has the type of accommodations travel writers dream of finding, and when they do, they hesitate to even whisper the address to their best pals for fear the great secret will get out. The location is perfect: it's a corner building on a quiet cobblestone street in Malá Strana, only a five-minute walk from the Charles Bridge and close to many restaurants listed in *Cheap Eats in Prague, Vienna, and Budapest.* All of the apartments are lavishly furnished with authentic Italian and French antiques, lush imported fabrics, Oriental rugs, beautiful paintings, state-of-the-art marble bathrooms with stunning fixtures, and kitchens stocked with the latest word in cooking utensils and crockery. A full range of business services is also available, and on the ground level is a smart wine bar where you can entertain guests or just stop by for a quiet drink before going out for the evening. I could move in today and never want to leave any of the ten magnificent apartments, which range in size from a studio to a three-bedroom penthouse flat, called Hradčanské, which has not only a master bathroom with a deep corner tub and crystal chandeliers but a baby grand piano and terrace. I also like Rudolpho because it has a fireplace, a divine bathroom with lots of lights and mirrors, and a gleaming glass dining table set on two stone columns. During my long stay here, nothing seemed to be too much trouble for the management team, from the owner, Mr. Bonelli, to the manager, Lucie Svobodová, the cordial desk staff, and the willing housekeeper Lilli. Prague is a city I plan to return to many times in the future, and when I do, I will be staying at the Residence Nosticova.

ENGLISH SPOKEN Yes

FACILITIES AND SERVICES Bar, direct-dial phone, fitted kitchens, laundry service, linens changed weekly, maid service extra, cable TV, room safe

NEAREST TOURIST ATTRACTIONS Malá Strana, Charles Bridge, Kampa Park

(27) HOTEL UNGELT $
Malá štupartská 1, Prague 1
9 apartments, all with shower, toilet, and kitchen

Unless you go in the off-season or are staying long enough to negotiate a better rate, a flat at the Ungelt in Staré Město could easily fall into a Big, Big Splurge category. So why bother to include it? Several reasons. The location is not only central but quiet, and if it is space you want, many of the modernly fitted flats redefine the word huge. Originally a cloister in the eleventh century, the building was redeveloped into nine flats: three very large two-bedroom units, and six they call small, but are far from it. For instance, take No. 5. It is a mystery to me how the management can consider this unit *small* when it contains a living room holding a seven-seat sectional, a wall of bookshelves, two double windows, and a big television set; an equally large bedroom with two more windows, bedside tables with drawers and three shelves, plus a double armoire with even more shelves; an eat-in kitchen with a four-burner electric stove and oven; and a bathroom with a tub and hand-held shower over it and a separate enclosed toilet. If you really want big, I suggest No. 4, which is a corner flat. It has a large, rustically furnished sitting room with an extra bed, an eat-in kitchen (but no oven), two bedrooms, a bathroom with two rolling racks of baskets for your toiletries, and a view from the window of the Church of Our Lady before Tyn. It also has a balcony on the back where you can step out and gaze at the neighborhood and the twin towers of the Tyn church, which is topped by what look like witches' hats.

The size and location of the flats—plus the lower rates for longer stays or in the off-season—make the

TELEPHONE
2481 1330

FAX
23 19 505

METRO
B, Náměstí Republiky

CREDIT CARDS
AE, MC, V

RATES
Single 5,410Kč, double 6,330Kč, triple 7,910Kč, and fourth person free; lower off-season rates and for longer stays

BREAKFAST
Continental included

Ungelt worth consideration. There is, unfortunately, a downside. No one ever said you would get style to go with your accommodation. Units 7, 8, 9, and 10 are not serviced by the lift, but Nos. 7 and 9 do have a little view of the church. Finally, the reception desk shuts down completely from 9 P.M. to 7 A.M., so you will be up a creek if you have any sort of problem or need something at night.

ENGLISH SPOKEN Yes

FACILITIES AND SERVICES Bar, direct-dial phone, hair dryer available, fitted kitchens, lift to five units, free parking, cable TV

NEAREST TOURIST ATTRACTIONS Old Town, Jewish Quarter

(32) FLATHOTEL ORION
Americká 9, Prague 2
19 apartments, all with shower or bath and toilet

TELEPHONE
691 02 09

FAX
691 00 98

METRO
A, Náměstí míru

CREDIT CARDS
AE, MC, V

RATES
Studio 2,430Kč, one-bedroom 3,060Kč, two-bedroom 4000Kč; dog 200Kč; lower off-season rates and for longer stays

BREAKFAST
On request, 150Kč per person, per day

These exceptional flats are located in a quiet area of Prague called Královské Vinohrady (the Royal Vineyards). The walk to the underground is about five or ten minutes, and then it's only one stop to Wenceslas Square and three stops to Old Town. The hotel is run by a Finnish company that also operates a full-service travel agency in the building and can provide sightseeing tours, tickets to cultural events, air tickets, and rental cars. The comfortable flats are outfitted with trim, black, rather masculine ASKO furniture, a Finnish company with a style similar to IKEA. From the smallest studio to an apartment for four, everything is sleekly modern and in good taste. No. 42, a studio, has a very nice kitchen with enough space to eat a meal. The largest, No. 54, can sleep four and looks like an office. A huge ten-person sectional couch provides seating in a workspace that has a TV and a chest of drawers. There is a separate bedroom, a big kitchen, and a very nice bathroom with a tub, free-standing sink, and a separate enclosed toilet. For a minimal charge, all guests are welcome to relax after a hard day in the authentic Finnish sauna.

ENGLISH SPOKEN Yes

FACILITIES AND SERVICES Direct-dial phone, hair dryer available, fitted kitchens, lift to five floors (walk to sixth), parking 250Kč per day in nearby building, satellite TV, office safe, sauna

NEAREST TOURIST ATTRACTIONS None, must use public transportation

Camping

For one of the cheapest Cheap Sleeps in Prague, consider sleeping under the stars in a campsite. While not central, the camps listed below are within a half an hour to an hour commute by public transport into central Prague. All charge an additional camp tax of 20Kč per person, per day, and do not take credit cards.

AUTOCAMP TROJSKA
Trojská 375/157, Prague 7

This campground has a garden setting as well as a restaurant and a snack bar.

TELEPHONE 68 86 036

FAX 85 42 945

METRO C, Nádraží holešovické, then bus No. 12

OPEN April–Oct

RATES Tent 95Kč per person, caravan 175–200Kč, bungalow 225Kč per person; children under age 6 are 35Kč, children 6–15 are 65Kč

ENGLISH SPOKEN Some

FACILITIES AND SERVICES Telephone, common kitchen, snack bar, restaurant, washing machine

NEAREST TOURIST ATTRACTIONS None, must use public transportation

INTERCAMMP KOTVA BRANÍK
U Ledáren 55, Prague 4

This is Prague's oldest and prettiest campsite, beautifully situated south of Prague on the Vltava River, and you can stay in either the campsite or grab a bed in the hostel.

TELEPHONE 46 13 97

METRO Tram Nos. 3 or 17

OPEN April–Oct

RATES Tent 85Kč per person; cabin for four, 550Kč; hostel: double 600Kč, triple 700Kč, quad 800Kč

ENGLISH SPOKEN Some

FACILITIES AND SERVICES Bike rental, canoeing, communal kitchen, tennis court, showers, washing machine

NEAREST TOURIST ATTRACTIONS None, must use public transportation

Hostels

Staying in a hostel is definitely one of the best Cheap Sleeps in Prague, provided you have either youth on your side and/or a mighty slim budget. Always plan to pay in cash (no plastic accepted) and share the bathrooms. Some of the hostels are fly-by-night affairs with little security and only a nodding acquaintance with houskeeping standards. Many are located in the suburbs—far, far from action central, which means taking long bus, trolley, and underground trips that will use up too much of your time in Prague. For the very latest listings, contact the AVE agency in the main train station, or at one of their branch offices (see "Accommodation Agencies," page 67). Other possibilities are listed below.

CHARLES UNIVERSITY DORMITORIES
Voršilská 1, Prague 1
1,000 dorm rooms located throughout Prague

TELEPHONE 2431 1105, 2491 3692
FAX 2431 1107
METRO B, Národní Třída
OPEN June–Sept 15
RATES Double, triple, or quad, 200–400Kč per person
BREAKFAST Included
ENGLISH SPOKEN Yes
FACILITIES AND SERVICES None
NEAREST TOURIST ATTRACTIONS None, must use public transportation

DOMOV MLÁDEŽE
Dykova 20, Prague 10
80 beds

The neighborhood is lined with trees and beautiful turn-of-the-century homes, and the rooms are above average.

TELEPHONE 25 06 88
FAX 25 14 29
METRO A, Jiřího z Poděbrad
OPEN Year-round
RATES Double, triple, quad 400Kč per person; dorm room for five, 280Kč per person
BREAKFAST Not included
ENGLISH SPOKEN Yes
FACILITIES AND SERVICES Garden, parking, restaurant, and safe

NEAREST TOURIST ATTRACTIONS None, must use public transportation

TRAVELLER'S HOSTELS
Reservations taken at Midulandská 5, Prague 1

Traveller's Hostels is a chain of five hostels run by expat Americans. If you want to spend your time in Prague surrounded by Americans, stay here; otherwise look elsewhere. There is no curfew, and the laid-back attitude shows. There is a place to do laundry and a bar to smooze with your compatriots.

TELEPHONE AND FAX 2491 0739

EMAIL xlipe01@use.cz

METRO B, Národní Trída

OPEN June 15–Sept 1

RATES 200–350Kč per person

BREAKFAST Included

ENGLISH SPOKEN Yes

FACILITIES AND SERVICES Bar, laundry

NEAREST TOURIST ATTRACTIONS None, must use public transportation

---

Private Home Accommodations

(9) PENSION U ČISTERCÍAKŮ
Plaská 8, Prague 5; PO Box 96
6 rooms, 2 with shower and toilet, 2 with kitchens

The place is in a good location in Malá Strana, but it definitely is not for everyone. However, if you are a Cheap Sleeper in Prague who is curious how the average Czech citizen lives in the capital city, then perhaps one of Alena Paterová's two apartments or one of the four rooms she rents in her apartment will be for you. When you first arrive at the address, there is no sign other than the word "accommodation" written by a buzzer. Press it and someone will let you in, then you must hike up four flights to the style-free rooms. Guests must not be in the market for any services or deep comforts: the beds are narrow and the kitchens could use some modern touches.

ENGLISH SPOKEN Very limited, but some French

FACILITIES AND SERVICES No elevator (four flights), parking 250Kč a day, radio

NEAREST TOURIST ATTRACTIONS Malá Strana, Kampa Park, Charles Bridge

TELEPHONE
9000 1500

FAX
9000 1497

METRO
A, Malostranská, or Tram Nos. 12 or 22 to Vitenzá

CREDIT CARDS
AE, MC, V

RATES
780Kč per person in a room without facilities; 1,960Kč for two in a room with facilities and limited kitchen

BREAKFAST
50–80Kč per person; price depends on size of breakfast

Glossary of Vocabulary Terms

The Czech language is difficult, and no one in Prague expects you to have mastered its finer points. However, it is always appreciated if you know a few basic words and phrases, and the following should get you started.

General Phrases

yes/no	*ano/ne*
I do not know/ I do not understand	*Nevím/Nerozumím*
Do you speak English?	*Mluvíte anglicky?*
I do not speak Czech	*Nemluvím česky*
Please/Thank you	*Prosím/Děkuji vam*
You are welcome	*Prosím*
Sorry	*Pardon*
Hello	*Dobry den/Ahoj*
Good evening	*Dobry večer*
Good night	*Dobrou noc*
Good-bye	*Na shledanou*
How are you?	*Jak se máte?*
Very well	*Velmi dobře*
Excuse me	*Promiňte*
Help!	*Pomoc!*
How much does it cost?	*Kolik to stojí?*
morning	*ráno*
evening	*večer*
today	*dnes*
tomorrow	*zítra*
yesterday	*včera*

At the Hotel

hotel	*hotel*
I would like . . .	*chci*
a single/double	*jednol žkové pokoj/dvojl žkové pokoj*
the key	*klíč*
The bill, please	*Dijte mi učet, prosím*
or, Can we pay, please	*prosím zaplatíme*

Signs

men (WC)	*muži/pani*
women (WC)	*ženy/dami*
entrance	*vchod*
exit	*východ*

no smoking	*kouření zakázáno*
open	*otevřeno*
closed	*zavřeno*
danger	*pozor*
metro station	*stanice*
bus or tram stop/ bus/tram	*zastávka/autobus/tramvaj*
railway station/train	*nádraží/vlak*
on the right	*na pravo*
on the left	*na levo*
straight ahead	*rovně*
street	*ulice*
square	*náměstí*
bridge	*most*
pull (sign on a door)	*sem*
push (sign on a door)	*tam*

Days of the Week

Monday	*pondělí*
Tuesday	*úterý*
Wednesday	*středa*
Thursday	*čtvrtek*
Friday	*pátek*
Saturday	*sobota*
Sunday	*neděle*
today	*dnes*
tomorrow	*zítra*
yesterday	*včera*
day before yesterday	*předevčírem*
day after tomorrow	*pozítří*
week	*tyden*

Numbers

0	*nula*
1	*jedna*
2	*dva*
3	*tří*
4	*čtyří*
5	*pět*
6	*šest*
7	*sedm*
8	*osm*
9	*devět*
10	*deset*
11	*jedenáct*
12	*dvanáct*

13	*třináct*
14	*čtrnáct*
15	*patnáct*
16	*šestnáct*
17	*sedmnáct*
18	*osmnáct*
19	*devatenáct*
20	*dvacet*
30	*třicet*
40	*čtyřicet*
50	*padesát*
60	*šedesát*
70	*sedmdesát*
80	*osmdesát*
90	*devadesát*
100	*sto*
1,000	*tisíc*

VIENNA

Baroque Vienna knows that an illusion which makes you happy is better than a reality that makes you sad.
—*Alan Whicker in* The Best of Everything
by William Davis (1980)

Vienna is more than Strauss waltzes, whipped cream, *Sachertorte*, ruffled dirndls, and overpriced opera tickets. What makes it so special? Vienna was the seat of the Holy Roman Empire from 1558 until 1806, and it is where more than six centuries of Habsburg rule have left their indelible mark on the city's music, art, literature, and architecture. The Austro-Hungarian monarchy is gone, but the word *Imperial* has lost none of its glamour here. Vienna is a city of music, enchanting us with superb orchestras, celebrated conductors, and the world-famous Staatsoper, which gives forty sold-out opera performances during the season. Beethoven, Haydn, Mozart, Schubert, and Strauss lived, performed, and died in Vienna. Besides listening to their music, you can visit their homes and grave sites. Vienna has given us Sigmund Freud, Gustav Klimt, Gustav Mahler, Erich von Stroheim, Hundertwasser, and Billy Wilder. Its museums house some of the most magnificent collections of art on the continent. The jewels and riches of the Hapsburgs are on display at the forty-seven-acre Hofburg, which served as the Imperial Palace in Vienna for six hundred years. The Kunsthistorisches Museum displays old masters and has the finest collection of Brueghels in the world. The Belvedere Palace, where Franz Ferdinand lived before his assasination in 1914, is composed of two Baroque mansions facing each other across formal gardens, and it has three art galleries with works of leading Austrian painters from the late seventeenth century to modern times, including works by Oskar Kokoschka, Gustav Klimt, and Egon Schiele. Just outside of Vienna is the Schönbrunn Palace, the summer home of the Hapsburgs, and its 1,441 rooms set in acres of gardens is as it was in Empress Maria Theresa's days. On the grounds is the Imperial Menagerie, the world's oldest zoo.

It is often enough just to soak up the beauty of Vienna itself and its simpler delights. The massive St. Stephen's Cathedral, Vienna's signature landmark and most important Gothic building, serves as the focal point of the city. Radiating from it is the Kärntner Strasse and various pedestrian streets, where stylish citizens promenade, visiting the elegant Viennese shops and sitting in outdoor cafés. Coffeehouses serve twenty varieties of coffee and sinfully rich pastries, and each is fondly regarded by its regular clientele as a combination second home, office annex, literary work place, and discrete meeting ground. Trips to the Vienna woods,

VIENNA

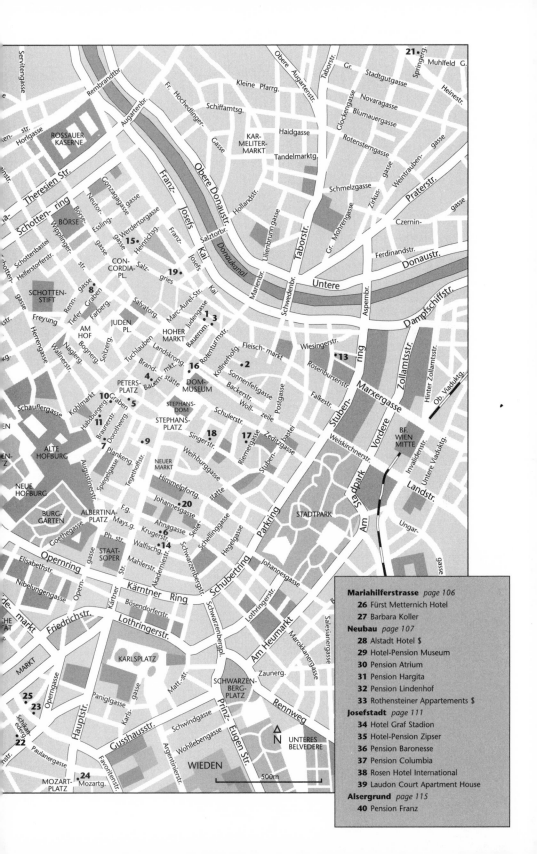

attending performances of the Vienna Boys Choir or the Royal Lippenzanner Horses at the Spanish Riding School, ordering *Wiener Schnitzel* at Figmüller, sampling a plate of sweets at Demel's, or enjoying an evening of wine and camaraderie at a wine tavern (*Heurige*) in the hills surrounding Vienna are only a few of the many pleasures magical Vienna offers its visitors.

Unless you stay in one of the five-star hotels, your hotel stay in Vienna will not be imperial in style or scope. The majority of the hotels in the Cheap Sleeps category come wrapped in an aura of changelessness, where modern meets ornate and a faded glow casts its light. The rooms are larger than in most other European capitals, and they are either bland or hopelessly frilly, always spotlessly clean, warm and toasty in the winter, and steaming in the summer if there is a heat wave. They are outfitted with trappings such as a duvet, those wonderful covered quilts that replace a top sheet and blanket, a television, and a telephone. Other amenities can be as scarce as the toiletries in your bathroom. Service is polite and correct and bill padding is very rare. A buffet breakfast is usually included in the room rate, and if it is hearty enough, all you will need for lunch is a marvelous pastry and a steaming cup of Viennese coffee. Unlike Budapest and Prague, Vienna does not lack for acceptable hotel rooms. Still, it is very important to make advance reservations, secure them with a deposit, and get a written confirmation to avoid any mix-ups.

True Viennese are always *gemütlich*, an untranslatable word that means good-natured, and that is how you will find them. They are truly charming, and their courtesy and good fellowship go a long way to making travelers feel at home and at ease in their city.

General Information

When to Go

Peak tourist season in Vienna is from April through October and again at Christmastime. While accommodation shortages are not as serious as they are in Prague and Budapest, it still makes sound Cheap Sleeping sense to book as far ahead as possible and arrive with confirmed reservations in hand. Musical festivals are an integral part of the cultural life of Vienna, starting with the *Silvesterkonzert* on New Year's Day. The main cultural festival combining the opera and theater is the *Wiener Festwochen* from May through the middle of June. The Mozart Festival leads up to the Christmas season, which is highlighted with the *Christkindlemarkts* held throughout the city (see "Cheap Chic in Vienna," page 194, for locations).

Holidays

On public holidays, banks, offices, and schools are closed, most stores are shut, and museums and galleries operate on limited schedules. Restaurant closing policies vary, so it is always advisable to call ahead if you have a specific place in mind. Some museums are closed on January 1, Easter Sunday, Whitsunday, Corpus Christi Day, November 1, and December 24 and 25 and for general elections. Vienna's municipal museums are free on Friday mornings.

January 1	New Year's Day
January 6	Epiphany
Easter Sunday/Monday	Dates vary
May 1	Labor Day
Sixth Thursday after Easter	Ascension Day
Sixth Monday after Easter	Whit Monday
May 29	Corpus Christi
August 15	Assumption Day
October 26	National Day
November 1	All Saints' Day
December 8	Immaculate Conception
December 24–26	Christmas

Money

The currency in Austria is the Austrian schilling, abbreviated as *öS*, or AS in English. The exchange rate at press time is 12.77AS to $1, but that is subject to fluctuation. Banking hours vary somewhat but are generally Monday to Friday 8 A.M. to noon and 1:30 to 3 P.M., and on Thursday until 5:30 P.M. The banking hours at the American Express office at

Kärntner Strasse 21–23 (tel: 515 400) are from Monday to Friday 9 A.M. to 5:30 P.M. and Saturday 9 A.M. to noon. There is a twenty-four-hour exchange office at the post office at Fleischmarkt 19.

A better way to get money is at an ATM machine. Plus and Cirrus machines are all over Vienna, but remember that your PIN has to be only four digits. The following banks have twenty-four-hour exchange machines: Bank Austria, Stephansplatz 2; Creditanstalt, Kärntner Strasse 7; and Die Erste Banke, Graben 21. For more information, see "Money Matters," page 17.

Tipping

There is usually a service charge included on your restaurant and hotel bill, thus you are not expected to leave any additional tip. In restaurants, however, it is customary to round off the total, and in hotels, leave 25 to 30AS per day for the maid if you have stayed a long time or if the service has been exceptional. If someone handles your luggage, that will be worth 20 to 25AS per bag. In the hair salon, the shampoo girl appreciates 20 to 30AS, and the hairdresser should get 10 percent—if he or she didn't completely ruin you. Toilet attendants expect you to leave 5 or 6AS in their saucers, and coatroom attendants are pleased with 10AS. Taxi drivers should have their fares rounded up to the next 10AS, and if they carry bags, an extra 10AS.

Safety and Security

Vienna holds no particular dangers to the traveler, but as always, be aware of your surroundings, don't venture into dark alleys alone at night, and wear a money belt. The most reported crimes against foreigners are purse snatching around St. Stephen's Cathedral and gypsy children picking pockets.

Telephones

The telephone system in Vienna is stable and not experiencing the upheavels of those in Prague and Budapest. It does have, however, some of the highest telephone charges in Europe. There is no such thing as a free telephone call in Austria. If you call next door, you pay to do so. In Vienna the numbers vary in length; some have seven numerals, others six. If you see a number followed by -0, you do not have to dial that final 0. It means that it is a line with extension numbers, and if you know the extension, dial it after dialing the six- or seven-digit number.

In hotels, sometimes there is an additional telephone surcharge, and you can almost depend on it if you are making an international call. Therefore, if you are trying to trim telephone costs, use pay telephones, which are dark green booths with bright yellow roofs. You can also make calls at any twenty-four-hour post office and use their direct phone service. If you are calling collect, you should use a post office telephone. To simplify matters, buy a telephone card (*telefonkarte*) from a tobacco shop or any post office.

Useful Telephone Numbers and Addresses

Emergency and Medical Numbers

Ambulance	144
Dentists (nights, weekends)	512 2078
Emergency doctors	144
Fire	122
Hospital	Allgemeines Krankenhaus, Währinger Gürtel 18–20, A-1090; tel: 404-00
Pharmacies	In every district, one pharmacy is always open twenty-four hours a day; after business hours, a sign on the door will give the address of the nearest one that is open
Police	133

Useful Numbers

To call Austria from the U.S.	dial 011 + 43 + 1 + the local number
To call the U.S. from Austria	dial 001 + area code + the local number
To call Vienna from within Austria	dial 0222 + the local number
Information	For Austria, 1611 For Europe, 1613 Abroad, 1614
Operator-assisted calls	1616
American Consulate for lost passports and emergencies	Gartenbaupromenade 2–4, A-1010; tel: 313 39; open Mon–Fri 8:30 A.M.–noon and 1–3:30 P.M.
American Embassy	Boltzmanngassse 16, A-1090; tel: 313 39
American Express	Kärntner Strasse 21–23, A-1010; tel: 515 40 0; open Mon–Fri 9 A.M.–5:30 P.M., Sat till noon
Lost property	Zentrales Fundamt, Wasagasse 22, A-1090; tel: 313 44 0 or 313 44 9211; open Mon–Fri 8 A.M.–noon
Lost property on U-Bahn or trolley	Zentrale Fundstelle; tel: 7909 105
Lost or stolen credit cards or traveler's checks (local call in Vienna)	American Express, 515 110 Diners Club, 512 350 MasterCard, 717 010 Visa, 711 110

Post Office	Main office: Fleischmarkt 19, A-1010; open daily, 24 hours
	Other 24-hour post offices are at the Westbahnhof, Südbahnhof, and Franz-Josefs-Bahnhof
	Branch offices are open Mon–Fri 8 A.M.–noon, 2–6 P.M., Sat 8 A.M.–noon
Vienna Tourist Office	Kärntner Strasse 38, A-1010; open daily 9 A.M.–7 P.M.; tel: 513 8892; fax: 216 8492; Internet: wtv.magwien.gv.at/
Austrian National Tourist Office	Margaretenstrasee 1, A-1040; tel: 58 86 60 In the U.S., 500 Fifth Avenue, Suite 800, New York, NY 10110; tel: 212-944-6880; fax: 212-730-4568

Transportation

The heart of Vienna is best seen and appreciated on foot. For trips farther afield, you can rely on the public transportation system, which is clean, efficient, fast, on time, and easy to use. If you arrive by car, my advice is to follow the lead of the Viennese and park it in a secure garage and forget about using it to get around the city. Otherwise, you will be faced with a difficult traffic system of one-way streets, limited and restricted parking zones, ticketing, and in dire cases, towing. Who needs this on a vacation? On the public transportation system, children under six travel free and those under fifteen ride free on Sunday, public holidays, and during Vienna school holidays. You can buy single-trip tickets or twenty-four- or seventy-two-hour tickets (*Netzkarte*) from tobacco shops, newsstands, and the machines and ticket windows in all U-Bahn stations. The Vienna Card is a seventy-two-hour ticket valid on all forms of public transportation, with additional discounts and benefits at more than one hundred participating establishments. It comes with an information brochure and can be purchased at the ticket office in most underground stations. If you plan on being in Vienna longer than a few days, buy a weekly card (*Wochenkarte*), which is valid from Monday to Monday and allows unlimited travel on all buses, trams, and U-Bahn trains. These weekly passes are sold *only* at ticket windows inside U-Bahn stations.

When the public transportation shuts down, night buses run every thirty minutes from 12:30 A.M. to 4 A.M., and supplemental tickets are required. If you want to circumnavigate the Ringstrasse, you can do it on tram No. 1 or No. 2. There are few transportation inspectors, but if you are caught without a ticket, the fine will be 500AS plus the price of the ticket you should have bought in the first place. Information, tickets, and maps are available at Vienna's Transportation Office on Karlsplatz or at St. Stephen's underground station as well as at several other major underground stops. Hours are Monday to Friday 6:30 A.M. to 6 P.M., Saturday, Sunday, and holidays 8:30 A.M. to 4 P.M.

Taxis are safe, drivers are honest, and fares are reasonable. You can go to a taxi rank, flag one down, or call ahead at 313 00, 401 00, 601 60, or 814 00. If you are going to the airport, ask for a reduced rate taxi. Fares run according to the time of day, with additional charges for more than one passenger and reserving by telephone.

Fiaker, or horse-drawn carriages, have been carrying people around the central part of the city for centuries. These carriages are driven by costumed drivers, last about twenty minutes, and cost around 650AS, but before you get in, be sure to determine the price. You can find them at Stephansplatz by St. Stephen's Cathedral, at Heldenplatz near the Hofburg, and at Albertinaplatz.

Discounts

Senior Citizens

It is not hard to get a discount in Vienna if you are a senior citizen. If you are over sixty-five (men) or sixty (women), you are entitled to half fares valid on the Austrian Federal Railways and the bus systems of the Federal Railways. As a prerequisite to purchasing half-fare tickets, a Railway Senior Citizens Identification has to be obtained, and it is issued at all major Austrian railroad stations. For the ID card, you need a passport photo and your passport. The price of the ID card is 350AS and it is *not* available in the United States. It is valid from January 1 to December 31. In addition, seniors should always ask for a senior rate at large hotels or when renting a car, and check with senior organizations in the States like AARP for their senior discount travel offers.

Students

Council Travel, part of the Council on International Educational Exchange (CIEE), is the largest American student budget travel organization. Through one of their offices worldwide you can get an International Student Identity Card (ISIC), issued to all enrolled students under twenty-six. The cost is under $20, and it qualifies as a true bargain when you add up the discounts it affords, including travel insurance. If you are a teacher, you also qualify for a discount card. Council Travel also sells discounted air tickets, Eurorail passes, package tours, and can make hostel and hotel arrangements. The main office is at 205 East 42nd Street, 16th floor, New York, NY 10017; tel: 212-822-2600, 800-438-2643, or 888-COUNCIL; email: info@ciee.org. Call for further information and the location nearest you.

Dedicated Cheap Sleeping budgeteers should join Hostelling/International IYHF. For the details, contact their headquarters at Hostelling Information/American Youth Hostels (HI-AYH), 733 15th Street, NW, Washington, DC, 20005; tel: 202-783-6161.

The Vienna Card

Holders of the Vienna Card get free travel on all forms of public transportation for three days. They also get discounts on entry fees at the Hofburg and Schönburnn palaces in addition to reduced prices at participating museums, restaurants, and shops. For further details, see "Transportation," page 88.

Disabled Travelers

All public buildings are required by law to provide wheelchair access, but that does not mean that they do. Only the U-3 and U-6 U-Bahn lines are equipped for handicapped travelers. Whenever a hotel renovates, usually they add a room or two with handicapped facilities. For more information, get the English-language booklet *Vienna for Guests with Handicaps* from the Austrian Tourist Board, 500 Fifth Avenue, 20th floor, New York, NY 10110; tel: 212-944-6880; fax: 212-730-4568. In Vienna, contact them at Margaretenstrasse 1, A1040; tel: 58 86 60.

Hotels in Vienna
by Area

No matter where you are staying in Vienna, a good street map is essential for negotiating the fifteen hundred miles of narrow, winding streets. Those given away are worth what you pay for them—nothing. Instead arm yourself with a Falk or a Hallwag map, available in U.S. travel book stores and in larger news kiosks and most bookstores in Vienna. Finding the address is the next hurdle, but not a difficult one once you understand the system. Vienna is divided into twenty-three postal districts. Street addresses start with the number of the district, followed by the name of the street and the number. Residential addresses also include the apartment number separated from the street number by a slash. The number of the district appears in either of two ways: as a four-digit number preceded by the letter A or as a single number. In the four-digit number, the district is represented by the two middle digits.

For example, an address in the first district might appear as either Am Fleischmarkt 17/4, A-1010, or as Am Fleischmarkt 17/4, 1. In the eighth district, the address could be Alser Strasse 20/1, A-1080, or Alser Strasse 20/1, 8.

INNERE STADT (INNER CITY) ⸺

The Innere Stadt (Inner City), otherwise known as the first district, is the historic heart of Vienna. It is characterized by a labyrinth of crisscrossing, small winding streets, many of them zoned for pedestrians. The district centers around Stepansdom, Vienna's magnificent Gothic cathedral, and within walking distance of this are the city's major museums, including the Kunsthishorisches (which houses one of the world's finest art collections), the opera house, the Hofburg (former imperial palace of the Habsburgs), hotels and restaurants in all price categories, historic coffeehouses, and wonderful shopping along pedestrian-zoned promenades.

HOTELS

OTHER OPTIONS
Apartment Rentals and Residence Hotels
Private Home Accommodations
Seasonal Accommodations
Note: A dollar sign ($) indicates a Big Splurge.

(1) HOTEL AUSTRIA
Am Fleischmarkt 20, A-1011
46 rooms, 42 with shower or bath and toilet

TELEPHONE
515 23

FAX
515 23/506

EMAIL
hotelaus@ping.at

U-BAHN
1, 4, Schwedenplatz

CREDIT CARDS
AE, DC, MC, V

RATES
Single without private facilities 790AS, with private facilities 1,190AS; double without private facilities 1,140AS, with private facilities 1,750AS; suite 2,360AS; extra bed 460AS; child's cot 230AS; lower off-season rates

BREAKFAST
Buffet included

The Hotel Austria is an excellent choice, located on a quiet cul-de-sac off the Fleischmarkt, Vienna's old meat market. Almost all the important sightseeing destinations in the inner city are within a five- to twenty-minute stroll, and restaurants, coffeehouses, and *Konditoreien* (bakeries) in all price categories are plentiful. As you enter this very pretty hotel, a formal sitting area with two crystal chandeliers and live green plants is on your left. On your right is the reception desk, which is staffed by a pleasant, multilingual crew. Breakfast is served in a large room with a flower-accented fountain in the center.

For assured quiet and more space, ask for Room 118, which has a small entryway and a couch, table, and two chairs in the bedroom. Room 111 is a good single; the bathroom has plenty of shelf space, plus a bathtub and shower. Room 101, a double right by the elevator, has high ceilings, two large windows, and a bathroom with a separate enclosed toilet. Those looking to trim costs should ask for one of the four rooms without en suite facilities. There is one on each floor, and the good part is that the hall toilet and bathroom on each floor are specifically reserved for guests occupying these rooms, so they are in essence private, just outside the room.

ENGLISH SPOKEN Yes

FACILITIES AND SERVICES Direct-dial phone, hair dryer available, lift, minibar, parking garage, porter, radio, satellite TV, office safe

NEAREST TOURIST ATTRACTIONS St. Stephen's Cathedral, Kärntner Strasse and excellent shopping, easy walk to almost everything else

(2) HOTEL KÄRNTNERHOF
Grashofgasse 4, A-1011
43 rooms, 41 with shower or bath and toilet

For almost two centuries a member of the Nagel family has been at the helm of this quiet hotel located minutes away from St. Stephen's Cathedral and central Vienna. Other pluses include a roof garden, a large breakfast buffet served in a no-smoking dining room, and a very friendly staff. Drawbacks for some could be the hand-held showers over tubs with no curtains, mixed decor, and some dingy views, especially in the single rooms. Families looking for more space should ask for one of the sixth-floor rooms with a glimpse of the spire of St. Stephen's. Two friends traveling together would be happy in No. 307, a twin-bedded nest with a built-in desk.

ENGLISH SPOKEN Yes

FACILITIES AND SERVICES Direct-dial phone, hair dryer available, lift to fifth floor, walk to sixth, parking available, satellite TV, office safe

NEAREST TOURIST ATTRACTIONS St. Stephen's Cathedral, Kärntner Strasse and excellent shopping, easy walk to almost everything else

TELEPHONE
512 19 23

FAX
513 22 28 33

EMAIL
kaerntnerhof@netway.at

U-BAHN
1, 4, Schwedenplatz

CREDIT CARDS
AE, DC, MC, V

RATES
Single without private facilities 600AS, with private facilities 1,080AS; double without private facilities 900AS, with private facilities 1420–1,720AS; triple 2,250AS; two-room suite 2,800AS; lower off-season rates

BREAKFAST
Buffet included

(3) HOTEL POST
Am Fleischmarkt 24, A-1010
107 rooms, 90 with shower or bath and toilet

Thank goodness the rooms at the centrally located Hotel Post are a quantum leap ahead of the dull exterior and lobby. Renovation of the rooms was completed in 1998, making them uniformly modern with polished wooden floors and spackled, sponge-painted walls in light lemon. Above all, they are clean. Room 528 is a

TELEPHONE
515 830

FAX
515 83 808

U-BAHN
1, 4, Schwedenplatz

CREDIT CARDS
AE, DC, MC, V

larger twin with two chairs by a desk, good luggage and closet space, and a bathroom complete with tub, curtain, and a grip to hold onto. Room 507 is a quiet choice facing a large interior courtyard. Single travelers will appreciate No. 418, which has a workspace facing a window and a stall shower in the bathroom. An added advantage of the Post is its restaurant, which is open daily until midnight and which provides room service if you feel like cocooning in your room.

ENGLISH SPOKEN Yes

FACILITIES AND SERVICES Direct-dial phone, hair dryer, lift, parking available, restaurant, room service, satellite TV, seminar rooms, PC-modem socket, office safe

NEAREST TOURIST ATTRACTIONS St. Stephen's Cathedral, good shopping, most other tourist sites within a thirty-minute stroll

(4) HOTEL SCHWEIZERHOF $
Bauernmarkt 22, A-1010
55 rooms, all with shower or bath and toilet

The long narrow sitting area of the Schweizerhof has brown sectionals leading to another lounge area with two sofas and armchairs, a huge fake wisteria tree in one corner, and a pine tree in another. Fortunately, Cheap Sleepers are not going to spend much time in this dated area. The hotel offers more amenities than most—such as a scale in some bathrooms so you can monitor your visits to Demel's pastry shop, drying racks in others in case you need to do a bit of laundry, and candy on your pillow at night.

Some rooms are definitely better than others, and without going into full detail, I can tell you to avoid No. 613, with its high windows out of which you can't see, and No. 504, a double or triple on the street side that had the only bathroom in the hotel with mold—a serious no-no in my book. Which rooms should you request? Room 525 facing the street is a good single with space to spread out some work. No. 520 on the back has no view, but the dark modern furniture, Oriental rugs, and corner sitting space make the room pleasant in spite of its drab outlook.

You begin your day at the Hotel Schweizerhof in the large seventh-floor breakfast room, which has rooftop views of Vienna. During the week the buffet includes hard-boiled eggs, assorted cheeses and meats, six cereal choices, plus the usual breads, juices, and warm drinks.

RATES
Single without private facilities 530AS, with private facilities 850AS; double without private facilities 800–870AS, with private facilities 1,320–1,430AS; triple without private facilities 1,110AS, with private facilities 1,750AS; lower off-season rates

BREAKFAST
Buffet included

TELEPHONE
533 19 31 or 32

FAX
533 02 14

U-BAHN
1, 3, Stephansplatz

CREDIT CARDS
AE, MC, V

CLOSED
Jan 11–Feb 19

RATES
Single 1,250AS, double 1,800AS, triple 2,100AS; lower off-season rates

BREAKFAST
Buffet included; champagne and salmon served on Sunday

On Sunday the addition of champagne and salmon turn the meal into a festive occasion.

Also under the same ownership is the Hotel zur Wiener Staatsoper; see page 96 for description.

ENGLISH SPOKEN Yes

FACILITIES AND SERVICES Direct-dial phone, some hair dryers, lift, satellite TV, room safe 50AS per stay, scale in some rooms, drying racks in some rooms

NEAREST TOURIST ATTRACTIONS St. Stephen's Cathedral, shopping, all of central Vienna within a thirty-minute stroll

(5) HOTEL WANDL
Petersplatz 9, A-1010
138 rooms, 134 with shower or bath and toilet

The Wandl is a Cheap Sleeper's dream: a full-service hotel in an excellent location that looks and acts much more expensive than it is. Automatic doors lead guests into a reception area defined by a stained-glass ceiling and tufted, dusty rose–colored velvet chairs. An inside courtyard is enhanced by a lovely multicolored fountain. For those seeking quiet, Room 321, overlooking this fountain court, is a good choice, but I would avoid No. 322, which is quiet but has a pebbled window staring at a wall. Room 408, a modernly furnished double with a balcony, has enough space in its four-drawer armoire and double three-drawer bedside chests to unpack and stay for weeks. The small entry, nice bathroom, and view of St. Peter's Church make this a popular selection. Oriental area rugs on wooden floors and wide, white, textured wall coverings set the stage for No. 409, a twin with a blue tiled bathroom with its own window.

A buffet breakfast is served in a regal room crowned with crystal chandeliers and featuring comfortable seating around tables overlaid with pink and white tablecloths.

ENGLISH SPOKEN Yes

FACILITIES AND SERVICES Bar, direct-dial phone, hair dryer available, lift, cable TV, office safe, porter, laundry service

NEAREST TOURIST ATTRACTIONS Within a ten-minute walk of almost everything in central Vienna

TELEPHONE
534 55 0

FAX
534 55 77

U-BAHN
1, 3, Stephansplatz

CREDIT CARDS
AE, DC, MC, V

RATES
Single without private facilities 775AS, with private facilities 925–1,475AS; double without private facilities 1,225AS, with private facilities 1,575–2,000AS; suite 2,125AS; extra bed 300AS; free baby cot; lower off-season rates

BREAKFAST
Buffet included

(6) HOTEL ZUR WIENER STAATSOPER $
Krugerstrasse 11, A-1010
22 rooms, all with shower or bath and toilet

TELEPHONE
513 12 74

FAX
513 12 74 15

U-BAHN
1, 2, 4, Karlsplatz

CREDIT CARDS
AE, MC, V

RATES
Single 1,250AS, double 1,800AS, triple 2,100AS; lower off-season rates

BREAKFAST
Buffet included

When I lived in Prague in the early 1980s, this hotel was my address whenever I came to Vienna, not so much for the size of the rooms, but for the premier location, which is just off the Kärntner Strasse on a pedestrian-zoned street that can only be described as perfect. From the front door guests can walk three minutes to the opera, five to St. Stephen's Cathedral, and to everything else that lies in the heart of this beautiful city.

The hotel's entry has a lovely old cocoa and white tiled floor with gold trimmed accents, and the reception desk is on your right. All the rooms (one single and the rest doubles) face front. The bathrooms have been renovated, and the rooms on the first floor have new wallpaper. While the rooms are not large, they are well appointed, featuring decent light and pleasant furnishings. The hotel enjoys a dedicated following, requiring reservations months in advance.

ENGLISH SPOKEN Yes

FACILITIES AND SERVICES Direct-dial phone, hair dryer available, lift, special parking rates in public garage, satellite TV, room safe 50AS per stay

NEAREST TOURIST ATTRACTIONS Ideally located, three-minute walk to the opera

(7) PENSION ACLON
Dorotheergasse 6-8, A-1010
28 rooms, 14 with shower or bath and toilet

TELEPHONE
512 79 400

FAX
513 87 51

EMAIL
office@nethotels.com

U-BAHN
1, 3, Stephansplatz, or 3, Herrengasse

CREDIT CARDS
None (must pay in cash, but can reserve with credit card)

RATES
Single 500–730AS, double 860–1,200AS, triple 1,230–1,620AS, quad 2,000; dogs free

BREAKFAST
Continental included

The Michlmayer family, along with their Hungarian hunting dog Emma, run this top-drawer pension in the heart of Vienna. Featuring original Biedermeier decor and furnishings, the twenty-eight-room pension covers two floors and is located next to Café Hawelka, one of the oldest and most famous coffeehouses in the city (see *Cheap Eats in Prague, Vienna, and Budapest* for a description).

At the Aclon, breakfast is served in a dining room with large crystal chandeliers and an Art Deco marble buffet. Seating is around a communal table or at four other smaller tables. All the rooms are nice, especially No. 301, which has the advantage of a marble bathroom. Dedicated Cheap Sleepers can ask for No. 416, a sweet, light room, or No. 304, which has bright coordinating curtains and chair covers: both rooms have sinks but no other private facilities. For those demanding quiet, ask for No. 421, which is rented either as a single or double and looks onto an inner courtyard. The bathroom has a shower, good lighting, and a large mirror.

ENGLISH SPOKEN Yes

FACILITIES AND SERVICES Direct-dial phone, hair dryers available in rooms with private facilities, no elevator, minibars in rooms with private facilities, satellite TV, office safe

NEAREST TOURIST ATTRACTIONS Walking distance from everything in the heart of Vienna

(8) PENSION LERNER
Wipplingerstrasse 23, A-1010
7 rooms, all with shower or bath and toilet

Cheap Sleepers looking for a good location, most amenities, and a pleasant, English-speaking owner/manager should consider the seven-room Pension Lerner. The rooms are basic, with duvets on the beds and a satellite TV to keep you abreast of breaking news stories around the globe. The only room I would try to avoid is No. 101, which is on the back side with four types of tile in the bathroom, none of them matching, and a grim view facing gray walls. If you are looking for more space, ask the owner, Hans Schöll, about the four apartments he has, which are located just behind St. Stephen's Cathedral on Schulerstrasse.

ENGLISH SPOKEN Yes

FACILITIES AND SERVICES Direct-dial phone, hair dryer available, lift, satellite TV, office safe

NEAREST TOURIST ATTRACTIONS St. Stephen's Cathedral, all other sites within an easy walk

TELEPHONE
533 52 19

FAX
533 56 78

U-BAHN
1, 3, Stephansplatz

CREDIT CARDS
AE, DC, MC, V

RATES
Single 670–900AS, double 980–1,220AS

BREAKFAST
Cold buffet included

(9) PENSION NEUER MARKT
Seilergasse 9, A-1010
37 rooms, 28 with shower or bath and toilet, 9 with shower only

Aside from the central location, the Pension Neuer Markt offers guests the option of being served lunch and/or dinner in their dining room. Another important feature is the exceptional desk staff, one of whom is celebrating more than thirty years on board, another twenty-five. In the fickle hotel business, this is impressive. There is no lounge or sitting room. Instead, guests

TELEPHONE
512 23 16

FAX
513 91 05

U-BAHN
1, 3, Stephansplatz

CREDIT CARDS
AE, DC, MC, V

Single without private facilities 640–740AS, with private facilities 720–900AS; double without private facilities 970–1,100AS, with private facilities 1,400AS; extra bed 320AS; half board 180AS per person; full board 280AS per person; lower off-season rates

BREAKFAST
Buffet included

congregate around tables in the dining room for cups of tea and the exchange of travel tips. The long, windowless laminated halls give the odd feeling of being aboard a ship, but fortunately, the rooms have outlooks, dispelling any feelings of claustrophobia. The hotel does not honor special room requests, but all are comfortable and pleasing, with pink as the color of choice, which is carried out in the rose velvet upholstery and pink tiles in many of the bathrooms.

ENGLISH SPOKEN Yes

FACILITIES AND SERVICES Direct-dial phone, hair dryer available, lift, satellite TV, room safe, full or half board available

NEAREST TOURIST ATTRACTIONS St. Stephen's Cathedral, and everything else in the core of Vienna

(10) PENSION NOSSEK
Graben 17, A-1010
26 rooms, 22 with shower or bath and toilet, 4 with shower only

TELEPHONE
533 70 41-0

FAX
535 36 46

U-BAHN
1, 3, Stephansplatz

CREDIT CARDS
None

RATES
Single without private facilities 520–670AS, with private facilities 820AS; double without private facilites 720–820AS, with private facilities 1,120–1,520AS; extra bed 370AS

BREAKFAST
Contintental included

The building, which is in the center of Vienna's shopping district, was the home of Wolfgang Mozart from 1791 to 1792. Today it is an apartment/office building with the Pension Nossek occupying the second floor. Run by two sisters, it is a popular choice for shopoholics and anyone else wanting to be in the thick of things on the pedestrian-only Graben. The public areas welcome guests with bowls of fruit and an eclectic mixture of furniture, including a writing desk. The high-ceilinged rooms are sprinkled with Art Deco furnishings and are large enough to move about. Those on the front have a direct view of the Graben. Some have polished wooden floors with Oriental accent rugs, and those without a toilet provide robes for the trek down the hall.

ENGLISH SPOKEN Yes

FACILITIES AND SERVICES Direct-dial phone, hair dryer, lift, some minibars, TV 40AS per day, office safe, robes provided in rooms without private toilet

NEAREST TOURIST ATTRACTIONS Shopping along and near Graben, St. Stephen's Cathedral, walking distance to all in the center of the city

(11) PENSION PERTSCHY
Habsburgergasse 5, A-1010
43 rooms, all with shower or bath and toilet

For a quiet, center-city location, the Pension Pertschy is a perfect choice. Housed in the Palais Cavriani, a historical landmark dating from the early 1700s, the pension wanders around several floors of an apartment building. The Old Viennese style of decoration is a bit dowdy by today's tastes, but modern comforts and the prime site far outweigh any dislike of the pink velvet decorating theme. Many rooms have high ceilings, ornate crystal chandeliers, and ceramic-tiled heaters. Everyone likes No. 220, a large double with two dusty rose armchairs, a sofa bed, and a bathroom with a tub and enclosed shower and plenty of towels. Several singles have narrow closet space and limited sitting space, but if you are going to be here for a short stay and plan to spend little time in your room, these are very small drawbacks. For Cheap Sleepers with families, the large rooms with corner kitchens are ideal.

ENGLISH SPOKEN Yes

FACILITIES AND SERVICES Direct-dial phone, lift, mini-bar, parking, cable TV, office safe

NEAREST TOURIST ATTRACTIONS Ideal location in the heart of Old Vienna

TELEPHONE
534 49 0

FAX
534 49 49

U-BAHN
2, Herrengasse

CREDIT CARDS
DC, MC, V

RATES
Single 720AS, double 1260AS; extra bed 300AS; two rooms with kitchens, rates on request; lower off-season rates

BREAKFAST
Buffet included

(12) PENSION RESIDENZ
Ebendorferstrasse 10, A-1010
15 rooms, all with shower and toilet

Pension Residenz, a popular pension run for two decades by Herr Ziegler, is officially listed in Vienna's first district, but it is actually just beyond the Inner Ring on a small street next to the Rathaus. Ziegler, an accommodating host, says, "Even our friendliness is included in the price of your stay." And so is the soothing classical music he plays all day long in the reception area. He also rolls out the red carpet—literally—along the hallway, which leads guests to traditionally furnished rooms with bathrooms offering enclosed stall showers (but no tubs). Room 20, either a double or triple, has gray-toned Louis XVI reproduction furnishings, plenty of space, and light from two windows. Single travelers will appreciate the good layout in Room 34, but avoid No. 33 with its two ugly barrel-like chairs. Nos. 31 and 32 are also good picks, thanks to their window light and wood furnishings.

TELEPHONE
406 47 86-0

FAX
406 47 86-50

EMAIL
vienna@pension-residenz.co.at

U-BAHN
2, Schottentor

CREDIT CARDS
MC, V

RATES
Single 720AS, double 1050AS; extra bed 200AS; lower off-season rates

BREAKFAST
Buffet included

ENGLISH SPOKEN Yes

FACILITIES AND SERVICES Direct-dial phone, hair dryer available, lift, minibar, parking can be arranged, TV, office safe

NEAREST TOURIST ATTRACTIONS Rathaus, Parliament, Museums, Burgtheater

(13) PENSION RIEDL
Georg Coch-Platz 3, A-1010
8 rooms, all with shower and toilet

TELEPHONE
512 79 19
FAX
512 79 19-8
U-BAHN
1, 4, Schwedenplatz, or 3, Stubentor
CREDIT CARDS
DC, MC, V (only for stays of two or more nights)
RATES
Single 570–870AS, double 940–1,220AS, triple 1,520AS, quad 1,820AS
BREAKFAST
Continental served in the room

If there is a more loquacious hostess in Vienna than Maria Felser, I have yet to meet her. Maria takes a personal interest in her guests, from serving them breakfast in bed if they ask for it to providing tips on what to see and do in Vienna. Her small pension has only eight rooms; it's on a *platz* overlooking the ornate Postsparkasse, a marble Art Deco building designed by Otto Wagner. From No. 7 you can step out on the balcony and have a direct view of the angel on the Post Bank across the street. This is the largest room, but the bathroom is on the small side. The bath and toilet for No. 8 are in the hall, but they are private for these guests only. Despite this inconvenience, I would choose it in the summer because of its flower-filled balcony. Any group of three voyagers will appreciate Room 6. Originally two small rooms, it is now one big room with modern furniture and two showers.

ENGLISH SPOKEN Yes

FACILITIES AND SERVICES Direct-dial phone, hair dryer available, lift, parking in the same building 200AS per day, office safe, laundry service

NEAREST TOURIST ATTRACTIONS On the edge of the Inner Ring; about a ten-minute walk to St. Stephen's Cathedral, twenty to the opera

(14) PENSION SUZANNE
Walfischgasse 4, A-1010
25 rooms, all with shower or bath and toilet

TELEPHONE
513 25 07
FAX
513 25 00
U-BAHN
1, 4, Karlsplatz
CREDIT CARDS
AE, DC, MC, V
RATES
Single 900AS, double 1,110–1,325AS; extra bed 500AS; lower off-season rates

A stay at the Pension Suzanne puts opera fans a mere block away from the magnificent Staatsoper. If it's *Sachertorte* that you adore, the Hotel Sacher where this famed Viennese treat began is less than a five-minute walk away. The pension is small, with every inch given to the rooms—there is no lounge or sitting area. Breakfast is served in a room with pink-covered tables and gold-trimmed white chairs covered in gray-blue damask.

Room 14 is off this dining area and done in deep rose velvet. Lacy curtains cover a picture window overlooking a terrace below. The armoire provides shelf and hanging space, and a large bathroom offers a stretch tub with a hand-held shower over it. No. 13 is a quiet backside single. The bathroom has an elongated tub and mirror plus good lighting. Room 12 has twin beds positioned in the shape of an L. A built-in closet is a welcome asset, as are the two armchairs. The only minus I could spot was the somewhat dated stall shower. Another good selection is Room 28, a double with a sitting area that has two armchairs, a sofa bed, and a wall-mounted television. A four-drawer dresser in addition to an armoire insures pleasant unpacking. The bathroom has double sinks, a lighted mirror, and a separately enclosed toilet.

ENGLISH SPOKEN Yes

FACILITIES AND SERVICES Direct-dial phone, hair dryer, lift, satellite TV, office safe

NEAREST TOURIST ATTRACTIONS Opera, museums, St. Stephen's Cathedral, Kärntner Strasse

BREAKFAST
Continental included

(15) SCHWEIZER PENSION
Heinrichgasse 2, A-1010
11 rooms, 6 with shower or bath and toilet

Monica and Anita, two charming sisters, preside over the Schweizer Pension, which was started by their grandparents more than 150 years ago. The location on Rudolfsplatz puts guests within walking distance of all the major attractions in the Inner City. The eleven rooms are modern in tone, spotlessly clean, and generally quiet. The communal bathroom (used by five rooms), with a tub on feet and stall shower, is perfectly acceptable. At Christmastime and other major holidays, the dining room is gaily decorated, creating a welcoming and homey feeling without being corny. Breakfast is generous, and as Monica said, "No one leaves the house hungry." Thanks to Monica and Anita's friendliness and the reasonable rates for Vienna, the pension is booked months in advance, so please make your arrangements as soon as you know your dates.

ENGLISH SPOKEN Yes

FACILITIES AND SERVICES Direct-dial phone, hair dryer available, lift, street parking tickets available, radio, cable TV, office safe, laundry service

NEAREST TOURIST ATTRACTIONS Everything in central Vienna is within a ten- to thirty-minute walk

TELEPHONE
533 81 56
FAX
535 64 69
U-BAHN
2, 4, Schottenring
CREDIT CARDS
None
RATES
Single 450–800AS, double 700–980AS; extra bed 280AS; lower off-season rates
BREAKFAST
Included

LEOPOLDSTADT

Leopoldstadt, or the second district, is separated from the rest of Vienna by the Danube Canal. Its main drawing card for visitors is the Prater, the huge city park. Also here is Vienna's trade fair exhibition hall. The area is inhabited largely by immigrants from Turkey, and it has some taudry areas devoted to sex shops and the red-light trade.

HOTELS

(21) Hotel Reichshof $ **102**

Note: A dollar sign ($) indicates a Big Splurge.

(21) HOTEL REICHSHOF $
Mühlfeldgasse 13, A-1020
73 rooms, all with shower or bath and toilet

TELEPHONE
214 31 78

FAX
214 31 78-66

EMAIL
reservation@reichshof

U-BAHN
1, Praterstern/Wien Nord

CREDIT CARDS
AE, DC, MC, V

RATES
Single 1,000–1,400AS, double 1,500–1,900AS, triple 1,300–1,900, apartment 2,500–2,700AS; lower off-season rates

BREAKFAST
Large buffet included

What a hotel! When you arrive, you are likely to be greeted by Axel, the beautiful Dalmation dog who enthusiastically welcomes everyone. Built in 1887 in a classical style, the Reichshof has always been family owned, and it has a wide spectrum of devoted guests who have grown to love and appreciate this very special address in Vienna. What began as a traditional hotel has evolved into one of the most creative imaginable, with the operating strategy saying it all: "Your individuality is our philosophy." This is not just a marketing slogan; it is the driving force that propels present owner Rainer Scheithauer, who encourages young artists and architects to design and develop at least four new room concepts every year.

Guests have a choice of either standard rooms, which are traditional, or superior rooms, which play on the fantasies of "managers, lovers, psychiatrists, astronomers, and dreamers." If you have any occasion to celebrate, do it here in any one of his thirty or more superior rooms. Lovers will want No. 101, done in salmon and azure blue with a drape over the bed, a mirror across from it, and nudes painted on the wall. The beige and brown marble bathroom has a free-standing sink and a tub for two. Astronomers and dreamers will request No. 304, the Star Room, with its ceiling depicting the northern sky aglow with 520 lights. This knockout room has a blue bedspread and backdrop accented with aqua chairs facing a fabulous built-in blue desk and an Art Nouveau crystal lamp. In addition there is a large wardrobe and luggage area. The bathroom has a big tub, full mirror, and a place to put everything. Room 208 could suit a single psychiatrist. Located on the back of the hotel, it is rather stern in tone, with a large desk, a collection of vintage lamps, and a black-and-white tiled bath. Dreamers will love the Laura Ashley Room, done in yellow; its pine furniture mixes well with the Art Deco yellow armchairs and seed prints on the walls. The Italian-style floral bathroom has a stall shower. Room 202 is called the Manager's Room. The strong burgandy color theme, large desk, photos of old cars, a dressing area, and wonderful bathroom tell you why. One of the apartments, No. 206, displays a valuable collection of Villeroy and Bosch UNICEF children's plates. If you try to take one with you, there will be a big, black "?" on the wall where the plate hung.

There is nothing wrong with the standard rooms, but after you have seen the superior rooms and apartments, they pale by comparison. The public areas of the hotel receive a mixed review. The collection of Oriental rugs used throughout is impressive, and so is the breakfast area along the street with black channel tufted bench seating and red Art Deco chairs positioned around gray marble tables. The lavish breakfast buffet, which is available to guests anytime during the day, includes champagne and cake plus five types of rolls, three or four breads, cereals, assorted fruit, more than a dozen cheese and sausage varieties, and six tea choices. Complimentary tea and coffee are served throughout the day, either here or in the summer garden. Unfortunately, the lobby with Indian throws tossed over some of the sofas and chairs does not reflect the imagination and attention to detail shown in the rest of the hotel, but given the setting and mood elsewhere, this is indeed a small blip in the big picture.

ENGLISH SPOKEN Yes

FACILITIES AND SERVICES Bar, direct-dial phone, hair dryers and minibars in deluxe rooms, lift, parking 120AS per day, cable TV, office safe, computer and fax hookups in deluxe rooms and apartments, eight nonsmoking rooms

NEAREST TOURIST ATTRACTIONS Not much, but very close to U-Bahn; three stops to St. Stephen's Cathedral, direct connection to airport

WIEDEN

The small fourth district lies just south of the Opera House and centers around Karlsplatz and Karlskirche. Also here is the Vienna Technical University and the Südbahnhof railway station.

HOTELS

(22) Carlton Opera Hotel $		**104**
(23) Hotel Drei Kronen		**105**
(24) Hotel Papageno		**105**

OTHER OPTIONS

Private Home Accommodations

(25) Frau Hilde Wolfe	**122**

Note: A dollar sign ($) indicates a Big Splurge.

(22) CARLTON OPERA HOTEL $
Schikanedergasse 4, A-1040
52 rooms, all with shower or bath and toilet

TELEPHONE
587 53 02-0

FAX
581 25 11

EMAIL
carlton@ping.at

U-BAHN
1, 2, 4, Karlsplatz, exit Session, Weinerhauptstrasse

CLOSED
Dec 22–26 and Jan 8–28

CREDIT CARDS
AE, DC, MC, V

RATES
Single 1,030–1,370AS, double 1,260–1,890AS; apartment with kitchen 2,200AS; extra bed 370AS; lower off-season rates

BREAKFAST
Buffet included

The Carlton Opera Hotel is in a well-preserved Jugendstil building not far from the big outdoor market and Saturday flea market. The Viennese Art Nouveau style begins at the door as you enter the lobby with its original beveled-glass and wood-frame elevator. Rooms display not only style but character and are customized with matching fabrics and coordinating colors. All have good bathrooms with decent towels, plus the small perks we all like to find, such as tea and coffee makers. The largest double, No. 502, has bare wooden floors and a sofa. Sheer curtains frame the two large windows, which let in plenty of daylight. I like No. 605, a comfortable single under a mansard roof. The addition of a comfortable chair and shelf space in the bathroom with a stall shower are welcome touches. The apartments with kitchenettes are good choices for families or those wanting a bit more space. Owner Ruth Dauber has plans to create more studios nearby, so if this sort of accommodation is for you, be sure to inquire if she has completed this project.

ENGLISH SPOKEN Yes

FACILITIES AND SERVICES Air-conditioning (except in four singles), direct-dial phone, hair dryer, lift, minibar, parking 120AS per day, cable TV, office safe, tea and coffee makers

NEAREST TOURIST ATTRACTIONS Easy walking distance to opera, museums, Kärntner Strasse, large outdoor market and Saturday flea market; good underground connections

(23) HOTEL DREI KRONEN
Schleifmühlgasse 24, A-1040
41 rooms, all with shower or bath and toilet

Ada Adler is a friendly owner who enjoys welcoming guests to her completely renovated Jugendstil hotel. The entrance is up a few steps and through a set of beautiful original brass-accented, beveled-glass swinging doors. Many of the rooms have their lovely, old wooden ceilings intact. Framed Gustav Klimt prints add a decorative note, and writing desks and luggage racks are conveniences that count. The location is just outside the Inner Ring, but it's close enough to walk to Kärntner Strasse, the opera, the famous museums, and to wander through the Saturday morning flea market on Linke Wienzeile.

ENGLISH SPOKEN Yes

FACILITIES AND SERVICES Direct-dial phone, hair dryer available, lift to all but top floor, cable TV, some room safes, office safe

NEAREST TOURIST ATTRACTIONS Opera, museums, Kärntner Strasse, St. Stephen's Cathedral, good underground connections

TELEPHONE
587 32 89, 587 82 84

FAX
587 82 84/11

U-BAHN
1, 2, 4, Karlsplatz, exit Session, Weinerhauptstrasse

CREDIT CARDS
AE, MC, V

RATES
Single 800–950AS, double 1,000–1,400AS; extra bed 250–350AS, mention *Cheap Sleeps* and receive a 10% discount

BREAKFAST
Buffet included

(24) HOTEL PAPAGENO
Wiedner Hauptstrasse 23-25, A-1040
39 rooms, all with shower or bath and toilet

The Papageno Hotel is named after Papageno in Mozart's opera *The Magic Flute,* which was first performed in Vienna in 1791. The hotel is just outside the Inner Ring, but it's still within walking distance to the opera and the underground station at Karlsplatz. Dedicated walkers will not find it too far to most of the museums, the Spanish Riding School, or the Imperial Palace. The well-maintained, older-style hotel has white halls with tiled floors topped with Oriental runners. Guests are treated to a breakfast buffet served in a room with a waterfall and a cage of live birds happily singing. Rooms are big, but they occupy different positions in the pecking order. For instance, No. 32 is a double with cream-colored duvet and pillow covers, an inlaid floor, armoire, extra sofa bed, one armchair, two desk chairs (but no desk), and a crystal chandelier. The white and

TELEPHONE
504 67 44

FAX
504 67 44 22

EMAIL
papageno@atnet.at

INTERNET
www.nethotels.com/papageno

U-BAHN
1, 2, 4, Karlsplatz

CREDIT CARDS
AE, DC, MC, V

RATES
Single 960–1,400AS, double 1,180–1,800, triple 1,520–2,180AS; discount for children and for longer stays; lower off-season rates

BREAKFAST
Included

blue tiled bathroom with a tub and shower is one of the best. No. 52 is a two-room suite with an entry hall leading to two bedrooms. The first has two twin beds with absolutely no view. In fact you can't even see out of it. The second small bedroom has a double bed, and again no view. Single guests fare well in No. 31. While it doesn't have a view, it does have a glass-topped writing desk, two chairs, and a stall shower in a bathroom with a small shelf and two hooks.

ENGLISH SPOKEN Yes

FACILITIES AND SERVICES Bar, direct-dial phone, hair dryer available, lift, minibar, office safe, satellite TV

NEAREST TOURIST ATTRACTIONS Ten-minute walk to the opera and the underground at Karlsplatz, about thirty to St. Stephen's Cathedral

MARIAHILFERSTRASSE _____

Vienna's busiest shopping street, Mariahilferstrasse, is the borderline between the sixth district and the seventh (Neubau). Starting at the Kunsthistorisches Museum and running more than two kilometers to the Westbahnhof, it is lined with every shopping possibility imaginable and has the crowds to prove it. The Naschmarkt, the city's outdoor food market and location of the Saturday morning flea market, is a colorful place to spend an hour or two soaking in the atmosphere and people-watching.

HOTELS

OTHER OPTIONS
Private Home Accommodations

(26) FÜRST METTERNICH HOTEL
Esterházygasse 33, A-1060
55 rooms, all with shower or bath and toilet

TELEPHONE
588 70

FAX
587 52 68

EMAIL
metternich@astrotel.at

U-BAHN
3, Neubaugasse

The building looks like an ornate, pink-frosted, multitiered wedding cake. In its heyday it must have been something with its sweeping marble entry, but now the hotel is fading around the edges and showing its age. If Cheap Sleepers can get past the dull halls and tacky red-and-black satiny bedspreads (which someone wearing blinders and dark glasses must have selected), then there is some merit left here, especially if you are a solo traveler looking for a larger space, a family with children under six years old, or can take advantage of the lower weekend rates.

Since all the rooms are doubles, singles have the advantage of staying in any double but paying the single rate. Room 32, facing the street, is a narrow room with modern furniture and a blue leather barrel chair. The bathroom houses a tub with a hand-held shower hose, but no curtain, a typical omission in a large percentage of Viennese hotels. Room 39 on the back is a quiet room with no view, but it does have space. I would avoid No. 31. Even though you have a peek at Mariahilferstrasse, the indoor-outdoor carpet needs changing, and so does that red satin flounce around the bed. Club Barfly, the hotel's American bar, seems to be a popular gathering spot and evening watering hole, which some guests will need to use frequently if they land in the wrong room.

ENGLISH SPOKEN Yes

FACILITIES AND SERVICES Bar, direct-dial phone, hair dryer available, lift, minibar, cable TV, pay videos, office safe

NEAREST TOURIST ATTRACTIONS Nothing, must use public transportation

NEUBAU

Neubau (the seventh district) is an expansive area between Josef Stadt and Mariahilf, and in itself it's rather dull. The most interesting part is Spittelberg, a small neighborhood of eighteenth- and nineteenth-century cobblestoned streets running between Siebensterngasse and Burggasse, which borders the Museum Quarter of the Inner City. This area has had a checkered past, having been an artistic and working-class area as well as a district known for prostitution. In the late 1960s it was ready for demolition, but a group of foresighted citizens banded together and managed to save the area and its Baroque and Biedermeier houses, which have almost all been restored. Spittelberg is now one of the most popular and charming areas in Vienna for boutique shopping, romantic strolling, interesting dining, and café hopping. At Christmastime one of the best Advent/Christmas markets is held here, and at other times

CREDIT CARDS
AE, DC, MC, V

RATES
Single 1,500AS, double 1,700AS; extra bed 350AS; special weekend rates; children up to age 6 are free in parent's room, children 6–12 pay half price

BREAKFAST
Buffet included

during the year there are street fairs and holiday celebrations. Please see "Cheap Chic in Vienna," page 194, for further details about shopping in Spittelberg.

HOTELS

OTHER OPTIONS

Apartment Rentals and Residence Hotels

Note: A dollar sign ($) indicates a Big Splurge.

(28) ALTSTADT HOTEL $
Kirchengasse 41, A-1070
29 rooms, all with shower or bath and toilet

TELEPHONE
526 33 99-0; toll-free from U.S., 800-365-3346

FAX
523 49 01

EMAIL
alt.vie@magnet.at

INTERNET
members.magnet.at/users/alt.vie/

U-BAHN
3, Neubaugasse

CREDIT CARDS
AE, DC, MC, V

RATES
Single 1,500AS, double 1,980AS; two-person suite 2,380AS, each additional person 400AS

BREAKFAST
Buffet included

There is no question that one of the most successful small hotels in Vienna is the Altstadt, which is owned and run by Otto Wiesenthal. For many years he traveled extensively with his computer business, gathering worldwide hotel experience. Finally in 1991, he decided to open his own hotel based on the information he had amassed in his travels. The result is nothing short of stunning. From the moment you arrive until you finally walk out the door, management's focus is on providing personalized service to each guest. A friendly, multilingual staff is always available to obtain opera tickets, book ongoing travel, arrange for business services, or help guests in any other way. Nothing seems to be too much trouble.

The hotel displays a smart, eclectic mixture of antiques and art, mixed attractively with reproduction and contemporary furniture styles. Guests are drawn to the beautiful salon with a wood-burning fireplace glowing on cold Vienna days. Mr. Wiesenthal's enviable collection of art lines the halls and is showcased in the crisp, Art Nouveau–style rooms, all of which have nicely tiled baths, two telephones, and videoplayers. Many have views of the Ulrichsplatz and the picturesque St. Ulrich Church, one of the oldest in Vienna. The suites are individually decorated and designed to meet the needs of longer-term guests who want working and living space apart from their bedroom. Another advantage is that three of them are equipped with a microwave, small stove, and refrigerator in case you want to go to the market and cook in during your stay. The largest apartment is the Angela, facing the back with two bedrooms plus a living room with one wall lined with books. The only disadvantage I could find was that you must walk through one bedroom to get to the other and through both of them to get to the bathroom. No. 33, a junior suite with no cooking facilities, is a large room with a sitting area and a view of St. Ulrich Church.

ENGLISH SPOKEN Yes

FACILITIES AND SERVICES Two direct-dial phones in each room, hair dryer, lift, minibar, parking 250AS per day, cable TV, videos, office safe, nonsmoking rooms available, limousine service to/from airport at additional charge

NEAREST TOURIST ATTRACTIONS Must use public transportation; three underground stops to St. Stephen's Church

(29) HOTEL-PENSION MUSEUM
Museumstrasse 3, A-1070
15 rooms, all with shower or bath and toilet

"Your splendid hospitality made our visit to Vienna an absolute joy" and "You have made certain that Vienna will remain a very special place" are only two of the laudatory reviews guests have written in the hotel's hospitality book. Originally the home of an aristocratic family going back to the seventeenth century, the pension has been owned for more than twenty-five years by Frau Scheyrer. Her guests, many of whom are associated with the nearby museums, have been coming back for years. The large rooms are old-fashioned without apologies, but many have superb views from large windows or private balconies. Bathrooms fall into the vintage category. You could hold a dance in Room 31, and the wardrobe is big enough to hang your ballgown. From here you can look out on St. Stephen's Cathedral, the Natural History Museum, and the Fine Arts Museum and Volkstheater. The furniture doesn't match the regal style of the house, but it is serviceable. Red-carpeted No. 34 is another big choice, with a small balcony and a shower in the bathroom. Room 33 is not as big, but the view is great and the decor more appealing. For a quiet

TELEPHONE
523 44 26-0, 523 51 27-0

FAX
523 44 26 30

U-BAHN
2, 3, Volkstheater

CREDIT CARDS
AE, DC, MC, V

RATES
Single 860–1,180AS, double 1,450–1,600AS; extra bed 250AS; lower off-season rates

BREAKFAST
Buffet included

single choice, book No. 38, which has a view of vine-covered walls and one of the better bathrooms done in pink tile.

ENGLISH SPOKEN Yes

FACILITIES AND SERVICES Direct-dial phone, hair dryer available, lift, parking 100AS per night, satellite TV, office safe

NEAREST TOURIST ATTRACTIONS All the major museums, Rathaus

(30) PENSION ATRIUM
Burggasse 118, A-1070
18 rooms, all with shower or bath and toilet

TELEPHONE
523 31 14, 526 51 04

FAX
523 31 14-9

U-BAHN
3, 6, Westbahnhof; Bus No. 48 and Tram No. 5 stop near the hotel

CREDIT CARDS
None

RATES
Single 600AS, double 880–980AS; extra bed 200AS; lower off-season rates

BREAKFAST
Continental included, served in rooms only

For Cheap Sleepers wanting to be near Westbahnhof Station, Herr Wagner's Pension Atrium is a good choice. He has been running the place since 1968 and takes great pride in his well-maintained eighteen-room pension. Although the neighborhood is not close to much on a visitor's must-see list, it does provide a good look at middle-class city living. All but two of the clean rooms have a balcony, and I think the best are those with tubs in the bathroom. The plain furniture is streamlined, windows are double-glazed to buffer the noise, closet space is generous, and most of the bathrooms have good shelf space, light, and heated towel racks. There is no breakfast room, so you can enjoy breakfast in bed or on your balcony.

ENGLISH SPOKEN Yes

FACILITIES AND SERVICES Direct-dial phone, hair dryer available, lift, parking 120AS, TV (satellite planned), office safe

NEAREST TOURIST ATTRACTIONS None, must use public transportation

(31) PENSION HARGITA
Andreasgasse 1, A-1070
10 rooms, 1 with shower and toilet; 6 with sink and shower; 3 with sink only

TELEPHONE
526 19 28

FAX
526 04 92

U-BAHN
3, Neubaugasse

CREDIT CARDS
None

RATES
Single 420–475AS, double 580–840AS, triple 945AS; lower off-season rates

The Pension Hargita is a perky little cutie, perfect for Cheap Sleepers who don't mind being a few underground stops away from tourist central. It is, however, convenient to the Westbahnhof and around the corner from all the shopping that lines Mariahilferstrasse. The collection of Austrian wood carvings, Tyrolean chairs, and ceramic plates displayed in the hotel adds authentic

character to the public areas, and it tells you that someone is paying attention to detail. The rooms are done in
bleached pine with simple duvet covers and bare floors. I
think the best buys are the rooms with only a sink.
Those with a shower have portable units resembling
airless phone booths stuck in the corner. However, there
is nothing wrong with No. 10, the only one that has the
works: that is, a soft blue bathroom with a shower and
toilet.

ENGLISH SPOKEN Yes

FACILITIES AND SERVICES No elevator (first-floor walk-
up), TV, office safe

NEAREST TOURIST ATTRACTIONS Mariahilferstrasse, otherwise must use public transportation

BREAKFAST
40AS per person

(32) PENSION LINDENHOF
Lindengasse 4, A-1070
19 rooms, 6 with shower or bath and toilet

Many years ago the pension was a place where young
girls and their chaperones stayed when visiting Vienna.
For the past two decades, George Gebrael, his daughter
Zara, and the rest of the family have been running the
show here. The hallway to the reception area, which is
backed by Mrs. Gebrael's postcard collection, is a veri-
table jungle of houseplants. There is no mandate on
luxury in the thirties-style furnishings that grace the
rooms. For best results, ask for something with a view
and avoid Rooms 7 through 15 and No. 19, unless you
are willing to accept a grim wall view in exchange for
less noise.

ENGLISH SPOKEN Yes

FACILITIES AND SERVICES Lift that only goes up (you
walk down), office safe

NEAREST TOURIST ATTRACTIONS Walk to the Volkstheater, but need public transportation for everything
else

TELEPHONE
523 04 98

FAX
523 73 62

U-BAHN
3, Neubaugasse

CREDIT CARDS
None

RATES
Single 370–470AS, double
620–840AS, triple 920–
1,250AS; extra person 300–
410AS; lower off-season rates

BREAKFAST
Continental included

JOSEFSTADT _____

Josefstadt, in the eighth district, is named after Emperor Josef I and is the smallest of Vienna's twenty-three
districts. The area, located toward the back of the
Rathaus (city hall), is largely a middle-class residential
neighborhood with many good restaurants and a few
good hotels.

HOTELS

OTHER OPTIONS

Apartment Rentals and Residence Hotels

(34) HOTEL GRAF STADION
Buchfeldgasse 5, A-1080
34 rooms, all with shower or bath and toilet

TELEPHONE
405 52 84

FAX
405 01 11 84

U-BAHN
2, Rathaus

CREDIT CARDS
AE, DC, MC, V

RATES
Single 870AS, double 1,400, triple 1,600, quad 1,780; lower off-season rates

BREAKFAST
Buffet included

The management is on its toes at this friendly hotel in a renovated nineteenth-century Biedermeier building close to the Rathaus, Vienna's city hall. For best results, ask for a room on the third floor either facing front or overlooking the courtyard. Rooms on the first floor tend to be noisy, and on the second, some of the windows are frosted and you can't see out at all. None of the rooms have double beds, either an advantage or a disadvantage depending on your traveling companion. Most come equipped with a desk, good lighting, and modern tiled baths.

During the off-season, rates are especially attractive.

ENGLISH SPOKEN Yes

FACILITIES AND SERVICES Direct-dial phone, hair dryer, lift, satellite TV, office safe

NEAREST TOURIST ATTRACTIONS Rathaus, museums, four underground stops to Karlsplatz

(35) HOTEL-PENSION ZIPSER
Lange Gasse 49, A-1080
47 rooms, all with shower or bath and toilet

TELEPHONE
404 540

FAX
408 52 66 13

U-BAHN
2, Rathaus

CREDIT CARDS
AE, DC, MC, V

RATES
Single 860AS, double 1,310–1,440AS; extra bed 390AS; lower off-season rates

There isn't much zip at the Zipser, but the surprise-free, clean, modern rooms offer guests uniform comforts. The nonthreatening browns and beiges work well with the plain built-in modular furniture. Singles have a desk with good working light, a closet with a safe, and a bathroom with shelf and hook space. Some of the larger rooms have sofa beds and double sinks in the bathrooms. Many rooms overlook a private garden, ensuring guests a calm night's rest. The location is not very central, but the underground whisks you to Karlsplatz and the Kärntner Strasse in minutes.

ENGLISH SPOKEN Yes

FACILITIES AND SERVICES Direct-dial phone, hair dryer available, lift, two parking places at 170AS per night, TV, room and office safe

NEAREST TOURIST ATTRACTIONS Rathaus, museums, otherwise must use public transportation

(36) PENSION BARONESSE
Lange Gasse 61, A-1080
39 rooms, all with shower or bath and toilet

The pension is located on a busy thoroughfare lined with shops catering to this middle-class area. Each room has its own individual touches, but they are all on the ruffly and frilly side, decorated in an older style with floral prints on both the carpets and fabrics. The brightest rooms face the front, but there is some street noise. One of these, No. 335, has a cream-colored bed and night stands. The striped wall covering coordinates with the dusty rose–colored flowered paper behind the bed. Rooms on the back are definitely more quiet, but the view is uninspiring. The best of these are No. 004, in shades of beige, orange, and brown, and No. 006, with three windows and a high tub in the bathroom that might be hard for some to step over.

ENGLISH SPOKEN Yes

FACILITIES AND SERVICES Direct-dial phone, some hair dryers, lift, minibar, satellite TV, office safe

NEAREST TOURIST ATTRACTIONS Rathaus, otherwise must use public transportation; good tram connections a half block away

(37) PENSION COLUMBIA
Kochgasse 9, A-1080
8 rooms, 1 with shower or bath and toilet

The Columbia is one of Vienna's oldest pensions, attracting a clientele who value a slower, Old World pace and who don't mind sharing hall facilities. When it opened more than a century ago, it was a full-fledged pension serving formal sit-down meals to guests who came for months at a time. It has always boasted some of the most reasonable rates in Vienna, even sixty years ago when a room with full board went for 10 to 12AS per day, or the equivalent of $1.25 to $1.75. It's definitely more expensive today, but the prices are still fair. Many

BREAKFAST
Buffet included

TELEPHONE
405 10 61

FAX
405 10 61 61

U-BAHN
2, Rathaus

CREDIT CARDS
DC, MC, V

RATES
Single 720AS, double 1,140AS, triple 1,420AS, quad 1,700AS; lower off-season rates

BREAKFAST
Buffet included

TELEPHONE AND FAX
405 675 7

U-BAHN
2, Rathaus

CREDIT CARDS
MC, V

RATES
Single 350–400AS, double 700–900AS, triple 1,050AS; sometimes lower off-season rates

BREAKFAST
Buffet included

signs of the pension's former grand life remain—the pretty staircase, high ceilings, a tile-and-brick fireplace, and many framed prints of old Vienna. The rooms are definitely not modern, but they are clean and you feel at home in them. Some have crystal chandeliers and great armoires. Room 8 has a matched pair of bird's-eye-maple twin beds, white lace curtains, and three Oriental rugs warming the old wooden floors. Hall baths and toilets are well maintained.

ENGLISH SPOKEN Yes

FACILITIES AND SERVICES No elevator (up two flights), office safe, free washing machine

NEAREST TOURIST ATTRACTIONS Not much, but good underground and tram connections

(38) ROSEN HOTEL INTERNATIONAL
Buchfeldgasse 8, A-1080
54 rooms, all with shower or bath and toilet

TELEPHONE
403 52 91 0

FAX
403 52 91 62

U-BAHN
2, Rathaus

RATES
Single 895 AS, double 1,790 AS, triple 1,950 AS

BREAKFAST
Buffet included

The hotel is part of a small chain with other properties in Vienna, Graz, and Salzburg. All the standard-issue rooms are identical, compactly designed around built-ins and one or two chairs, depending on the configuration. A small entry with coat hooks and a luggage rack gives the feeling of more space. The bathrooms provide stall showers, a sliver of soap, and decent towels. The one so-called extra I found odd was the gas mask that was in every room. None of the staff could explain their presence other than to say they have always had them, but never needed them. Strange.

ENGLISH SPOKEN Yes

FACILITIES AND SERVICES Bar serving light snacks, direct-dial phone, lift, minibar, parking 70 AS per night, radio, TV, room safe

NEAREST TOURIST ATTRACTIONS Rathaus, public transportation for everything else

ALSERGRUND

Alsergrund, the ninth district, is where you will find the University of Vienna, many medical facilities, the Freud Museum on Berggasse, modern art in the Palas Liechtenstein, and the Franz-Josef Bahnhof.

HOTELS

(40) Pension Franz   **115**

(40) PENSION FRANZ
Währinger Strasse 12, A-1090
25 rooms, all with shower or bath and toilet

The Pension Franz dates from the time our great-grandparents packed their trunks and left for Europe to do the Grand Tour. In those days, this pension was known as "a boarding house in a good situation in one of the most elegant districts of Vienna . . . with a fine view of the Ring and gardens of the Votive Church." The pension boasted "home comforts united with the advantages of a first class hotel, guaranteed to satisfy the most exacting visitor." Facilities included an elegant dining room with first-class cuisine, a luxurious drawing room, separate reading and music rooms, and a writing room with a typewriter. There were bathrooms, hot and cold water in every room, and central heating. In addition they offered a safe for guests, a vacuum cleaner, electric lights, a lift, an international telephone line, plus a resident doctor and dentist. The most expensive rooms were the two-room suites on the first floor. In other rooms, the prices ranged from 2AS a day for a single to 12AS for a corner double with a balcony. Full board cost 7AS a day and consisted of a Continental breakfast, a four- or five-course dinner served at 1 P.M., and a three-course supper at 8 P.M. A full bath cost 2AS, a hip bath 1AS, and a foot bath was half a schilling. Ah, those were the days.

Amazingly enough, not much has changed in the public areas of this Viennese relic. The impressive reception and lobby area still has a massive stone fireplace and sweeping stairway. Oriental rugs cover the inlaid floors. The breakfast room is hung with large oil paintings of anonymous ancestors and red-carpeted hallways lead to the twenty-five guest rooms. The rooms are a mixed bag, and some frankly fall short. Best bets include No. 201,

TELEPHONE
34 36 37

FAX
34 36 37 23

U-BAHN
2, Schottentor

CREDIT CARDS
AE, DC, MC, V

RATES
Single 700–800AS, double 1,000–1,200AS, triple 1,300–1,400AS; extra bed 200-300As

BREAKFAST
Buffet included

with three windows opening onto the Votive Church. The cream-colored lacquered furniture does justice to its surroundings, and still leaves plenty of living space. In addition to four armchairs in the center of the room, there is a double bed, double armoir, writing desk, and a mirrored dressing table. The blue tiled bathroom has everything including a bidet. Depending on your taste, you will either love or hate No. 204, done in uniquely sixties blond furniture with gold accents. There is some noise, but the view is good and so is the natural light. You do not want to reserve No. 110, which has hideous, viewless pebbled windows, or No. 204, a claustrophobic single facing a wall. As you can see, this hotel is not for every Cheap Sleeper, but if nostalgia is high on your list, and you get a good room, it can be a trip. When you go, be sure to ask to see the Visit Book, with entries as early as 1905 from guests from Odessa, Berlin, Prague, New York, Cairo, Bucharest, and Paris.

ENGLISH SPOKEN Yes

FACILITIES AND SERVICES Direct-dial phone, hair dryer available, lift to main floor only, minibar, cable TV, office safe

NEAREST TOURIST ATTRACTIONS None, must use public transportation

Other Options

Accommodation Agencies

VILLAS INTERNATIONAL
950 Northgate Drive, Suite 206, San Rafael, CA 94903

David Kendall runs Villas International, a company that provides clients with a full range of rental properties throughout Europe, including Vienna. I have used their services in Italy and in Austria and found them to be very service-oriented and a pleasure to deal with. When contacting them, be sure to state your needs, dates, and budget. Office hours are Monday to Friday 9 A.M. to 9 P.M., Pacific Standard Time.

TELEPHONE
415-499-9490; toll-free in U.S., 800-221-2260

FAX
415-499-9491

EMAIL
villas@best.com

INTERNET
www.villasintl.com

CREDIT CARDS
None

RATES
Vary by location, time of year, and level of luxury, but prices generally start at $650 per week for two in a studio

Apartment Rentals and Residence Hotels

Apartments rentals in Vienna are professionally run, and you won't run into the ghastly, garage-sale decor you sometimes find in Prague and Budapest. Apartments also tend to be big, but they will only be cheaper than hotels if you stay for two weeks or more. As always, assess your needs (length of stay, location, kitchen, elevators, and so on) so you get the kind of place that best suits you.

(16) APARTMENT-PENSION SACHER
Rotenturmstrasse 1/7, A-1010
8 apartments with kitchens and private facilities

You simply cannot beat this location—it is A+ perfect. Besides, a stay at the charming Apartment-Pension Sacher says, This *is* Vienna! Situated in the first district in the center of Old Vienna, most of the well-equipped and attractively furnished flats have a spectacular view of St. Stephen's Cathedral, and those that do not have a view are still miles ahead of the competition. The pension is owned by Claudia Sacher, the great-great-granddaughter of the chef who created the original *Sachertorte* in 1832, and his picture hangs in her tiny office behind

TELEPHONE AND FAX
533 32 38

U-BAHN
1, 3, Stephansplatz

HOURS
Office open Mon–Sat from 7:30 A.M.–1 P.M.

CREDIT CARDS
None

RATES
Single 850–1,050AS, double 980–1,270AS; extra bed 250AS; lower rates for longer stays

BREAKFAST
Not served

her desk. *All* of the flats are recommendable, thanks to their traditional Austrian furnishings, ample closet space, and comfortable layout. If you have flat No. 2, you will see the horse-drawn carriages that stand by the cathedral and have a bird's-eye view into the office and palace of the Archbishop of Vienna. No. 4 is one of the largest, with a huge sitting area and separate bedroom. The view of St. Stephen's is super, and so is the closet space. Both Nos. 5 and 6 are smaller, but still very, very nice and adaptable for a short or long stay. Because there are so few flats, it is easy to get acquainted with your neighbors, all of whom are interesting and loyally de-voted to this very special place. As you can imagine, reservations should be made as far in advance as possible.

ENGLISH SPOKEN Yes

FACILITIES AND SERVICES Fully fitted apartments with kitchens, linens, and daily maid service (except Sundays and holidays); direct-dial phone, fax and answering ma-chines on request, lift, cable TV, room safe, laundry service available

NEAREST TOURIST ATTRACTIONS Heart of the Inner City, everything within walking distance

(17) APPARTMENT PENSION RIEMERGASSE $
Riemergasse 8, A-1010
14 apartments with kitchens and private facilities

TELEPHONE
512 72 200

FAX
513 77 78

EMAIL
otto@otto.co.at

U-BAHN
3, Stubentor, or 1, 3,
Stephansplatz

CREDIT CARDS
None

RATES
Apartments start at 920AS per night for one person and go to 4,300AS per night for seven people; no weekly discounts, but 20% discount for monthly stays

BREAKFAST
66AS extra per day, per person

For a longer stay in Vienna, the Appartment Pension Riemergasse is on my very short list of preferred picks. The location in the first district is great. Nothing is more than twenty or thirty minutes by foot, and for longer journeys, you have the choice of two underground stops. The apartments are located in a wonderful old building that was originally built for a countess, and it was one of the few in the neighborhood not destroyed during World War II. The building is now owned by the Otto family, who for twenty-five years ran it as a pension. Now under the helm of one of the sons, Dr. Eugen Otto, it has been completely refitted into smart apartments with all the modern comforts and conve-niences. One of the smallest units, No. 31 has a compact kitchen with a microwave, nice bathroom with a long tub, and from the living room a view of St. Stephen's Cathedral, which is only a five-minute walk away. Apart-ment 2 has a large living room with a dining room table, a built-in extra bed, two sofas, two armchairs, and a huge master bedroom with loads of closet space and a second television set. There is a smaller twin bedroom with its own full bath, complete with tub and enclosed stall shower. Another advantage is the eat-in kitchen with a four-burner stove, refrigerator and freezer, dishwasher, and clothes washer and dryer. A stay here can be seductive, and should you decide to make more permanent arrangements, Dr. Otto can help you, as he runs his Vienna real estate office from here.

ENGLISH SPOKEN Yes

FACILITIES AND SERVICES Fully-fitted apartments with kitchens and all linens provided; direct-dial phone, hair dryer, lift to all but top floor, parking 190AS per day, cable TV, iron, office safe, daily maid service, twenty-four-hour reception, dishwasher and laundry facilities in larger apartments

NEAREST TOURIST ATTRACTIONS Can walk to everything in the Inner City

(18) SINGERSTRASSE 21/25 APARTMENTS $
Singerstrasse 21/25, A-1010
77 apartments with kitchens and private facilities

The Singerstrasse Apartments are billed as "the smart place to reside in downtown Vienna." That is true, especially if you are here on business and need modern whistles and bells in your accommodation. The location is less than five minutes from St. Stephen's Cathedral. The units are modern, each with a marble bath, designer furniture, air-conditioning, and fax and PC connections. All have walk-in closets with a safe, and the kitchens are fitted with not only a dishwasher and microwave but electric coffee makers, toasters, and even a champagne cooler. There is an underground parking garage and an in-house self-serve laundromat for those who do not want to send things out to be laundered.

ENGLISH SPOKEN Yes

FACILITIES AND SERVICES Air-conditioning, direct-dial phone with answering machine, hair dryer available, lift, parking 130AS per day, satelite TV, room safe, stereo with CD player, PC and fax connections, laundromat for guests, video security system, kitchens have microwave and dishwasher, twice weekly cleaning, a final cleaning and utilities are extra

NEAREST TOURIST ATTRACTIONS Within a five- to thirty-minute walk to everything in the center of Vienna

TELEPHONE
514 49-0

FAX
513 16 17

U-BAHN
1, 3, Stephansplatz

HOURS
Office open Mon–Fri 8 A.M.–8 P.M.

CREDIT CARDS
AE, DC, MC, V

RATES
Four types of apartments from 8,740–12,960AS per week; one-week minimum stay required; lower off-season rates and for longer stays

BREAKFAST
Not served

(33) ROTHENSTEINER APPARTEMENTS $
Neustiftgasse 66, A-1070
35 apartments, all with kitchens and private facilities

TELEPHONE
523 96 43

FAX
523 96 43 17

U-BAHN
3, Zieglergasse

CREDIT CARDS
MC, V

RATES
Rates start at 750AS per person and go up to 2,200AS, depending on type of apartment, length of stay, and time of year; lower rates for longer stays

BREAKFAST
Buffet included, but can be deducted (80AS per person) if requested in advance

If you are looking for true Viennese charm, service, and serenity outside of the midcity whirl (in Neubau, the seventh district), do yourself a great favor and make your reservation now at the Rothensteiner Appartements. This advice, however, comes with a warning: One guest arrived ten years ago and is still there, so plan accordingly!

For five generations this gracious property has belonged to the Rothensteiner family, who thirty years ago turned it into an apartment residence par excellence. The sitting areas, hallways, and dining room are graced with their Austrian antiques, photos of old Vienna, a table with a basket of dried flowers atop a hand-crocheted cover, and big green potted plants. The apartments are all different, and all are wonderful in their own way. Some of those suitable for one or two people, such as No. 31, have a Murphy bed, which allows for more daytime living space. No. 35, another single, has a mansard window and terrace with a table and chairs. I like its walk-in closet, corner kitchen, and desk space with bookshelves. If you need more space, reserve No. 18, one of the largest. The spacious living room has a sofa and two easy chairs, an old ceramic heater (for decoration purposes only), and a turn-of-the-century breakfront. The bedroom accommodates a double bed, armoire, and walk-in closet, and the bathroom is large enough to have a washing machine—a real advantage, in my opinion, if you are staying for any length of time. No. 22 is also an exceptional choice, with an eat-in modern kitchen and a bathroom with a tiled shower. But wait until you see the bedroom, which has a complete matching set of antique furniture, including twin beds, an armoire, and two bedside tables.

Frau Rothensteiner told me, "Our leading principle is to offer our guests a Viennese home, and therefore our family and staff strive for your satisfaction." I can assure you they exceed their own expectations, and who could ask for more?

ENGLISH SPOKEN Yes

FACILITIES AND SERVICES Direct-dial phone, hair dryer, lift, fitted kitchens, parking 120AS per night, TV, video player on request, office safe, some larger apartments have washing machines, laundry service, babysitting available, free use of bicycles, daily maid service; restaurant open Mon–Fri for dinner from Sept–June (closed for summer)

NEAREST TOURIST ATTRACTIONS None, must use public transportation

(39) LAUDON COURT APARTMENT HOUSE
Laudongasse 8, A-1080
39 apartments, all with fully fitted kitchens, shower, bath, and toilet

Laudon Court, located in a quiet residential quarter in the eighth district and close to the Rathaus, was my Vienna address, and I would definitely choose it again for many reasons. Within a five- to ten-minute walk from the front door are all the things one needs to set up and maintain housekeeping: a small supermarket and excellent greengrocer, two tempting bakeries, a full-service bank, drugstores, hairdressers, several outstanding restaurants (see *Cheap Eats in Prague, Vienna, and Budapest*), dry cleaners, assorted shops, and easy tram and underground connections to all parts of the city. Otherwise, taxis are only a block or so away. The four types of functional apartments are sparely modern. I appreciated the work space provided by the executive-style desk and comfortable black leather chair, being able to stay abreast of world news on CNN, the closets and drawer space, and the white tiled bathroom with plenty of shelves. Maid service was thorough and attentive, and the young desk staff efficient, helpful, and always friendly. All in all, Laudon Court adds up to a stellar Cheap Sleep in Vienna.

ENGLISH SPOKEN Yes

FACILITIES AND SERVICES Direct-dial phone, lift, fitted kitchens, radio, CD player, cable TV, maid service Mon–Sat, free washer and dryer in basement

NEAREST TOURIST ATTRACTIONS Rathaus, good public transportation connections to evertyhing else

TELEPHONE
407 13 70

FAX
407 13 71

U-BAHN
2, Rathaus

HOURS
Office open daily 8 A.M.–9 P.M.

CREDIT CARDS
AE, MC, V

RATES
From 1,000–2,000AS per day; crib 100AS; extra bed 200AS; final cleaning fee 700AS; prices depend on type of apartment and length of stay, with very good rates for one month or more

BREAKFAST
Not served

Private Home Accommodations

Private home accommodations in Vienna are not much different than those in Prague or Budapest. They are an old-fashioned type of lodging, and they are best-suited to those not needing to live in the fast lane. Rooms can be overfurnished, the bed spreads may not match, and the decor may not be to your taste, but they are usually presided over by friendly matrons and patrons who will be glad to see you. This type of accommodation provides a great window on the lives of working-class Viennese, whom you will meet and get to know during your stay.

(19) FRAU ADELE GRÜN
Gonzagagasse 1, Apartment 19, Third Floor, A-1010
4 private rooms, none with private facilities

TELEPHONE
533 25 06

U-BAHN
1, 4, Schwedenplatz

CREDIT CARDS
None

RATES
Single 500AS, double 800AS; extra bed 100AS

BREAKFAST

Almost three decades ago, Adele Grün found herself alone, but she decided she wanted to remain active and work a little, so she opened her home to paying guests. She told me, "My old lady friends have pills, aches, and pains, can't sleep, always complain. That's not for me. I take a little nap, do some grocery shopping because I still cook for my family. Then I go to the coffeehouse, meet my old lady friends and listen to their sad tales." Obviously she has the right approach to life because she has been going strong all these years and shows no signs of slowing down. Frankly speaking, hers is a basic budget choice with furnishings past their prime. The exception is the entryway, where she has some remarkable pieces of furniture. When I asked about them, she said they were all she had left after the Russians looted Vienna during World War II. She doesn't serve breakfast, but guests can make a cup of tea or coffee in her kitchen. The neighborhood in this part of the first district is interesting, especially Ruprecht's Church, which is just around the corner and one of the oldest in the city.

ENGLISH SPOKEN Yes

FACILITIES AND SERVICES Lift, public parking under the building

NEAREST TOURIST ATTRACTIONS Just off the Inner Ring, about a fifteen- to thirty-minute walk to most tourist destinations

(25) FRAU HILDE WOLFE
Schleifmühlgasse 7, A-1040
3 rooms, none with private shower or bath and toilet

TELEPHONE
586 51 03

U-BAHN
1, 2, 4, Karlsplatz

CREDIT CARDS
None

RATES
Single 400AS, double 550AS, triple 800AS, quad 1,035AS

If staying as a guest in a Viennese home appeals to you, this choice in the fourth district is one of the better options for Cheap Sleepers. When you arrive, there is no name outside to indicate where you should go in the building, but just walk up one flight of stairs and you will see the name on the door. Frau Wolfe is delightful, the perfect granny we all wish we had. She lives here with her husband and grandson, who is a teacher. Her daughter and her family occupy a flat upstairs. When I visited her on a cold, drab late-December day, she brought me into her kitchen and fixed me a big cup of hot chocolate. After my visit ended, she was the first person in Vienna to wish me a Merry Christmas.

Her rooms are far from modern; in fact, some of them feel plucked from an antique shop. One of her rooms has a marble fireplace and a wall of bookshelves behind glass doors. The Art Deco china cabinet displays the pieces she has collected over the many years she has lived in this flat. In another she has a large display of Austrian crystal. She has a larger room, suitable for two to four people, with an antique chest of drawers, love seat, several nice paintings, and a better closet situation. The room next to the bathroom is much more modern. The two hall toilets are excellent and the communal bathroom adequate. Frau Wolfe serves breakfast in her kitchen, and is available for babysitting duties. She also has a washing machine guests may use for a small charge.

ENGLISH SPOKEN Yes

FACILITIES AND SERVICES Lift

NEAREST TOURIST ATTRACTIONS Can walk to the opera, outdoor food and Saturday flea market, and to Karlsplatz, the biggest underground station in Vienna

BREAKFAST
35AS extra per person

(27) BARBARA KOLLER
Schmalzhofgasse 11, first floor, A-1060
5 rooms, all with shower or bath and toilet

This better be good, I thought, as I arrived at this sixth-district address, a dull building dating from the last century with the name J. M. Hammer etched across the front. To reach the guest house, I entered through the main door, walked to the end, and turned right to an iron gate that led to stairs going to the first floor. Spry Barbara Koller met me and showed me the five rooms she has been renting to visitors since 1971. I had frankly expected to be underwhelmed . . . but it was just the opposite. In addition to the affordable Cheap Sleeping price, all the rooms have something to offer, especially No. 5, where we are talking space with a capital S. The entryway, with a separate toilet off of it, is bigger than many hotel rooms. The room itself adjoins a large, sparsely furnished sitting room that overlooks the garden area for

TELEPHONE AND FAX
597 29 35

U-BAHN
3, Zieglergasse, or 3, 6, Wesbahnhof

CLOSED
Nov

CREDIT CARDS
None

RATES
390AS per person

BREAKFAST
Continental included

the Indian restaurant below. Two armoires and a luggage rack mean you can unpack and shake the wrinkles out of your clothes. Room 2 has the best layout and view of the garden. The bathroom has a tub and shower, plus a separate toilet and sink. Two windows let in plenty of light in Room 4, which has fifties-style furniture, a table and three chairs, and a great old two-tiered marble washstand. Even though the neighborhood is hardly exciting, you are only four stops from St. Stephen's Cathedral and five to the City Air Terminal.

ENGLISH SPOKEN Limited

FACILITIES AND SERVICES No elevator, room safe

NEAREST TOURIST ATTRACTIONS None, but public transportation is nearby

---

Seasonal Hotel Accommodations

Seasonal hotels are actually student dormitories that operate from July through September when the universities are not in session. While the accommodations are sparse, they do provide clean Cheap Sleeps for those on a limited budget. For the most part, credit cards are not accepted, groups are favored, and reservations should always be made as far in advance as possible. The Studentenwohnheimn der Wiener Musikhochschule, described below, is the most centrally located seasonal accommodation, and it is typical of what is offered. If you cannot get in here, the easiest thing to do is call or fax Rosenhotels (tel: 911 49 10; fax: 910 02 69), which operates several locations in Vienna, or contact the central reservation number for the Albertina student residences (tel: 521 74 93; fax: 521 19 68).

(20) STUDENTENWOHNHEIM DER WIENER MUSIKHOCHSCHULE
Johannesgasse 8, A-1010
85 rooms, 10 with shower or bath and toilet

TELEPHONE
514 84 48

FAX
514 84 49

U-BAHN
1, 4, Karlsplatz, or 1, 3, Stephansplatz

OPEN
July 1–Sept 30

CREDIT CARDS
None

Up to two hundred Cheap Sleepers can stay in eighty-five one-bed to four-bed rooms. All rooms are equipped with sinks, a telephone for incoming calls, and a minibar. Some have private facilities. The best deal is the apartment with two double rooms, a bathroom, a kitchen, and a living room, all for under 400AS per person, per night. During the year, the hostel operates as a dorm for music students who are studying in Vienna. Please note, the hostel is open to the general public only from the first of July through September.

An added bonus for Cheap Eaters is the student cafeteria, which is open for breakfast and lunch on weekdays only. Prices are definitely Cheap Eater friendly and wine and beer are served.

ENGLISH SPOKEN Yes

FACILITIES AND SERVICES Lift, small lockers, minibars

NEAREST TOURIST ATTRACTIONS Heart of Inner City, can walk to everything

RATES
All rates are per person: single without private facilities 320AS, with private facilities 500AS; double without private facilities 220AS, with private facilities 390AS; triple with private facilities 280AS; quad 260AS; apartment with kitchen and private facilities 370AS. Student rates for any room without private facilities 170AS; special student rates in September; all with private facilities, single 240AS, double 210AS, extra bed 160AS. Group discounts for twenty or more people.

BREAKFAST
Included for rooms with private facilities; lunch and dinner for groups on request

Glossary of Vocabulary Terms

In Austria, German is spoken with an accent, and the Viennese have their own dialect. This just adds to the fun of trying to unscramble this very difficult language. Don't worry, though, as no one expects you to be conversant. However, it is always nice to recognize a few words and to extend greetings. Below is a list of a few words and terms to help you.

General Phrases

yes/no	*ja/nein*
Please/You are welcome	*Bitte schön*
Thank you very much	*Danke schön*
Excuse me	*Entschuldigen sie*
Good day	*Grüss got*
Good morning	*Guten morgen*
Good evening	*Guten abend*
Good night	*Guten nacht*
Good-bye	*Auf wiedersehen*
How are you?	*Wie ghet is ihnen?*
Very well, thank you	*Sehr gut, danke*
And you?	*Und ihnen?*
Pleased to meet you	*Sehr erfreut*
Mr./Mrs./Miss	*Herr/Frau/Fräulein*
large/small	*gross/klein*
a little	*wenig ein bisschen*
a lot	*sehr viel*
all	*alles*
good/bad	*gut/schlecht*
hot/cold	*heiss/kalt*
with/without	*mit/ohne*
open/closed	*offen, auf/geschlossen*
right/left/straight ahead	*rechts/links/gerade aus*
Where are the toilets?	*Wo sind die toiletten bitte?*
Do you speak English?	*Sprechen sie Englisch?*
I do not speak German	*Ich spreche kein Deutsch*
I do not understand	*Ich verstehe nicht*
I understand	*Ich verstehe*
Where is . . .?	*Wo ist . . .?*
What is this?	*Was ist das?*
Do you have?	*Haben sie?*
How much does that cost?	*Wieviel kostet das?*
It is expensive/cheap	*Es ist teuer/billig*

At the Hotel

a room	*ein zimmer*
I would like a room for two	*Ich hätte gern ein zimmer für zwei*
I would like a single room	*Ich hätte gern ein einzelzimmer*
with shower, bath, toilet	*mit dusche, bad, toilette*
the key	*den schlüssel*
The bill, please	*Die rechnung bitte*

Signs

women's toilets	*damen/frauen*
men's toilets	*herren/männer*
entrance	*eingang*
exit	*ausgang*
attention	*achtung!*
beware	*vorsicht!*
no smoking	*nicht rauchen*
no entrance	*kein eingang*
push/pull	*drüken/ziehen*
vacant/occupied	*frei/besetzt*

Days of the Week

Monday	*Montag*
Tuesday	*Dienstag*
Wednesday	*Mittwoch*
Thursday	*Donnerstag*
Friday	*Freitag*
Saturday	*Samstag*
Sunday	*Sonntag*
today	*heute*
yesterday	*gestern*
tomorrow	*morgen*
holidays	*ferien*
bank holiday	*feiertag*

Numbers

1	*eins*
2	*zwei*
3	*drei*
4	*vier*
5	*fünf*
6	*sechs*
7	*sieben*
8	*acht*
9	*neun*

10	*zehn*
11	*elf*
12	*zwölf*
13	*dreizehn*
14	*vierzehn*
15	*fünfzehn*
16	*sechszehn*
17	*siebzehn*
18	*achtzehn*
19	*neunzehn*
20	*zwanzig*
21	*ein-un-zwanzig*
30	*dreissig*
40	*vierzig*
50	*fünfzig*
60	*sechzig*
70	*siebzig*
80	*achtzig*
90	*neunzig*
100	*hundert*
500	*fünfhundert*
1,000	*tausend*

BUDAPEST

To be Hungarian is a permanent joy.
—Joseph Wechsberg, The Lost World of
Great Spas, *1979*

Budapest is in fact three cities in one. In 1873 Buda, Pest, and Óbuda were officially joined to form the capital city we know as Budapest. The three still have distinct atmospheres of their own. Buda, on the western bank of the Danube, is the site of the Castle District and the famous Hotel Gellért. It is wooded and mainly residential. Across the river is Pest, which is as flat as Buda is hilly, a bustling and noisy metropolis with pedestrian-zoned shopping streets, businesses and banks, and wide boulevards. Linking the two are nine bridges over the Danube. Óbuda, which is on the northern Buda side of the river, is distinguished by blocks of housing projects and is not very interesting.

Budapest has been called the "Pearl of the Danube," but its many attractions make it a diamond as well. With two million inhabitants, it is not only the largest city in Hungary but the administrative, political, economic, commercial, tourist, and cultural center of the country. The city is famous for its spa baths, where the tradition of bathing in thermal and medicinal waters dates from Roman times. Some of the spas go back as far as the Turkish occupation in the sixteenth century and are still in use today, and many more are decorated with the colors and forms of Art Nouveau. Aside from the thermal waters, the many-sided city has Old World charm, the elegance of the West, the mystique of the Orient, and the Mediterranean flair of the south. There are art galleries, museums, a beautiful opera house, concert halls, historical buildings, consumer goods, interesting handcrafts, and lavish coffeehouses—all for prices that are less than almost anywhere else in Europe.

Since the fall of Communism in 1989, the city has a new entrepreneurial spirit, Western goods are available, and Budapest seems to be on the move again. But not everything is changing at the same pace. For many, city life can still be drab, utilitarian, and grim, and some feel threatened by the changes and how they are affecting their lives. While I was in Budapest, I was told by one pundit, "In the past, it took five people to do a job. Now, management expects us to actually work, and produce!" Hello, capitalism.

During the years Hungary was under the thumb of a socialist government, millions of visitors still came, attracted by the low cost of having a good time here. They are still coming, especially to Budapest, and their numbers are expected to reach fifteen million a year in the near future. While this influx has stretched the hotel industry to the limit, finding a hotel room in the city is still not that difficult—what's hard is finding

BUDAPEST

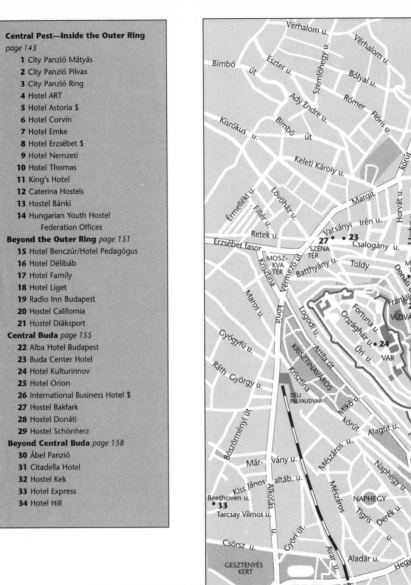
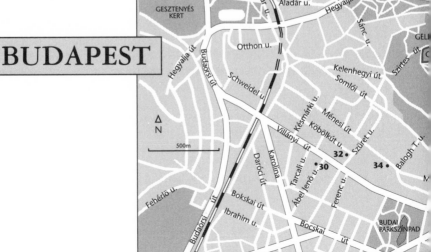

one that's suitable. Due to a lack of funding capital, renovation and rebuilding projects are moving at a snail's pace, a direct opposite of the boom going on in Prague. With few exceptions, the socialist-era hotels have little curb appeal and offer unimaginative rooms done in the drabbest of colors. More often than not, staff act as if they are doing you a favor just by acknowledging your presence, let alone actually helping you. When it is convenient for them, they will get around to serving you, but only after they have completed their personal business, eaten their snack, or completed unimportant paperwork.

Cheap Sleepers should watch out for the minihotels and pensions that are pushed by touts at the railway stations and airports, promoted by some booking agencies, and even sold by unknowing U.S. travel agents. These minihotels sound promising at the outset, but believe me, I saw enough of them to know that promises are *all* they offer. Minihotels usually are a series of five or six rooms in some grimy block of depressing flats. The beds are mere cots, wardrobe space laughable, upkeep is minimal, cleanliness suspect, and comfort and security big, fat zeros. There is a communal bathroom and sometimes a hot plate and sink the owner labels as a kitchen. Payment is required up front and there are no refunds. Forget all about anyone being on site to help you. . . . Why would the owners want to spend time in these dumps? They sit in their offices, where you are required to go to get your keys, pay any additional costs, and then find the address of the minihotel the best way you can. Another warning is in order about the locals, or their representatives, cruising the railway stations offering rooms in their homes for breathtakingly low prices. There are tales of both success and woe with these arrangements. You may luck out, but chances are greater that you won't. To avoid getting stuck east of Mars in rooms with unacceptable, unsafe conditions, ask to see the room *before* accepting the offer or agreeing on the price. If this request is refused, you should refuse the offer.

Minihotels and locals aside, there are decent Cheap Sleeps in Budapest, from cheap and cheerful to luxurious and lavish Big Splurges. Armed with this book, you should not have a problem finding something to suit your taste and budget. To be assured of getting what you want, always make advance reservations and insist on a written confirmation in return. Many Budapest Cheap Sleeps have great off-season rates, so if cost is a main factor, avoid the peak times from April to June and August to October. Most rates are quoted in German marks, Austrian schillings, or U.S. dollars, although payment can be made in cash in Hungarian forints. No matter what type of Cheap Sleep you have, expectations should be kept in perspective. Rooms will be clean, and larger than you would find in Paris, but charming, coordinated decorating schemes, soft carpeting, and baskets of toiletries are in short supply. Beds are good but sometimes low to the ground. They are made up with a sheet laid over the mattress and a covered duvet on top of that. There is no top sheet or blanket, but don't worry. Once you get used to sleeping under a duvet, you will be out shopping for some to have at home.

General Information

When to Go

Spring is one of the loveliest times to visit Budapest and so is the early fall. By late October, there is a definite chill in the air, but the compensation for many is that the opera season is in full session. The summers are hot and air-conditioning is not prevalent. Other than a ten-day ballet and opera festival (in July or August, dates vary from year to year) the cultural life revolves around organ concerts and a week-long rock, folk, and jazz festival held on Óbuda Island. The winters are cold, long, and dark. The winter pollution from the use of brown coal for heating can be debilitating for those with lung problems. Between Christmas and New Year's Day, many shops, restaurants, and offices close. For a complete listing of yearly events in Budapest, contact Tourinform at Sütro u. 2, 1052 Budapest, tel: 317-9800; fax: 317-9578.

Holidays

Shops, museums, banks, and many restaurants are closed on holidays. By 2 P.M. on December 24, everything in Budapest is closed and this includes all forms of public transportation. On December 25 and 26, businesses are still shuttered, but public transportation runs on a limited schedule. Things pick up slightly after that, but not until January 2 or 3 can you count on the city returning to a normal work and transportation schedule.

January 1	New Year's Day
March 15	National Holiday (Commemorates 1848 Revolution)
Easter Sunday	Dates vary
Easter Monday	Dates vary
May 1	Labor Day
Sixth Monday after Easter	Whit Monday
August 20	St. Stephen's Day
October 23	Remembrance Day (Memorial day for 1956 uprising, and anniversary of the birth of the Republic in 1989)
December 24–26	Christmas

Addresses

For first-time visitors, the Budapest system of addresses can be confusing and lead to many hours of wandering the city searching in vain for your destination. What unknowing visitors quickly realize in dismay is that many streets in different parts of the city have the same name.

Therefore, it is crucial to know which district the address is in. Buda and Pest are divided into twenty-three districts, called *kerület* and abbreviated as *ker*. Five are in Buda: I, II, III, XI, XIII. District I is the area around the Castle and the most important from a visitor's standpoint. Seventeen of the remaining districts are in Pest, and XXI is for Csepel Island. In Pest the most important district is the fifth, or V, which is the center of the city. Every address states the number of the district either as a roman numeral preceding the address—such as, V. Váci utca 3—or as a four-digit numerical code with the district represented by the middle two numbers—such as, 1053 Váci utca 3. The above address is in the fifth district; the number 1120 would mean an address in the twelfth district. After determining the *kerület*, the next step is to know what type of street you are looking for. A common mistake is with *utca*, which means "street" and is often abbreviated as *u*. This should not be mixed up with *út*, which means a wide street or an avenue. To help you find your way with as little confusion as possible, please refer to the address terms given below.

To add to the fun, Hungarians address their envelopes in backward order from the way Americans do. Hungarians put their family name first and their first names last. The address line begins with the postal code, then the city, the street name, the house number, and the floor and flat numbers. We would place this information in the center, or to the right of center, of the envelope. In Hungary, it is written in the bottom left-hand corner. If you are dating your correspondence, the order is year/month/day.

fasot	alley
híd	bridge
körút (krt.)	boulevard or ring road
körtér	circle
köz	lane
liget	park
part	riverbank
pályaudvar (pu.)	railway station
rakpart	embankment
sétány	walk
sziget	island
sor	row
tér	square
tere	square of
udvar	arcade, passageway
utca (u.)	street
út	wide road or avenue
útja	road of

Money

The Hungarian unit of currency is the forint (Ft). Because it is not a convertible currency, changing it back into a hard currency is costly; therefore you should estimate your cash-on-hand needs carefully, exchange only what is necessary, and use credit cards whenever possible. Inflation is climbing at an alarming rate, and the forint is constantly being devalued. This means that dollars and other hard currencies are worth more, and as a result, most hotel rates are quoted either in German marks, Austrian schillings, or U.S. dollars. At press time, the exchange rate was 223Ft to $1.

To avoid credit card tampering, always write the amount you are paying on the credit card slip with a numerical figure and by spelling it out. For example: write 2,400Ft in the money column, write two thousand four hundred forints across the face of the credit card slip, and be sure to draw lines through all the empty boxes. Every hotel and shop listing in *Cheap Sleeps in Budapest* tells you which credit cards are accepted. Because the business establishment has to pay a commission to the credit card issuing company, sometimes discounts are given for cash transactions, so it always pays to ask. ATM machines have arrived in Budapest to a limited degree. Cash machines are more popular. With these, you insert a foreign note and get Hungarian forints back. American Express has a twenty-four-hour cash machine, and so do both the Nyugati and Kelti railway stations. Banks will give better rates than commission kiosks, but shop around because rates do vary. Banks are open on Monday from 8:30 A.M. to 6 P.M., Tuesday through Thursday until 4 P.M., and Friday until 1 P.M. In addition to exchanging traveler's checks and cash, most banks and American Express offices can advance money on a credit card. Below are some convenient money-changing addresses.

NOTE: Changing money on the black market or doing your banking on the street is just plain stupid. You will be cheated, no matter how sweet the deal sounds.

Banks: Ibusz Bank, V. Petőfi tér 3. Open twenty-four hours a day. Will exchange cash and traveler's checks and advance money on Visa or Diners Club credit cards.

Cash machines: V. Károly körút 20; V. Sas u. 3; V. Váci u. 40; VI. Andrássy út 49.

Exchange machines: Budapest Bank, VI. Király u. 16; accepts MasterCard and Visa. Postabank, Nyugati railway station underpass; accepts Visa. OTP, V. Deák Ferenc u. 7-9; accepts MasterCard.

American Express: V. Deák Ferenc u. 10. Open Monday to Friday 9 A.M. to 6 P.M., Saturday until 2 P.M. Currency exchange, money grams, cash advances, mail and fax delivery for cardholders, travel services.

Tipping

The rules are vague in Budapest, but as a general rule, tip 10 percent or round off the total. In restaurants, if a service charge has been added, this *is* the tip. Otherwise, tell the bill-collecting waiter the total you are paying, including the tip, and hand it over to him or her. Never leave the tip on the table. Taxi drivers expect to get a 10 percent tip, but don't do it if they have cheated you (see "Taxis," page 140). Hairdressers, coat-check ladies, repairmen, attendants in changing rooms at baths and swimming pools, and even doctors and dentists all expect tips. No matter how grim the toilet may be, the restroom attendant gets 20Ft, and you will see the saucer prominently placed on the counter. Many visitors find that a bundle of hard currency notes in small denominations solves the tipping problem nicely. Use either U.S. dollars or Austrian schillings for this purpose. You will be amazed at the positive response.

Safety and Security

For the most part, visitors need only employ common sense and the usual awareness of their surroundings while in Budapest. Lock up your valuables in the hotel safe, carry as little as you think you need in a money belt hidden in your clothes, and leave expensive jewelry and clothing at home. While violent crimes are rare, pickpockets, purse snatchers, and scam artists are working especially well in some parts of the city. The metro is a favorite spot for petty thieves, and so are the escalators leading in and out of them. Watch out on Line No. 2. Popular targeted trams are Nos. 4 and 6. Margaret Island (Margitsziget) is the domain for purse snatchers. Other crime hot spots are the Castle District and Mathias Church, Heroes' Square, and the pedestrian shopping street Váci utca, which is ripe with pickpockets, prostitutes, and other illicit dealings. If young, beautiful girls suddenly befriend you along Váci utca, watch out! These girls work for specific restaurants, bars, or nightclubs, and they will invite you to accompany them for drinks or a meal. They get a commission and you pay a sky-high price. Stay out of District VIII around Rákózi tér at night, which operates as a red-light district after the sun sets.

The law states that every person must carry proper identification at all times. Police can check, but they rarely do. However, they do warn visitors not to be fooled by plainclothes men or women posing as "tourist police" who will ask to see your ID, then ask to check how much money you are carrying in your wallet—and then in a flash and by slight of hand remove most of it. If you are black, Asian, or Middle Eastern, exercise additional caution. Sadly, Budapest has racist gangs who hang around metro stations and the fringes of the city center, and the police often look the other way or dismiss incidents altogether. If it is dark, you are alone, and you are going to an outlying area, consider taking a taxi.

Telephones

The antiquated telephone system in Budapest is currently undergoing privatization. This means that ultimately the service should improve, but the process is and will be difficult. Don't be alarmed if you are cut off in the middle of a call, and remember not to believe every busy signal you hear—always redial the number several times. At present, all telephone numbers in Budapest are subject to change. The numbers given in *Cheap Sleeps in Budapest* have been checked, and rechecked, and were correct as of press time. However, you must expect some changes. If you experience difficulty and cannot get a connection, call 317-0170 for directory assistance in Budapest.

Most public telephones accept coins and phone cards. For each 10Ft coin you will get from two to six minutes of time. Go with the phone card if you plan to make many calls, especially long-distance ones.The cards can be purchased in denominations of 50 to 120 units and are available at post offices, metro stops, newsstands, tobacco shops, and street vendors.

Hotel surcharges on all long-distance calls are positively frightening, so make sure to use public telephone booths, which are in many hotel lobbies, the telephone office, or the post office. At the main telephone office (V. Petőfi Sándor u. 17; tel: 317-5500; M3, Ferenciek tere), you can make telephone calls and send faxes worldwide. Credit cards are not accepted. The hours are Monday to Friday 8 A.M. to 8 P.M., Saturday and Sunday 9 A.M. to 3 P.M. A telephone guide in English is available from the main desk.

To make an international call from Budapest, dial 00, listen for the second dial tone, then dial the country code, the city code, and the number. For example, to call a number in the United States, you would dial 00 + 1 + the area code + the number. To call other cities in Hungary from Budapest, or to call Budapest from anyplace else in the country, dial 06, wait for the second tone, and then add the city code and then the number. International rates are the same night and day; there is no low rate.

To call Budapest from the United States, dial 011 + 36 (the country code) + 1 (the city code) + seven-digit number.

Useful Telephone Numbers and Addresses

Emergency Numbers

These numbers can be called free from any telephone.

Ambulance	104
Fire	105
Police	107
Twenty-four-hour English-speaking emergency service	318-821
Alcoholics Anonymous (call for meetings in English)	VII. Kertész u. 28, first floor; tel: 168-5426; M2, Blaha Lujza tér

IMS, a private medical
clinic with English-
speaking doctors   XIII.Váci út 202; tel: 129-8423, 149-9349;
M3, Újpest Városkapu; open Mon–Fri
8 A.M.–8 P.M.; AE, MC

SOS Emergency
Medical Service   VIII. Kerepesi út 15; tel: 318-8288, 24-hour
number 318-8212; M2, Keleti; open 24-
hours daily; AE, MC

Dental Co-op   XII. Zugligeti út 60; tel: 376-3600; Bus 22;
open Mon–Wed, Fri 9 A.M.–6 P.M., Thur 1–
6 P.M.; AE, MC, V

SOS Dental Clinic   VI. Király u. 14; tel: 322-0602, 322-7010;
all lines, Deák Ferenc tér; open 24-hours
daily; AE, DC, MC, V

Pharmacies (look for a
green cross outside)   I. Szénsa tér, tel: 202-1816
VII. Rákózi út, tel: 39-114-3694

Useful Numbers

Hungary country code	36
Budapest city code	1
Directory Assistance	In Budapest, 317-0170
	International, 267-5555
American Embassy	V. Szabadság 12, tel: 267-4400
American Express	V. Deák Ferenc utca 10; tel: 266-8680; fax: 267-2028; all lines, Deák Ferenc tér. Open Mon–Fri 9 A.M.–6:30 P.M., Sat until 2 P.M. Currency exchange and full travel agency. Cardholders can use their mail service; address letters to you at: American Express Travel Service, Client Mail, Deák Ferenc utca 10, 1052 Budapest
Lost property	Talált Tárgyak Osztálya, VII. Akácfa u. 18; tel: 322-6613; M2, Blaha Lujza tér. Open Mon–Thur 7:30 A.M.–3 P.M., Wed until 7 P.M., Fri until 2 P.M.
Lost property at airport	357-9123
Post Office	Magyar Posta, V. Petőfi Sándor u. 17-19; all lines, Deák Ferenc tér; open Mon-Fri 8 A.M.–8 P.M., Sat until 3 P.M.
Public Toilets	For public toilets, bring your own toilet tissue. The best toilets are found in McDonald's, Burger Kings, or in fancy hotels

Tourist Information

Budapest Tourism Office	V. Dorottya u. 4; tel: 132-6565; M1, Vórósmarty tér; and at the Nyugati railway station; open Mon–Fri 9–5:30, Sat until 12:30
Hungarian National Tourist Office	150 E. 58th Street, New York, NY 10155; tel: 212-355-0240
Hungarian Hotel Sales Office	6033 West Century Boulevard, Suite 670, Los Angeles, CA 90045; tel: 310-649-5808, 800-448-4321
Ibuz (National Tourism Agency)	V. Petőfi ter 3; tel: 318-5707; metro: M3, Ferenciek tere; open 24 hours daily; Visa. Best for accommodations; other tourist info as well
Tourinform	V. Súto u. 2; tel: 317-9800; all lines, Deák Ferenc tér. Best office for information; also reservations for sightseeing tours and cultural programs and map sales
Central Ticket Office (theater, opera, musicals)	VI. Andrássy út 18; tel: 322-7914; M1, Opera; open Mon–Thur 9 A.M.–6 P.M., Fri until 5 P.M.
Filharmónia Office (tickets for classical concerts, opera)	V. Vórósmarty tér 1; tel: 318-0441, 317-6222; M1, Vórósmarty tér; open Mon–Fri 10 A.M.–1:30 P.M., 2–6 P.M.

Transportation

Budapest has two hundred bus routes, fifteen trolley buses, thirty-three tram lines, and a three-line metro, which conveniently intersects at Deák Ferenc tér in central Pest. There is also a funicular railway going to the Castle, a cog-wheel railway, boats on the Danube, and bicycles for people to use in City Park and on Margaret Island (Margitsziget). This web of public transportation is good, despite its overcrowding during morning and evening rush hour, lack of service to much in the Buda Hills, and its restricted service between 11:30 P.M. and 5 A.M., when the metro closes but night routes are in operation. However, the casual Budapest tourist will not be greatly affected by these few drawbacks. Most of the places on the must-see list are within a reasonably central area, where using the various different travel modes only adds to the enjoyment of a Budapest visit.

If you are traveling on one of the new buses, look at the lighted sign in back of the driver. This gives you the stop as well as other bus and metro connections at that stop. The most important thing to remember when using public transportation is that every time you change from one mode to another—that is, from metro to bus, from one bus to another, or from one metro line to another—it will cost you one ticket, and you must get the ticket punched for each leg of your journey. If you are caught by one of the plainclothes inspectors without a ticket, or not having it punched, the on-the-spot fines are 6,000Ft, about $32. It isn't worth it when you can buy a one-way ticket for 35Ft, a ten-trip booklet for 630Ft, an unlimited three-day pass for 1,120Ft, and a weekly one for 1,450Ft. Validate your ticket (which is not necessary for unlimited passes) in the orange boxes at metro entrances or the red, hand-operated punch slots on buses and trams. Put the ticket in with the arrow pointing downward and pull the black knob toward you.

Tickets can be purchased at metro ticket windows, newspaper kiosks, tobacco shops, and at some hotel desks. To buy a pass, take a passport-size photo to the Deák Ferenc tér metro station. To get the most out of the system, you will need a transportation map. The one published by the Budapest Transport Authority (BKV; tel: 317-5518, 342-2335) is good, and you can buy it for around 70Ft (65¢) at most metro ticket windows. The main transportation system runs from 5:00 A.M. to 11:30 P.M. After that you must rely on night buses. All of the hotel and shop listings in *Cheap Sleeps in Budapest* give the closest metro stop, noting both the number of the line and its name (such as, M3, Ferenc körút).

Taxis

The taxi situation in Budapest rivals that in Prague, only in Budapest the drivers have been dubbed *hyenas*. In many cases, that term is too delicate. Taxi fares are unregulated, and you can guess what that means, especially when a foreigner hops in. Indeed, most taxis seem to have two rates: one for locals and another for everyone else. The hyenas hang around the airport, train stations, and tourist areas and have fast-speed meters and return-trip charges. Never pay a return trip for the driver and never agree to pay in hard currency. If a driver demands either, you know he is unethical. At the airport or train stations, only use a dispatcher cab that belongs to one of the companies listed below. The best way to avoid an expensive incident is to call one of these taxi companies, or ask that the hotel receptionist do it for you, and find out ahead of time from the hotel what the ride should cost. Don't flag down a taxi on the street unless you are absolutely desperate, and then look for cabs with a large company logo and a yellow number plate. And don't assume that the taxis lined up outside your hotel are all legit—most often these are the worst offenders. However, if you do get a taxi from a taxi rank, you do not have to take the first one in line; it is up to you to select your own driver. No matter how you get the taxi, make sure the meter is turned on. Not all taxi drivers are crooks. Many are honest and pleasant, drive well-maintained cars, speak a little English, and try to practice their conversational skills with you. At the end of the ride, a receipt should be given on request, and a small tip is always appreciated.

Buda Taxi: 120-0200

City Taxi: 211-1111, dispatchers (usually) speak some English

Fő Taxi: 222-2222

6x6: 266-6666

Discounts

Senior Citizens

Seniors are not given any price breaks in Budapest. The situation is similar to Prague, where people retire early with a pension, have subsidized housing, and have limited needs and expectations. The best time to save money is before you leave home. Get a senior discounted airfare, negotiate a senior price if you are renting a car, and check with AARP on their travel discounts.

Students

Students do better in the discount department. No student under twenty-six should leave home without an International Student Identity Card (ISIC) or an International Youth Hostel Federation Card. Teachers also qualify for the FIYTO card, which gives them many of the same discount priviledges. If you did not purchase the cards at home, you can buy them in Budapest at Express, a student-based travel agency. It's located at V. Szabadság tér 16; tel: 131-6393; all lines, Deák Ferenc tér; open Monday to Friday from 8 A.M. to 4 P.M. You will need a passport-size color photo. An ISIC card and the FIYTO and IYHF youth hostel cards are sold through Council Travel, the largest student budget travel organization in the United States, with offices worldwide. The main office for Council Travel in the United States is at 205 East 42nd Street, 16th floor, New York, NY 10017; tel: 212-661-1414, 800-438-2643, or 888-COUNCIL. Office hours are Monday to Friday 9 A.M. to 5 P.M. These cards are sold for under $20 and entitle the holder to great discounts on air and rail travel as well as, depending on the particular country, discounts for hostel and hotel accommodations, reduced prices for museums, concerts, and cultural events, and certain travel insurance coverage.

The Budapest Card

Does the Budapest Tourism Office have a deal for you! This office has issued a new tourist card. The small plastic card gives free entry to fifty-five museums in Budapest, entitles the holder to travel without a ticket on the Budapest transportation system, offers reduced admission to three thermal baths and a swimming pool, and offers substantial reductions for many other tourist-related activities. It also comes with an information guide. The Budapest card is valid for three consecutive days and can be purchased in travel and information offices, museums, hotels, and major metro stations.

Disabled Travelers

Budapest is not well equipped for disabled travelers. There are a few hotels with handicapped bathrooms in ground-floor rooms, but few restaurants have facilities, and the public transportation system has none. That is not to say there is not help out there for the handicapped visitor in Budapest. The Hungarian Disabled Association (MEOSZ) does have a special bus available by advance arrangement. For further information on what to expect, contact them directly: III. San Marco u. 76; tel: 388-2388; Tram No. 1. They are open Monday to Friday 8 A.M. to 4 P.M.

In the States, the Society for the Advancement of Travel for the Handicapped has information about special tours for handicapped travelers. There is a yearly membership fee. Contact them at 347 Fifth Avenue, Suite 610, New York, NY 10016; tel: 212-447-7284; fax: 212-725-8253.

Hotels in Budapest by Area

Open door. Open hearts. Open minds. . . . Hungary.
—Anonymous

It is said that Budapest does not lie on the Danube, but that the river flows through the city, dividing Buda from Pest. Connecting the two sides are nine different bridges. For purposes of describing Cheap Sleeps in Budapest, I have arranged the listings by area in Pest and then in Buda.

PEST

CENTRAL PEST—INSIDE THE OUTER RING

Central Pest lies on the eastern side of the Danube, between the river and the boulevards forming the Outer Ring, which are named after former Hungarian monarchs: Ferenc körút, József körút, Erzsébet körút, Teréz körút, and Szent István körút. The Outer Ring road begins on the Pest side of the Petőfi híd in the southern part of the city and ends at the Margit híd in the north. The area is known for its shopping, luxury hotels, many restaurants, museums, and the opera. It is also where most of the Pest business and government work takes place. Also within Central Pest is Erzsébetváros, the Jewish Quarter, and in the southeast corner an area known as Józsefváros, a large neighborhood undergoing some urban renewal.

HOTELS

OTHER OPTIONS

Apartment Rentals and Residence Hotels

Note: A dollar sign ($) indicates a Big Splurge.

(1) CITY PANZIÓ MÁTYÁS

TELEPHONE
338-4711

FAX
317-9086

EMAIL
100324.235@compuserve.com

INTERNET
www.hungary.net/taverna

METRO
M3, Ferenciek tere

CREDIT CARDS
AE, DC, MC, V

RATES
Rates quoted in German marks; single 125DM, double 160DM, apartment 227–365DM; extra bed 37DM; lower off-season rates

BREAKFAST
Buffet included

V. Március 15. tér 8, H-1056 Budapest
55 rooms, all with shower or bath and toilet

The City Panzió Mátyás is part of the popular Taverna Hotel and Restaurant Company. This moderately priced midcity pick is housed in a meandering building that was once private apartments. Redone in 1995, the modern, cookie-cutter rooms have minimal blond furniture and small bathrooms. Those from the second floor up, on the front, are the best, but there will be some noise, especially in No. 501, a two-room apartment. Rooms on the first floor facing the back are below ground level and depressing. The location is excellent, and the hotel restaurant, Mátyás Prince, one of the most expensive and well-known in Budapest.

ENGLISH SPOKEN Yes

FACILITIES AND SERVICES Bar, direct-dial phone, hair dryer available, lift from second floor, minibar, restaurant, cable TV, office safe

NEAREST TOURIST ATTRACTIONS Danube, shopping, easy underground access to all Budapest

(2) CITY PANZIÓ PILVAX

TELEPHONE
266-7660

FAX
317-6396

EMAIL
pilvax@taverna.hu

INTERNET
www.taverna.hu

METRO
M3, Ferenciek tere

CREDIT CARDS
AE, DC, MC, V

V. Pilvax köz 1-3, H-1052 Budapest
32 rooms, all with shower and toilet

City Panzió Pilvax sits only fifty meters from the pedestrian shopping zone of Budapest. From the front door it is also an easy walk to the Jewish Quarter, and the underground is less than five minutes away. In addition, the hotel is quiet and the rooms display few surprises or flaws. Two of the best twin-bedded choices are Nos. 106 and 114. Both have luggage space, modern bathrooms, and windows looking onto the pedestrian shopping street in front. The worst choices include any room on the first or second floors that faces the back. The hotel is part of the Taverna group and offers guests two dining possibilities, one in a casual pub restaurant and another in a more formal, rather stiff dining room.

ENGLISH SPOKEN Yes

FACILITIES AND SERVICES Bar, direct-dial phone, hair dryer available, no elevator (two floors), restaurant, cable TV, office safe, restaurant

NEAREST TOURIST ATTRACTIONS Within a thirty-minute walk of almost everything in central Pest

(3) CITY PANZIÓ RING
XIII. Szent István körút 22, H-1137 Budapest
39 rooms, all with shower or bath and toilet

The City Panzió Ring, positioned on the Outer Ring of central Pest, offers reliable Cheap Sleeping in predictable quarters. Even though the blue rooms are universal in their sameness, they are bright with unadorned blond furniture and include at least one chair, luggage space, a desk, a framed picture or two, and full length mirrors. Bathrooms are tiled and towels monogrammed with the hotel's logo. A ring road in any city is bound to be noisy, so I recommend one of the ten rooms that face an interior courtyard. The management and desk staff at this Taverna group hotel are very friendly.

ENGLISH SPOKEN Yes

FACILITIES AND SERVICES Conference room, direct-dial phone, hair dryer available, no elevator, minibar, parking 1,500Ft per day, radio, cable TV, laundry service, office safe

NEAREST TOURIST ATTRACTIONS Close to Margitsziget Island and some shopping, otherwise must use public transportation

(4) HOTEL ART
V. Királyi Pal u. 12, H-1053 Budapest
32 rooms, all with shower or bath and toilet

For one of the best small hotels in Budapest, Cheap Sleepers can check into the Art Deco Hotel ART, where the small lobby radiates a subdued charm with its green plants and faux painted columns. Compact yet efficient corner built-in desks, minibars, bedside lights, and heated towel racks in the rooms display the extra attention to detail and welcome extras one seldom finds in moderately priced Budapest hotels. A soothing atmosphere is achieved with coordinated colors and fabrics and pleasing views. Room 51, a small twin on the top

RATES
Rates quoted in German marks; single 125DM, double 160DM, apartment 227DM; extra bed 37DM; lower off-season rates

BREAKFAST
Buffet included

TELEPHONE
340-5450

FAX
340-4884

EMAIL
ring@taverna.hu

INTERNET
www.taverna.hu

METRO
M3, Nyugati pályaudvar

CREDIT CARDS
AE, DC, MC, V

RATES
Rates quoted in German marks; single 125DM, double 160DM, triple 200DM; lower off-season rates

BREAKFAST
Buffet included

TELEPHONE
266-2166; toll-free from U.S., Best Western 800-528-1234

FAX
266-2170

METRO
M3, Kálvin tér

CREDIT CARDS
AE, MC, V

RATES
Rates quoted in German marks; single 150DM, double 185DM, suite 250DM; children under 12 free; lower off-season rates

floor, and No. 52, a double with more closet space and a view of the Liberty Statue, can be sold singly or together, making them good family choices. No. 53 is a two-room suite. In the living room is a large turquoise green leather sofa and two chairs, a desk, and built-in cupboards. The small bedroom has a double bed and a modern bathroom off of it. No. 44, also a two-room suite but with twin beds, has the best bathroom, a sitting room with natural light from two windows, and an oversized sofa and chair set that is typically Hungarian. Workout buffs will appreciate the fitness center, and everyone can relax after a day of sightseeing in the sauna. For those not wanting to stray far for dinner, there is the hotel restaurant.

ENGLISH SPOKEN Yes

FACILITIES AND SERVICES Air-conditioning, bar, two conference rooms, direct-dial phone, fitness center, hair dryers in most bathrooms, lift, minibar, restaurant, room service, satellite TV, office safe, free sauna, trouser presses in suites

NEAREST TOURIST ATTRACTIONS Danube, shopping along Váci u., excellent underground connections

(5) HOTEL ASTORIA $
V. Kossuth Lajos u. 19, H-1053 Budapest
130 rooms and 5 suites, all with shower or bath and toilet

TELEPHONE
317-3411, 317-3863
FAX
318-6798
EMAIL
astoria@hungary.net
INTERNET
www.justweb.com/hotel-astoria
METRO
M2, Astoria
CREDIT CARDS
AE, DC, MC, V
RATES
Rates quoted in German marks; single 145–190DM, double 190–250DM, suite 290–330DM; extra bed 60–70DM; half or full board available; lower off-season rates
BREAKFAST
Buffet included

The landmark Hotel Astoria is one of the most-loved hotels in the heart of Budapest. It was built in 1914 on the site of the medieval town walls, and in October 1918, the first democratic government, which declared independence from Austria, was formed here. Despite several renovations, the Empire style of the original building has been kept intact in the marble-lined, gilt-accented lobby and reception areas and in the elegant ground-floor coffeehouse. Other reminders of a bygone era are the long expanses of white hallways and the brass kick plates on the doors of the spacious rooms.

With 130 rooms and 5 suites, it is easy to compile a list of favorite rooms, especially among the renovated rooms. For instance, an at-home feeling is created in No. 414, a two-room corner suite outfitted in reproduction antiques, complete with two corner curio cabinets filled with ceramic pieces, figurines, and crystal. Soft beige wall coverings and a potted palm add to its appeal, as do the sofa and three chairs. Room 440, a double in soft yellow and green, has a new bathroom with sink space, a magnifying mirror, and good light. Room 304 lands in the Cheap Sleep reject file: its lime green bathroom has a bad shower, and it has foot-to-foot twin beds and too much old furniture. Because the hotel dates from a time when automobiles, trams, and buses were not noise polluters, light sleepers should bring earplugs or request a room on the back.

ENGLISH SPOKEN Yes

FACILITIES AND SERVICES Bar, direct-dial phone, some hair dryers, lift, minibar, free parking, restaurant, coffeehouse, cable TV, room or office safe

NEAREST TOURIST ATTRACTIONS Center of Pest, easy walk to shopping and business activities

(6) HOTEL CORVIN
IX. Angyal u. 31, H-1094 Budapest
40 rooms, all with shower or bath and toilet

The neighborhood is a redevelopment work in progress, and as always in an area being revitalized, some projects turn out better than others. The Hotel Corvin, with a brick-and-stucco exterior remiscent of Art Deco, is one of the best examples of how a building rising from the ashes can be a focal point in revitalizing an area. Unusual use of colors and textures creates an artistic entry and extends to the public areas, where a cheerful art exhibit will certainly charm even the most hardboiled art critic. Before opening in 1996, the hotel held a competition for children in Budapest from ages six to fourteen to draw chalk pictures depicting the life of King Corvin Mátáyas, the popular king the hotel is named after. From the more than one thousand entries, one hundred were selected, and the winning pictures, with each child's name on it, hang throughout the reception, lobby, and dining room. Simplicity sets the tone for the rooms. There are two on each floor similar to No. 208, which is large enough to have a small sitting area. There is also plenty of luggage, shelf, and closet space and a bigger bathroom. Room 202 and those like it have tiled baths with shelf space and enclosed showers.

ENGLISH SPOKEN Yes

FACILITIES AND SERVICES Bar, direct-dial phone, hair dryer available, lift, minibar, parking, restaurant for breakfast and dinner, TV, office safe

NEAREST TOURIST ATTRACTIONS Not much, must use public transportation

TELEPHONE
218-6566

FAX
218-6562

EMAIL
corvin@mail.datanet.hu

METRO
M3, Ferenc körút

CREDIT CARDS
None

RATES
Rates quoted in German marks; single 145DM, double 165DM; extra bed 40DM; lower off-season rates

BREAKFAST
Buffet included

(7) HOTEL EMKE
VII. Akácfa u. 1-3, H-1072 Budapest
76 rooms, all with shower or bath and toilet

TELEPHONE
322-9230

FAX
322-9233

EMAIL
emke@pannoniahotels.hu

METRO
M2, Blaha Lujza tér

CREDIT CARDS
AE, DC, MC, V

RATES
Rates quoted in German marks;
single 125DM, double 155DM,
suite 185DM; extra bed 35DM

BREAKFAST
Buffet included

Let's start with the list of positive points about the Hotel Emke. It is part of the Pannonia group of hotels in Hungary, thus assuring a certain standard of operation. Many American guests like the strictly nonsmoking rooms and the location, which is close to shopping, business activities, and an underground stop. The rooms on the seventh floor are definitely the ones you want. These are renovated, are high enough to escape traffic noise, and have rooftop views of the neighborhood. No. 708, a two-room suite, has plenty of wardrobe space, a large bedroom, and a curved sink in the bathroom. Room 709 is a rather narrow twin, but the newer bathroom saves the day. On the negative side, the lobby is definitely dated and in need of a quick fix, and so are all the rooms on the first four floors.

ENGLISH SPOKEN Yes

FACILITIES AND SERVICES Direct-dial phone, hair dryer, lift, minibar, parking, cable TV, office safe, nonsmoking rooms

NEAREST TOURIST ATTRACTIONS Shopping, business activities, good transportation connections

(8) HOTEL ERZSÉBET $
V. Károli Mihály u. 11-15, H-1053 Budapest
123 rooms, all with shower or bath and toilet

TELEPHONE
328-5700

FAX
328-5763

METRO
M3, Ferenciek tere

CREDIT CARDS
AE, DC, MC, V

RATES
Rates quoted in German marks;
single 220DM, double 270DM;
lower off-season rates

BREAKFAST
Buffet included

In name at least, the Hotel Erzsébet is as old as the Hungarian capital. Budapest dates from 1872 when three towns—Pest, Buda, and Óbuda—merged to become Budapest. The Hotel Erzsébet, named after the wife of the ruling monarch, opened that same year. By 1976, however, the hotel had fallen into a sad state and was eventually razed. A new hotel was erected in its place in 1985.

When you are here, be sure to see the interesting lobby display of historical pieces of china, porcelain, and old postcards that reflect the hotel's history. Today the hotel has a contemporary tone: all of its lookalike white bedrooms have white linen duvet covers and a small pillow hiding a piece of candy sitting atop the beds. Each room has a modern bath, work area, and wardrobe. The hotel restaurant, János Pince, resembles a beer cellar and serves predictable Hungarian food.

ENGLISH SPOKEN Yes

FACILITIES AND SERVICES Air-conditioning, direct-dial phone, hair dryer available, lift, minibar, radio, restaurant, cable and pay TV, videos, office safe, soundproofed rooms

NEAREST TOURIST ATTRACTIONS Easy walk to main shopping area of Pest, good public transportation connections

(9) HOTEL NEMZETI
VIII. József körút, H-1088 Budapest
76 rooms, all with shower or bath and toilet

In February 1998 all of the rooms in this century-old Art Nouveau–style hotel were renovated, making it one of the best in its category in the city. The lobby uses red velvet with abandon—on the tufted sofas and chairs and in the small bar in back. It is a good place to spend a few minutes sitting by the window and observing the passing stream of humanity. In the dining room, a detailed stained-glass skylight oddly blends well with modern wooden pillars and mezzanine seating. A lovely stairway leads to hallways dotted with vintage pieces and large mirrors. Air-conditioning and double windows buffer the incessant noise in the rooms facing the bustling Blaha Lujza square. It would be hard to quarrel with Room 212, done in burgandy and cream colors, with two large windows letting in plenty of daylight. Coordinated floral fabrics work well together in No. 102, a quiet double on the back with a tiled bath that has plenty of sink space plus a tub and shower. Good service and a pleasant reception team are further reasons that this is a desirable Cheap Sleep in Budapest.

ENGLISH SPOKEN Yes

FACILITIES AND SERVICES Air-conditioning, conference room, direct-dial phone, hair dryer, lift, minibar, parking 700Ft per day, restaurant, cable TV, some room safes, office safe, nonsmoking rooms

NEAREST TOURIST ATTRACTIONS Jewish Quarter, otherwise will need public transportation

TELEPHONE
303-9310

FAX
314-0019

EMAIL
nemzeti@pannoniahotels.hu

METRO
M2, Blaha Lujza tér

CREDIT CARDS
AE, DC, MC, V

RATES
Rates quoted in German marks; single 170DM, double 210DM; extra bed 55DM; half board available

BREAKFAST
Buffet included

(10) HOTEL THOMAS
IX. Liliom u. 44, H-1094 Budapest
45 rooms, all with shower or bath and toilet

The hotel is named after the director's son, Thomas, and the boy's picture is framed in the letter 0 of the word Thomas on the hotel's brochures and business cards. The

TELEPHONE AND FAX
218-5505/6/7/8

METRO
M3, Ferenc körút

CREDIT CARDS
AE, DC, MC, V

RATES
Rates quoted in German marks;
single 120DM, double 160DM;
lower off-season rates

BREAKFAST
Buffet included

area around the hotel is being redeveloped, and so far the changes have received mixed reviews, depending on whom you talk to. The hotel is a nonspecific contemporary building with rooms that could be in any hotel worldwide. The sixth floor is reserved for nonsmoking guests. No. 64 has a small sitting room and balcony. It is a good deal because you are not charged for the extra footage. The breakfast area displays a degree of flair, with its color-splashed glass table tops surrounded by black bentwood bistro chairs. Mirrored columns give it the illusion of spaciousness.

ENGLISH SPOKEN Yes

FACILITIES AND SERVICES Bar, direct-dial phone, hair dryer available, lift, minibar, parking, cable TV, room and office safe, five nonsmoking rooms on sixth floor

NEAREST TOURIST ATTRACTIONS Danube River, otherwise will need public transportation

(11) KING'S HOTEL
VII. Nagy Diófa u. 25-27, H-1074 Budapest
82 rooms, all with shower and toilet

TELEPHONE AND FAX
352-7675

METRO
M2, Astoria or Blaha Lujza tér

CREDIT CARDS
AE, V

RATES
Rates quoted in U.S. dollars;
single $50, double $60–80,
triple $120; lower off-season
and group rates

BREAKFAST
Continental included

The owner, Monica, and her husband lived in Israel for years until they returned to her birthplace and created this hotel. I was amused by two signs prominently displayed in the lobby: one threatens that "If you do not close these doors you will be charged $1," and the other advertises "complete dental work done in short time across from the hotel."

If you can laugh at these while overlooking the drab lobby filled with oversized, green, "pleather"-covered sandbag-style sofas and K-Mart plastic porch chairs, you will come to appreciate the spotless rooms in what is the only kosher hotel and restaurant in Budapest. The real difference in the rooms is size and location. Most are similarly equipped, with American mattresses backed by brass headboards, a small TV set, a one-drawer desk, two hard chairs, a mirror, and serviceable bathroom. The two I would absolutely reject are Nos. 212 and 222, which have one window at the ceiling level you can't see out of. Mehadrin kosher meals under the supervision of the Chief Rabbi of Budapest are served in the hotel's two knotty pine-paneled restaurants. According to high Jewish law, one is for meat and the other dairy, and both are open on all high Jewish holidays.

ENGLISH SPOKEN Yes

FACILITIES AND SERVICES Air-conditioning, direct-dial phone, hair dryer available, lift, kosher restaurant, cable TV, office safe

NEAREST TOURIST ATTRACTIONS Heart of Jewish Quarter, twenty-minute walk to shopping area, good public transportation connections

BEYOND THE OUTER RING ‒‒‒‒‒‒‒

Beyond the Outer Ring road of Pest are lovely old villas, many now occupied by embassy offices and residences, gracing wide tree-lined streets. Andrássy út leads to the Millennium Monument on Heroes' Square and the two art galleries that flank it: the Art Gallery on the right and the Fine Arts Museum on the left. Beyond is the City Park, which has an outdoor ice skating rink, zoo, amusement park, lake, castle, and the Szécheni Thermal Baths, whose outdoor thermal pool is usually anchored by old men sitting and playing chess on floating boards. Nearby is the world-famous Gundel restaurant, now owned by George Lang and Ronald Lauder, and its less expensive sister restaurant, Bagolyvár (see *Cheap Eats in Prague, Vienna, and Budapest*). Public transportation into the heart of Pest, and across the river to Buda, is quick and easy.

(15) HOTEL BENCZÚR AND HOTEL PEDAGÓGUS
VI. Benczúr u. 35, H-1068 Budapest

Hotel Benczúr

TELEPHONE
342-7970, 342-7975

FAX
342-1558

METRO
M1, Kodály körönd

CREDIT CARDS
MC, V

RATES
Rates quoted in German marks; single 135DM, double 160DM, triple 180DM, suite 200DM; half board available; lower off-season and group rates

BREAKFAST
Buffet included

Hotel Pedagógus

TELEPHONE
342-7970, 322-0821

FAX
322-9019

EMAIL
pedhotel.@mail.matav.hu

METRO
M1, Kodály körönd

CREDIT CARDS
MC, V

RATES
Rates quoted in German marks; single 106DM, double 117–130DM, triple 135DM, suites 145DM; lower off-season and group rates

BREAKFAST
10DM extra per person

Hotel Benczúr: **93 rooms, all with shower or bath and toilet**
Hotel Pedagógus: **60 rooms, all with shower and toilet**

The Hotels Benczúr and Pedagógus occupy the same plot of real estate in the attractive, diplomatic section of Budapest. While any location defined as "Beyond the Outer Ring" suggests a tourist Saturn, the hotels are actually not badly situated at all. Nearby is the famous City Park with an ice rink and thermal baths, Heroes' Square, and the city's Fine Arts Museum. The underground is five stops from the heart of the business and shopping district. The two hotels share facilities, which include Oriental massage, a restaurant serving à la carte and half-board meals, and the possibility of having dental surgery performed during your stay. Thanks to their diplomatic neighbors, the area is quiet and certainly safe. Across the street is an amazing yellow-and-white Victorian building that houses a private kindergarten.

While the rooms at the Pedagógus have an air of socialistic budget institutionality about them and are geared toward groups, they are among the best in the Cheap Sleeping game in Budapest: all very clean, with hardwood floors, matching fabrics, stall showers, enough closet space, and bedside lighting. Many of the upgraded and renovated rooms at the Benczúr look out on a leafy garden where guests can sit during the warm weather. Again, they are clean and display coordinated colors and fabrics. Some have walk-in closets and balconies. For more demanding guests, they are probably worth the extra outlay, but for true Cheap Sleepers in Budapest, the Pedagógus needs no apologies.

ENGLISH SPOKEN Yes

FACILITIES AND SERVICES Bar, conference room, dentist, direct-dial phone, garden, hairdresser, lift, masseuse, minibars (in Pedagógus, in suites only), parking, restaurant, TV, office safe

NEAREST TOURIST ATTRACTIONS Diplomatic area of Budapest, Hösök tere (Heroes' Square), Fine Arts Museum, City Park

(16) HOTEL DÉLIBÁB
VI. Délibáb u. 35, H-1062 Budapest
35 rooms, all with shower or bath and toilet

If you believe in ghosts, those occupying this once-grand mansion across from Heroes' Square must have many wonderful stories to tell about the past life of this dowager princess, which now is a Cheap Sleep in Budapest. The area is full of embassy residences and assorted diplomatic missions. Despite this, there is no getting around the fact that the hotel sits on a noisy corner and does not have either air-conditioning or double windows to muffle the noise. The clean, functional rooms are textbook examples of socialist-inspired interior decoration, with beige and brown colors, globe lights, and wooden floors. A small dining room with a brass fan light and fifties maple tables and chairs doubles as a bar from 5 to 10 P.M.

ENGLISH SPOKEN Yes

FACILITIES AND SERVICES Bar, direct-dial phone, lift to two floors, some radios, cable TV, office safe

NEAREST TOURIST ATTRACTIONS Heroes' Square and City Park, Fine Arts Museum, excellent public transportation connections

TELEPHONE
322-8763, 342-9301

FAX
342-8153

METRO
M1, Hősök tere

CREDIT CARDS
None

RATES
Single 8,400Ft, double 10,115Ft, triple 12,100Ft; lower off-season rates

BREAKFAST
Buffet included

(17) HOTEL FAMILY
XIII. Ipoly u. 8/b, H-1133 Budapest
13 rooms, all with shower or bath and toilet

Cheap Sleepers who can live with a short commute to action central will be rewarded by a stay at the Hotel Family, one of the nicest small hotels in Budapest. Not much space is devoted to the attractive lobby, but the modern Scandinavian-designed rooms have an easygoing, airy feel, and even the smallest is huge by anyone's standards. There are six rooms similar to No. 202, a two-level atelier with fifteen-foot windows dominating a downstairs living area complete with sofa bed, two chairs, double-mirrored closets, desk, and small powder room. Upstairs is a large bedroom with more space in a walk-in closet than many of us have at home. Room 201, another two-level suite, has a ground-floor twin with a sink and toilet off of it and a large double room upstairs with a full bath. The view over a parking area could be better, but a business center is planned for the area and hopefully will be completed very soon. There is not much of visitor interest in the immediate area, but it is

TELEPHONE
120-1284

FAX
129-1620

METRO
M3, Lehel tér

CREDIT CARDS
AE, DC, MC, V

RATES
Rates quoted in German marks; single 150DM, double 180DM, suite 200DM; half board available; lower off-season rates

BREAKFAST
Buffet included

close to Margitsziget Island, a beautiful vehicle-free island in the Danube known and loved for its many walking and bike paths, summer sports activities, and two beautiful spa hotels. Also nearby is a fascinating outdoor market on Váci út, where sweet old ladies sell handmade items and you can sample a pastry or a round of fried dough, see sauerkraut and pickled paprikas dipped from deep barrels, check out the seasonal produce, and try to guess the animal parts displayed in glass cases.

ENGLISH SPOKEN Yes

FACILITIES AND SERVICES Air-conditioning, bar, direct-dial phone, hair dryer available, lift to two floors, minibar, parking, restaurant, cable TV, office safe, sauna and masseuse

NEAREST TOURIST ATTRACTIONS Danube River, Margitsziget Island, large outdoor market on Váci út

(18) HOTEL LIGET
VI. Dózsa György út 106, H-1068 Budapest
139 rooms, all with shower or bath and toilet

TELEPHONE
269-5300, 269-5318

FAX
269-5329

EMAIL
100324.235@compuserve.com

INTERNET
www.hungary.net/taverna

METRO
M1, Hősök tere

CREDIT CARDS
AE, DC, MC, V

RATES
Rates quoted in German marks; single 210DM, double 225DM; extra bed 62DM; dogs 30DM; half board for groups of ten or more; lower off-season rates and in rooms without air-conditioning

BREAKFAST
Buffet included

The logo for the hotel is taken from the black metal sculpture on the building's corner of a woman in a see-through dress hanging backward from a tree. It is one of those go-figure pieces of art that no one wants to admit knowing how or why it is there.

There is nothing else unusual about this modern hotel, which has an impressive list of facilities and services. In the summer, there is a pleasant front terrace where guests are served drinks. The attractively done rooms are designed to appeal to a wide spectrum of folks. Their pleasing colors won't jar sensibilities, and tiled baths with sink space and good light will be welcome to everyone. The most-requested rooms are those that connect to make small suites and the ones with views of the City Park Zoo and Heroes' Square.

ENGLISH SPOKEN Yes

FACILITIES AND SERVICES Most rooms air-conditioned, bar, conference room, direct-dial phone, dogs accepted, hair dryer available, lift, masseuse, minibar, parking, radio, restaurant, cable TV, room and office safe, sauna and solarium

NEAREST TOURIST ATTRACTIONS Heroes' Square, City Park, Fine Arts Museum

BUDA

CENTRAL BUDA

From the Castle District and Gellért Hill on the Buda side of the Danube are spectacular panoramic views: they extend over both banks of the river, taking in the nine graceful bridges spanning it, to the buildings of downtown Pest. On Castle Hill—in addition to the Royal Palace, the dramatically beautiful Mátyás Church, and the Fisherman's Bastion guarded by the statue of St. Stephen—the historically protected area has nine museums, endless historic buildings and souvenir shops, herds of tourists, and the Hilton Hotel. Vehicular traffic is restricted, but access by Várbusz, which runs every few minutes from Moszkva tér, is efficient, or you can hike the steep hills and climb the steps from below. From the northeast side of the Castle District toward the Danube is the area called Watertown, which is one of Budapest's oldest. The main street is Fő út, and Batthyány tér is its main square, with the lovely Baroque Church of St. Ann on one corner.

The hills of Buda are dotted with beautiful homes; it is said that the higher the house is on the hillside, the richer the owner. On the Buda side of Szabadság híd is the most famous hotel in Budapest, the Hotel Gellért, an Art Nouveau masterpiece that's famous for its thermal baths and swimming pools. Even if you have no intention of going to the baths, it is worth the small fee just to see this ornate statement to a bygone era.

HOTELS

OTHER OPTIONS

Note: A dollar sign ($) indicates a Big Splurge.

(22) ALBA HOTEL BUDAPEST
I. Apor Péter u. 3, H-1011 Budapest
95 rooms, all with shower or bath and toilet

TELEPHONE
375-9244; toll-free from U.S.,
Utell, 800-448-8355
FAX
375-9899
METRO
M2, Batthyány tér
CREDIT CARDS
AE, DC, MC, V
RATES
Rates quoted in U.S. dollars;
single $95, double $125; lower
off-season rates and other
promotional rates
BREAKFAST
Buffet included

The rooms are sterile and there isn't much of a view, but if you want to be on the Buda side of the Danube, this is about as good as it gets for those Cheap Sleepers who need modern accommodations. To nail down the best price, it never hurts to shop. Start by calling the toll-free Utell number and ask for the lowest rate being promoted during your time in Budapest. Then check directly with the hotel to see if they can give you an even better deal. The rooms are all about the same in comforts, but I can't say that for the bathrooms. In the twins and larger doubles they are fine, with sink space, but don't look for toiletries. Those in the singles are often just a spout over a shower pan with a curtain to keep you from spraying water all over the place. The breakfast buffet is laid out in a nonsmoking room overlooking a small garden.

ENGLISH SPOKEN Yes

FACILITIES AND SERVICES Air-conditioning, bar, conference room, direct-dial phone, hair dryer, lift, minibar, parking, cable TV, office safe, laundry service

NEAREST TOURIST ATTRACTIONS Castle District

(23) BUDA CENTER HOTEL
II. Csalogány u. 23, H-1027 Budapest
37 rooms, all with shower and toilet

TELEPHONE
201-6333
FAX
201-7843
EMAIL
hotelbch@euroweb-hu
METRO
M2, Batthyány tér
CREDIT CARDS
AE, MC, V
RATES
Rates quoted in German marks;
single 100DM, double 120DM,
four-person suite 200DM; extra
bed 20DM; children under 6
free, children from 6–12 half
price; lower off-season rates
BREAKFAST
Buffet included

The Buda Center Hotel is located on the top four floors of a socialist-inspired office building. On the ground floor is an equally uninspiring Chinese restaurant and a pub that would be fine for a quick beer, but not much else. The neighborhood doesn't sparkle either, but it is reasonably close to Moszkva tér, where you can board the shuttlebus to Castle Hill. In most other cities, this hotel would not be considered at all, but given the present hotel situation in Budapest, anything that is clean is a contender, and the Buda Center Hotel is at least that. The identical rooms have blue indoor/outdoor carpeting and tiled bathrooms with waffle weave and No. 2 grade sandpaper toilet tissue. Those on the front have small balconies, while the ones on the back overlook a green space and the back of other similar buildings. I know it doesn't sound like much, but trust me . . . there is a lot out there that is much worse.

ENGLISH SPOKEN Yes

FACILITIES AND SERVICES Air-conditioning (30DM extra per day in high season), bar, direct-dial phone, hair dryer available, lift, minibar, parking 10DM per day, satellite TV, office safe

NEAREST TOURIST ATTRACTIONS Castle District

(24) HOTEL KULTURINNOV
I. Szentháromság tér 6, H-1014 Budapest
16 rooms, all with shower and toilet

For one of the best Cheap Sleeps in Budapest, and definitely tops in the Castle District, look no further than one of the sixteen rooms at the Hotel Kulturinnov. If you walk across the street to the Hilton, a single will start at $170 and a double at $270, both without breakfast. The Kulturinnov is part of a Gothic palace built in the early 1900s during the reign of Emperor Franz Joseph I and used as the Ministry of Finance until World War II, when it became a state library. Now the building is part of the Ministry of Culture and the hotel serves as one of its revenue makers, along with various offices and conference halls. The location on the central square atop Castle Hill and next to the Mátyás Church rates an A+. The building is equally as fabulous—the entry has marble pillars and arches and leads to a sweeping stairway.

The rooms . . . ah, yes. Frankly speaking, they are no match for their surroundings; they are dated and furnished in motel-modern. Nevermind, just focus on the prices, and besides, the rooms are also big, clean, and most face either the Hilton or a pretty courtyard. Only a few overlook the car park. However, the parking area is a real bonus for motorists, since there is no parking allowed on the surrounding streets and the entire area is restricted. The hotel issues a free permit that allows guests with cars entry and exit to the Castle District.

ENGLISH SPOKEN Yes

FACILITIES AND SERVICES Direct-dial phone, hair dryer available, no elevator, minibar, parking, office safe

NEAREST TOURIST ATTRACTIONS Perfect location in center of Castle District

TELEPHONE
355-0122, 375-1651

FAX
375-1886

METRO
M2, Moszkva tér, then take shuttle bus to Castle Hill

CLOSED
Christmas to Jan 5

CREDIT CARDS
AE, DC, MC, V

RATES
Rates quoted in U.S. dollars; single $60, double $75; lower off-season rates

BREAKFAST
Buffet included

(25) HOTEL ORION

I. Döbrentei u. 13, H-1013 Budapest

30 rooms, all with shower or bath and toilet

TELEPHONE
356-8583, 356-8933

FAX
375-5418

METRO
M2, Batthyány tér, then tram
No. 19 to Döbrentei tér

CREDIT CARDS
AE, DC, MC, V

RATES
Rates quoted in German marks;
single 150DM, double 200DM;
extra bed 40DM; lower off-
season rates

BREAKFAST
Buffet incuded

Decent rooms without a trace of flare await Cheap Sleepers at the Hotel Orion. The location is between the Danube and the southern part of the Castle District. The hotel restaurant is hardly gourmet, but for fast-food fixes, it will do. White textured wash-and-wipe walls in the bedrooms are set off by dark wood furniture and low lying beds. Guests have the usual perks, plus a free sauna, which is nice after a day scaling the hilly streets weaving around the Castle District. Room 46 on the back has a large corner picture window with a vista of the Tabani Church. Room 11 is a twin facing the street and has a sofa that can sleep two extra people.

ENGLISH SPOKEN Yes

FACILITIES AND SERVICES Air-conditioning, direct-dial phone, hair dryer available, lift, minibar, radio, restaurant, cable TV, office safe, sauna

NEAREST TOURIST ATTRACTIONS Between Danube River and Castle District

BEYOND CENTRAL BUDA ⸺⸺⸺⸺

The beautiful neighborhoods of the Buda Hills and the peace and tranquility they offer seem to be the drawing cards for visitors. If you are staying here, a car is a definite advantage. The public transportation is fine during the day, but some walking will be required. At night, the transportation system to this area of the city is poor.

HOTELS

OTHER OPTIONS

Hostels

(30) ÁBEL PANZIÓ
XI. Ábel Jenö u. 9, H-1113 Budapest
10 rooms, all with shower and toilet

The Ábel Panzió is a private guest house that has everything going for it except location. However, its quiet neighborhood setting and wonderful rooms are compensation enough for Cheap Sleepers who don't mind the safari into the city. Repeat guests are drawn to the restored 1930s–style villa with its comfortable rooms, tasteful furnishings, and lovely garden in the back. All of the well-kept rooms are large and have twin beds and a private tiled bathroom. Room 2 is one of the biggest. It has a little porch facing the quiet street and an antique desk with beveled glass doors sitting in one corner. Room 7 has a slanted ceiling with cross beams and modern furniture. On winter mornings, guests are served a buffet breakfast at a communal table in a pretty room with three big windows overlooking a porch and garden. In the summer, tables are set outside and lingering over another cup of coffee is encouraged. Management is exceptional, and reservations are suggested as far in advance as possible.

NOTE: To get to Ábel Panzió, go to the Deák Ferenc tér metro stop and take tram Nos. 47 or 49 to Móricz Zsigmond körtér (which is the third stop after the Szabadság bridge and Gellért tér). From Móricz Zsigmond körtér, take tram No. 61 and get off at the second stop. Ábel Panzió will be on the left on Ábel Jenö utca.

ENGLISH SPOKEN Yes

FACILITIES AND SERVICES Honor bar, direct-dial phone, no elevator, three free parking spaces

NEAREST TOURIST ATTRACTIONS None, must use car or public transportation

TELEPHONE AND FAX
385-6426, 209-2537, 209-2538

METRO
Take buses from Deák Ferenc tér metro stop; see note

CREDIT CARDS
None

RATES
Rates quoted in German marks; single or double 90–100DM; extra bed 30DM

BREAKFAST
Buffet included

Other Options

Accommodation Agencies

TRADESCO TOURS/HUNGARIAN HOTELS

TELEPHONE
310-649-5808; toll-free 800-833-3402
FAX
310-649-5852
EMAIL
tradesco@ix.netcom.com
INTERNET
www.TRADESCOTOURS.com
HOURS
Mon–Fri 6 A.M.–5:30 P.M. (PST)
CREDIT CARDS
MC, V

6033 West Century Boulevard, Suite 670, Los Angeles, CA 90045

Tradesco Tours is a California-based company that can arrange all or part of your trip to Budapest, or to any other destination in Hungary. It can be a service as simple as booking a week in a spa hotel, or as elaborate as arranging for escorted or private tours anywhere in the country. They also have useful information no matter how you are planning your Hungarian trip. Call the toll-free number and they will send you their free brochures. On a recent trip to Budapest, I used Tradesco Tours to book a stay at a spa hotel, and I was very impressed with their services and the prices they offered. In fact, my spa experience was a major highlight of the trip, and one I definitely plan to repeat—using Tradesco Tours to make all the arrangements.

TRAVELER'S POTPOURRI

TELEPHONE
913-341-6828;
toll-free 800-273-7133
FAX
913-341-1248
EMAIL
travpor@kcnet.com
INTERNET
www.travelsmarter.com/exciting
CREDIT CARDS
None

6724 West 83rd Street, #303, Overland Park, KS 66204-3955

Don and Marie Marsolek operate Traveler's Potpourri, which specializes in family B&Bs and apartment rentals in Budapest, Prague, Slovenia, and a limited number in Slovakia. Please see the description in Prague under "Accommodation Agencies," page 70.

Apartment Rentals and Residence Hotels

TÜNDE VARGA APARTMENT RENTALS

If you are staying a week or more in Budapest, one of the best Cheap Sleeping options is to rent an apartment. However, Cheap Sleepers take heed: this market is filled with a wide range of options that run the gamut from clean and acceptable to utterly ghastly. While I was in Budapest, I looked at dozens of possibilities and finally came to the conclusion that Tünde Varga and her sister, Dóra, have some of the best apartment rentals available. Tünde, a true capitalistic go-getter, works part-time as an Italian interpreter and German tour guide while studying for a degree in tourism. For the past eleven years she and her sister have slowly built up an inventory of centrally located apartments that they rent to tourists. In some cases they have remodeled them totally; in others they have maintained the status quo. The decor is nonthreatening, furnishings generally modern, and all are in desirable areas of Budapest with easy access to bus and underground lines. Sizes vary from a studio on the main pedestrian shopping street in Pest to modern, two-bedroom flats in the old Jewish Quarter. The word is out on these two delightful young ladies and what they have to offer, so if this appeals to you, make your plans as far in advance as possible.

ENGLISH SPOKEN Yes

FACILITIES AND SERVICES Depends on flat; all have weekly maid and linen service, cable TV; all have lift, parking, washing machine; pickup at airport or train station possible; no telephones for outgoing calls

NEAREST TOURIST ATTRACTIONS Depends on location of flat

TELEPHONE AND FAX
250-1874

MOBILE PHONE
06 30 9604 57 from within Hungary only

EMAIL
varga_aparts@compuserve.com

CREDIT CARDS
None, cash only

RATES
Depends on flat and length of stay, but rates generally start at $40 to $50 per night

(19) RADIO INN BUDAPEST
VI. Benczúr u. 19, H-1068 Budapest
31 apartments, all with shower or bath and toilet and fitted kitchens

Cheap Sleepers in Budapest here for more than a few nights and willing to stay a little off the tourist trail (beyond the Outer Ring in Pest) will be hard-pressed to beat the Radio Inn, which was once a hostel for employees and guests of the Hungarian National Radio. Because it is near the Academy of Music, it now attracts

TELEPHONE
342-8347, 322-8285

FAX
322-8284

METRO
M1, Hősök tere

CREDIT CARDS
MC, V

Rates depend on size of apartment, number of people, time of year, and length of stay; singles start from 8,000Ft and doubles from 11,000Ft; extra bed 3,000Ft

BREAKFAST
Served to groups only

music students from around the world. When I was there a large Japanese chamber music group filled the hotel and held their practice sessions in the dining room. Other frequent guests include official visitors to the Chinese embassy next door, to the Vietnamese mission across the street, and to the Bulgarian, Yugoslavian, or French embassies, which are also in the neighborhood. With this impressive lineup of guests you might think the Radio Inn would be rather posh, terribly chic, or just plain stuck on itself. Not at all. Instead it is an unpretentious place offering plain accommodations at very reasonable prices. Each floor has its own cleaning lady—and do they ever do their jobs well! The apartments are absolutely spotless. All the units are furnished with plain, easy-care pieces and have workable kitchens and nice bathrooms. Views are of the quiet residential street in front or on the back facing a garden. There just isn't a bad one in the lot.

ENGLISH SPOKEN Yes

FACILITIES AND SERVICES Direct-dial phone, lift, satellite TV, office safe, maid and laundry service

NEAREST TOURIST ATTRACTIONS Heroes' Square, City Park, Fine Arts Museum

(26) INTERNATIONAL BUSINESS HOTEL $
I. Donáti u. 53, H-1015 Budapest
12 apartments, fully furnished with fitted kitchens, shower, bath, and toilet

TELEPHONE
356-7198
FAX
214-3660
EMAIL
ibh9000@westel900.net
METRO
M2, Batthyány tér
HOURS
Office open Mon–Fri 9 A.M.–4 P.M.
CREDIT CARDS
AE
RATES
Rates quoted in U.S. dollars and depend on number of people, size of apartment, and length of stay; prices range from $100–$280 per day; lower weekly and monthly rates
BREAKFAST
$5 per person, per day

These apartments in central Buda are fabulous. Not only are they the hands-down winners in all of Budapest, but they are high on my short list of all-time favorites worldwide. Owner Peter Dietrich has spared no effort or cost in raising imagination and whimsical creativity to new heights. Style and attention to detail are apparent everywhere you look. It would be impossible to choose a favorite apartment because each flat is different in its unique theme and decoration, providing an environment similar to living in a fine contemporary art gallery. Take No. 7, which has both a theatrical and faintly western theme carried out by a top hat coat hanger suspended from the wall, an old railroad clock, and a graphically designed chess set. The view from the double windows is of the Castle, and from the bedroom, you see the Danube River and Pest. In the upstairs bedroom, an old steamer trunk has been turned into a wardrobe and a rolling rack added for hanging extra clothes. There is a

Jacuzzi in the bathroom. No. 3 is one of the smaller units, with a balcony and rooftop views across the river to Pest and of the nearby St. Anne onion-dome church. Steep stairs lead to a sloped-roof bedroom. In No. 8, the phrase "cooking in a closet" goes high style and high tech. Dietrich has taken an old marble breakfront and outfitted it with a working sink and pullout stove. Talk about being creative! Stained-glass doors lead to the master bedroom, which has a big double-mirrored wardrobe.

In other apartments, recessed lighting, Ikea and Italian furnishings, one-of-a-kind cocktail bars, amusing lamps, and fine works of art are used with marvelous results. Many have great balconies, most have postcard views. Nothing has been overlooked: the kitchens feature the latest designs and include attractive eating and cooking utensils plus a microwave, toaster, juicer, and coffeemaker. The large tiled bathrooms are up-to-the-minute with Jacuzzis in all but three. There are only a few apartments with washers and dryers, but a reasonably priced laundry service is provided. For some, the stairs that lead to a few of the mezzanine bedrooms might pose problems, but for everyone else, staying in any one of these dynamic apartments will be a special treat that will be hard to forget, or to top.

ENGLISH SPOKEN Yes

FACILITIES AND SERVICES Air-conditioning, direct-dial phone, fax and answering machine, lift, parking, cable TV, CD player, Jacuzzi in nine apartments, washing machines in largest apartments, laundry service, fitness room, solarium, maid service included, airport and train pickup by arrangement

NEAREST TOURIST ATTRACTIONS Castle District

Hostels

In Budapest, one of the Cheapest Sleeps possible is at a hostel. The only ones recommended here are those affiliated with Hostelling International or Travellers' Youth Hostels-Youth Way and university dorm accommodations. Private hostels can have a whole host of problems, including dirty facilities, rampant theft, questionable owners, and unsavory guest behavior. My advice is to avoid them at all costs. Relatively new on the Budapest hostel scene are beds in university dorms that are vacant when school is not in session. Roving touts work the Kelti railroad station to get business for them. Prices start around 900Ft for a dorm bed and go up to 2,600Ft for a double. You won't need an ISIC or International Youth Hostel card to stay here, but if you have one, you will get a discount.

Almost all of the hostels are open for only a short span, usually from June or July to September. If you arrive and haven't called ahead to reserve a place, look for hostel representatives at the Kelti railroad station. The city tourist offices do not book hostels. Unless otherwise stated, the hostels do not have private facilities, do not serve breakfast, do not accept credit cards, and do not have curfews. However, English is spoken, and bedding is included, though bath towels usually cost extra.

(12) CATERINA HOSTELS
VI. Andrássy út 47, H-1061 Budapest
30 beds, none with private facilities

In addition to its central location and year-round availability, the Caterina has a TV in each room, kitchen privileges, and a pay laundry. Accommodations are in dorm rooms or in a six-person apartment.

TELEPHONE 342-0804

TELEPHONE AND FAX 352-6147

METRO M1, Oktogon

OPEN Year-round

RATES Rates quoted in U.S. dollars; from $8 per person in dorm room; $15 per person in apartment for 6 which has private facilities, TV, and kitchen; towels 30Ft; use of laundry 700Ft

FACILITIES AND SERVICES Kitchen privileges, old lift, TV, office safe

NEAREST TOURIST ATTRACTIONS Everything in Central Pest

(13) HOSTEL BÁNKI
VI. Podmaniczky u. 8, H-1065 Budapest
160 beds in two- or four-person rooms and dormitories

TELEPHONE 312-5268

METRO M3, Nyugati pályaudvar

OPEN July 7–Aug 20

RATES 1,500–2,000Ft depending on room and how many beds are in it

FACILITIES AND SERVICES Kitchen privileges, pay laundry, communal TV

NEAREST TOURIST ATTRACTIONS Not many, need public transportation on Pest side

(14) HUNGARIAN YOUTH HOSTEL FEDERATION OFFICES
VI. Bajcsy-Zsilinszky út 31.11/3, second floor, H-1065 Budapest

This office handles group bookings *only*. They also have lists of hostels in Budapest and throughout Hungary. Contact by phone or fax.

TELEPHONE AND FAX 131-9705, 111-3297
METRO M3, Arany János utca
HOURS Mon–Fri 8 A.M.–5 P.M.

(20) HOSTEL CALIFORNIA
XIII. Váci út 21, H-1134 Budapest
120 beds in dorm rooms for six to eight people

TELEPHONE 140-8585
FAX 120-8425
METRO M3, Dózsa György út
OPEN June 14–Aug 20
RATES 1600Ft per person
FACILITIES AND SERVICES Kitchen privileges, pay laundry, parking, restaurant, sports area, communal TV
NEAREST TOURIST ATTRACTIONS Long walk to Heroes' Square, City Park; otherwise must use public transportation on Pest side

(21) HOSTEL DIÁKSPORT
XIII. Dózsa György út 152, H-1134 Budapest, enter from Angyalföld út
200 beds in one- to four-person rooms and dorms

Hostel Diáksport is known as the Party Hostel thanks to its air-conditioned bar, which serves twenty different beers, sandwiches, and other booze.

TELEPHONE 140-8585, 329-8644
FAX 120-8425
METRO M3, Dózsa György út
OPEN Year-round
RATES 1,500–2,000Ft per person
FACILITIES AND SERVICES Twenty-four-hour air-conditioned bar, kitchen priviledges, pay laundry, communal TV
NEAREST TOURIST ATTRACTIONS Heroes' Square and City Park in Pest

(27) HOSTEL BAKFARK
II. Bakfark u. 1-3, H-1027 Budapest
70 beds in dorm rooms

TELEPHONE 201-5419
FAX 120-8425
OPEN June 15–Aug 31
METRO M2, Moszkva tér
RATES 1,500–1,700Ft per person
FACILITIES AND SERVICES Kitchen privileges, laundry, communal TV, handicapped access
NEAREST TOURIST ATTRACTIONS Castle District in Buda

(28) HOSTEL DONÁTI
II. Donáti u. 46, H-1024 Budapest
60 beds in dorm rooms

TELEPHONE 201-1971
FAX 120-8425
METRO M2, Batthyány tér
OPEN June 15–Aug 31
RATES 1,500Ft per person
FACILITIES AND SERVICES Kitchen privileges, laundry, communal TV
NEAREST TOURIST ATTRACTIONS Castle District in Buda

(29) HOSTEL SCHÖNHERZ
II. Irinyi Joséf u. 42, H-1114 Budapest
300 beds in two- to four-person rooms, all rooms with showers

TELEPHONE 466-5460
FAX 120-8425
METRO M2, Blaha Lujza tér, then tram No. 4 to second stop after Petőfi Bridge
OPEN July 7–Aug 31
RATES 1,800–2,300Ft per person
FACILITIES AND SERVICES Kitchen privileges, laundry, communal TV, disco
NEAREST TOURIST ATTRACTIONS Nothing, must use public transportation from Buda

(31) CITADELLA HOTEL
XI. Citadella sétány, H-1114 Budapest

This is one of the most popular and Cheapest Sleeps in the capital city, even though it's outside of central Buda. You sleep in dorms with ten to fourteen others, and it's definitely nothing fancy.

TELEPHONE 466-5794

FAX 386-0505

METRO From Deák Ferenc tér metro stop, take tram Nos. 47 or 49 to Móricz Zsigmond körtér, then take bus No. 27

OPEN Year-round

RATES 900Ft per person

FACILITIES AND SERVICES Bar, office safe 100Ft per day

NEAREST TOURIST ATTRACTIONS Gellért Hotel, Danube on Buda side

(32) HOSTEL KEK
XI. Szüret u. 2-18, H-1114 Budapest
100 double rooms with sinks or sinks and showers

The hostel is in a quiet area close to the Citadel on Gellért Hill outside central Buda.

TELEPHONE 371-0066

FAX 120-8425

METRO From Deák Ferenc tér metro stop, take tram Nos. 47 or 49 to Móricz Zsigmond körtér, then take bus No. 27 (two stops)

OPEN July 1–Aug 20

RATES 2,000Ft per room

FACILITIES AND SERVICES Kitchen privileges, laundry, parking

NEAREST TOURIST ATTRACTION Gellért Hill on Buda side

(33) HOTEL EXPRESS
XII. Beethoven u. 7-9, H-1126 Budapest
132 beds in two- to six-person rooms, none with private facilities

The white-painted, clean rooms have bare floors and duvets on the beds. There is a sink in every room and the addition of a shower in others. The Buda neighborhood is upscale and quiet.

TELEPHONE 375-2528

FAX 375-3082

INTERNET www.hctnet.hu/hostels

METRO From M2, Moszkva tér, take tram No. 59 (3 stops). Look for white church on corner of Beethoven u., the second street on the left after tram stop.

OPEN Year-round

CREDIT CARDS AE, DC, MC, V (add 10% surcharge)

RATES 1,500–2,500Ft, depending on how many beds in room; discounts for IYHF members

BREAKFAST Included, but can deduct 350Ft if not taken

FACILITIES AND SERVICES Communal TV, office safe

NEAREST TOURIST ATTRACTIONS None, must use public transportation from Buda side

(34) HOTEL HILL
XI. Ménesi út 5, H-1118 Budapest
70 beds in double rooms, two doubles share a shower and toilet

This is the best-equipped hostel in Budapest.

TELEPHONE 385-2122

METRO From Keleti Pu. take bus No. 7 (red) to Móricz Zsigmond Körtér (3 stops)

OPEN July 1–Sept 6

RATES 2,800–3,400Ft, depending on how many beds in room

FACILITIES AND SERVICES Air-conditioned, kitchen privileges, laundry, indoor swimming pool, tennis courts, gym, handicapped access, restaurant

NEAREST TOURIST ATTRACTIONS Danube River on Buda side

Glossary of Vocabulary Terms

Even the natives agree that unless Hungarian is your mother tongue it is almost impossible to learn to speak it fluently. English is spoken more and more in Budapest, and in hotels and restaurants there is usually someone who can come to your aid. Even though no one expects a visitor to speak the language, it is useful to learn a few very basic words and phrases.

General Phrases

yes/no	*igen/nem*
Hello	*Szervuz*
Good morning	*Jó reggelt*
Good evening	*Jó estét*
Good night	*Jó éjszakát*
Good-bye	*Viszontlátásra*
Please	*Kérem*
Thank you	*Köszönöm*
You are welcome	*Szívesen*
Excuse me	*Bocsánat*
left/right	*balra/jobbra*
shop	*bolt, üzlet*
How much is it?	*Mennyibe kerül?*
good/bad	*jó/rossz*
Do you speak English?	*Beszél angolul?*
I do not speak Hungarian	*Ez nem tetszik Magyarul*
I am American	*Amerikai vagyok*
I do not understand	*Nem értem*
I do not know	*Nem tudom*
Where is the . . .?	*Hol van a . . .?*
railway station	*pályaudvar*
airport	*repülőér*
tourist office	*turista iroda*
restaurant	*étterem*
restroom (ladies/mens)	*wc/toalett (női/férfi)*
Help!	*Segítség!*

At the Hotel

hotel	*hotel*
reservation	*foglalás*
room	*szoba*
double/single room	*kétágyás/egyágyás*
passport	*útlevél*

theft	*lopás*
The bill, please	*Számla, kérem*

Signs

open/closed	*nyítva/zárva*
entrance	*bejárat*
exit	*kijárat*
no smoking	*tilos a dohányzás*
danger	*veszélyes*

Days of the Week

Monday	*Hétfő*
Tuesday	*Kedd*
Wednesday	*Szerda*
Thursday	*Csütörtök*
Friday	*Péntek*
Saturday	*Szombat*
Sunday	*Vasárnap*

Numbers

1	*egy*
2	*kettő*
3	*három*
4	*négy*
5	*öt*
6	*hat*
7	*hét*
8	*nyolc*
9	*kilenc*
10	*tíz*
11	*tizenegy*
12	*tizenkettó*
13	*tizenhárom*
14	*tizennégy*
15	*tizenöt*
16	*tizenhat*
17	*tizenhét*
18	*tizennyolc*
19	*tizenkilenc*
20	*húsz*
25	*húszonöt*
30	*harminc*
40	*negyven*
50	*ötven*
60	*hatvan*

70	*nyolcvan*
90	*kilencven*
100	*száz*
200	*ketöszáz*
300	*háromszáz*
1,000	*ezer*
10,000	*tizezer*

SHOPPING: CHEAP CHIC

Life is a great bundle of little things.
—Oliver Wendell Holmes

On a trip to Prague, Vienna, and/or Budapest, visitors cannot possibly spend all of their waking moments going to museums, visiting cathedrals, and admiring the sights. Sooner or later it will be time to shop. In these three cities, the possibilities are endless, with a wide variety of tempting stores and boutiques. However, this listing of Cheap Chic shops is by no means comprehensive, nor does it represent the cheapest goods available. This section is intended to start smart Cheap Chic shoppers on their great buying adventures. I begin with a few general tips of the trade, and then provide listings for each city of some of the best and most dependable shops for finding quality merchandise at the best value.

In Budapest and Prague, it is still possible to find a few bargains, but in Vienna your chances are very slim. The best buys in all three revolve around folk art and handcrafts, though in Budapest you can still find a few antique bargains. Clothing in all three cities is sometimes twice the price you would pay for it on sale at home, but in Vienna you can't fault the quality—that coat or suit will still be in good condition years after you are tired of it and it has gone out of style. If you only remember two essential truths, you will do fine: A bargain is only a bargain if you really like it and can afford it; and more importantly, there are no real bargains left, only lucky purchases. Good luck, and above all, have fun.

Cheap Chic Shopping Tips

1. When you see something that you like, want, and can afford, buy it. Do not plan to leave and come back another time because you probably won't, and even if you do return, the item may be gone. Worse yet is leaving the store and not being able to locate it again, or finding it closed, not to reopen until you have left town.

2. Pack an empty soft folding suitcase in your luggage so you can bring your purchases home with you. This is especially important in Prague and Budapest, where many stores do not ship. The postal system in these two cities is deeply entrenched in red tape, and the dependability of it is almost laughable. If the airline charges you an excess baggage fee (usually around $100), it will probably save you money, not to mention many wasted hours, and the near-migraines you'll experience, wading through the arcane postal rules and regulations.

3. Never change money in a store. Go to a bank or ATM for the best rate.

4. For larger purchases, ask if the store will give you a modest (3 to 5%) discount if you pay in cash.

5. When buying from a street merchant or a fleamarket stand, remember: Cash is king. Bargaining is expected, and the higher the price, the more room there is to deal. But be realistic and fair, especially if you are buying from sweet little grandmothers selling their handmade treasures in Budapest or Prague.

6. In Vienna you can expect a salesperson to wait on you until you have decided on your purchase. Sometimes in Prague and Budapest you will run into clerks who have not shed their socialistic attitude nor mastered the art of customer relations.

7. Use a pocket calculator to avoid asking, "How much is that in dollars?"

8. Inspect everything and buy with care. Nothing is returnable.

9. When shopping in Vienna and Budapest, take the time to do the paperwork for the value-added tax (VAT) refunds. See pages 195 and 207 for details on how to do it for both cities.

10. When returning to the United States, remember these points when clearing customs (see also Customs, page 175):
    - You and every member of your family on the trip, regardless of age, can bring back $400 worth of duty-free purchases.
    - Don't cheat, don't smuggle, and above all, don't do, or carry, drugs.
    - Be nice.

Customs

Every United States citizen, even a baby, is entitled to bring back $400 worth of duty-free merchandise acquired abroad, and you are legally supposed to include every purchase you bring back with you—even toothpaste and hand cream. Families can pool their duty-free buys, so savvy Cheap Chic shoppers can use what their spouse and children do not. After reaching the $400 limit, there will be a 10 percent charge on the next $1,000, and more as the amount increases. Have your receipts ready and make sure they coincide with what you filled out on the landing card. Customs officials have seen and heard it all, and they can spot a liar or cheater in a second—don't try to be clever or to beat the system. If you do, you and your luggage will undergo exhaustive searches, and that's just for openers.

Any purchase worth less than $50 can be shipped back to the States as an unsolicited gift and is considered duty-free, and it does not count in your $400 limit. You can send as many of these unsolicited gifts as you wish, but only one unsolicited gift per person for each mailing, and don't mail anything to yourself. If the worth of the package exceeds $50, duty will be charged, and you will have to pay it before you get your goods.

If you travel with expensive cameras, fancy watches, or valuable jewelry, carry copies of the receipts for them, or you could be questioned about them and even end up paying duty on them. Don't laugh—it has been known to happen.

People who look like hippies get routinely stopped and have their bags searched by customs officials of many countries, not just the United States. So do women who are bedecked and bejeweled, dragging furs and toting designer luggage.

For more information on the U.S. Customs rules and regulations, send for the free brochure, "Know Before You Go," available from the U.S. Customs Service, Box 7407, Washington, DC, 20044; tel: 202-927-6724.

Cheap Chic in Prague

Before 1989 and the Velvet Revolution, Prague was a shopping wasteland that limited visitors to buying crystal or browsing through the government-controlled shops, which displayed a variety of goods from other Communist countries. As for clothing, forget it: the styles were frumpy, the workmanship shoddy, and the colors hideous. After shedding the cloak of Communism, Prague's transformation by capitalism has been meteoric. Even though Prague is still catching up to other Western European cities, its marketplace has blossomed and shopping is now considered a national pastime. While few visitors go to Prague specifically to shop until they drop, designer clothes, French cosmetics, underwear at Marks and Spencer, imported wines and cheeses, bags by Louis Vuitton, and the latest word in electronics are all available for credit card purchase. Aside from all this merchandise—most of which is available at home and sometimes for considerably less money—you can find many treasures that reflect the city's rich cultural history, such as old books and prints, a variety of handcrafts (particularly puppets and wooden toys), and well-priced fine art in galleries and studios. Also look for turn-of-the-century antiques, garnets and beautiful amber jewelry, and Art Nouveau and Art Deco collectibles. If you are buying antiques, be aware that the Czech government requires permits for many objects to be taken out of the country, and to comply with this, most antique stores provide the necessary export permits. Shoppers should also be aware that unlike many other European countries, the Czech government does *not* refund the 22 percent VAT you will pay on everything you buy.

While giant strides have been made when it comes to retail merchandise, there is often a lingering socialist attitude about customer relations and service. The old time-wasting method of standing in line to buy something, then standing in another to pay for it, and queuing again to have it wrapped and given to you still exists in smaller shops, as does smoking on the job, which many consider not only a right but an entitlement. In the old days, most salespersons regarded customers as inconvenient intrusions and treated them with either rude indifference or downright neglect. Even though service has improved, it doesn't always come with a smile, and the customer is not always right.

Shopping Hours

Shops along the major tourist trails have longer hours. They are usually open Monday to Friday from around 10 A.M. until 6 P.M. in the winter and later in the summer. On Saturday they may close around 1 P.M., and they may reopen for a few hours on Sunday. Major department stores are open seven days a week, usually with shorter hours on the weekends.

Shopping Areas and Shopping Streets

Shopping Areas

The best shopping is found in the following areas, which are within walking distance of each other: Malá Strana, across the Charles Bridge from Old Town; Kampa, a picturesque corner by the Charles Bridge with art and craft galleries, tourist kitsch, and benches for the weary; Staré Město, with Old Town Square and the streets radiating from it; and Nové Město, where Prague does its business and shops in departments stores.

Shopping Streets

The major shopping streets are Celetná, Pařížská, Karlova, Na příkopé, Václavské náměstí, Mostecka, and Nerudova. Celetná connects Old Town Square with Náměstí Republiky and resembles any smart boutique-lined shopping street in the world. Along here you can look for glass, garnets, amber, and designer togs, and you will pay generally high prices. An address on Pařížská, a wide boulevard leading from Old Town to the Jewish Quarter and the river, carries with it the most prestige, and is considered by many to be the equivalent of New York's Fifth Avenue or the Champs Elyseé in Paris. That may be a stretch, but the designer shops and fancy airline offices are impressive.

Karlova, the strip of roadway winding from the Charles Bridge to Old Town, is definitely the most tourist trod in the capital, and the shops reflect this, selling the good, the bad, and the ugly. But you will inevitably find yourself here at least once during your visit, so just be on your guard and shop with care. Stores along the pedestrianized Na příkopé, which runs from Vaclavské náměstí (Wenceslas Square) to Náměstí Republiky, are geared to the Czech hunger for goods bearing well-known names from the West, such as the Body Shop, the Tie Rack, Next, Adidas, Bennetton, Levi, The Gap, DKNY, McDonald's, and even Planet Hollywood. There is no shortage of strategically located ATMs either.

When you cross the Charles Bridge to Malá Strana you will be on Mostecka, another tourist magnet with shops to match. From Mostecká, most visitors wend their way to Nerudova, part of the Royal Way leading to the Prague Castle (Hradčany). As you would expect, the shops along Nerudova are geared to enticing tourists to spend money.

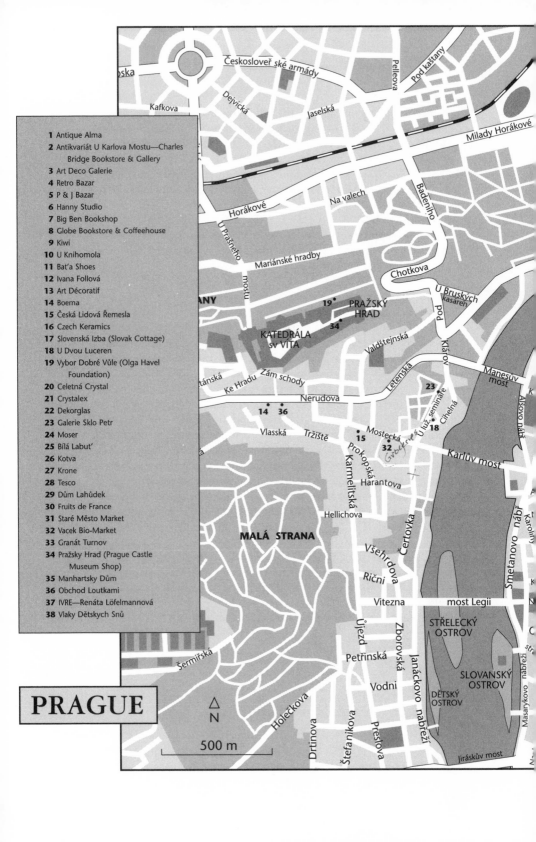

1 Antique Alma
2 Antikvariát U Karlova Mostu—Charles
   Bridge Bookstore & Gallery
3 Art Deco Galerie
4 Retro Bazar
5 P & J Bazar
6 Hanny Studio
7 Big Ben Bookshop
8 Globe Bookstore & Coffeehouse
9 Kiwi
10 U Knihomola
11 Bat'a Shoes
12 Ivana Follová
13 Art Décoratif
14 Boerna
15 Česká Lidová Řemesla
16 Czech Keramics
17 Slovenská Izba (Slovak Cottage)
18 U Dvou Luceren
19 Vybor Dobré Vůle (Olga Havel
   Foundation)
20 Celetná Crystal
21 Crystalex
22 Dekorglas
23 Galerie Sklo Petr
24 Moser
25 Bílá Labuť
26 Kotva
27 Krone
28 Tesco
29 Dům Lahůdek
30 Fruits de France
31 Staré Město Market
32 Vacek Bio-Market
33 Granát Turnov
34 Pražsky Hrad (Prague Castle
   Museum Shop)
35 Manhartsky Dům
36 Obchod Loutkami
37 IVRE—Renáta Löfelmannová
38 Vlaky Dětskych Snů

PRAGUE

△
N

500 m

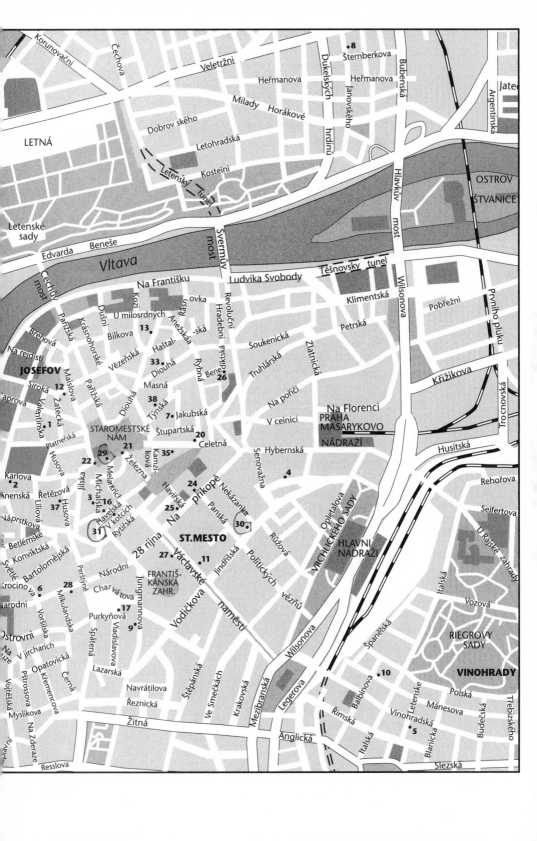

Antiques and Rare Books

(1) ANTIQUE ALMA
Valentinská 7, Staré Město, Prague 1

TELEPHONE 23 25 865
FAX 23 22 580
METRO A, Staroměstská
CREDIT CARDS AE, MC, V
HOURS Mon–Fri 10 A.M.–6 P.M.
ENGLISH SPOKEN Yes

You will find everything from top hats to tails—if you look long enough—in this wonderful jumble of antiques and just plain junk crammed onto two levels, which are just cluttered and messy enough to make them challenging. The help virtually ignores your presence as you sift through the displays: smaller pieces are upstairs, and furniture, rugs, paintings, light fixtures, and costumes are on the basement level. A bonus is their restaurant/wine bar, the Klub Belle Epoque, which also serves as the meeting place for the association of Prague antiques dealers. For more on the restaurant, please see *Cheap Eats in Prague, Vienna, and Budapest.*

(2) ANTIKVARIÁT U KARLOVA MOSTU—CHARLES BRIDGE BOOKSTORE & GALLERY
Karlova 2, Staré Město, Prague 1

TELEPHONE AND FAX 26 21 86, 2422 9205
EMAIL info@meissner.cz
INTERNET www.meissner.cz
METRO A, Staroměstská
CREDIT CARDS AE, DC, MC, V
HOURS Mon–Fri 10 A.M.–6 P.M., Sat 11 A.M.–4 P.M.
ENGLISH SPOKEN Yes

The prices are high and so is the quality. For rare books, original prints, drawings, and paintings, it is considered one of the best in Prague.

(3) ART DECO GALERIE
Michalská 21, Staré Město, Prague 1

TELEPHONE 23 16 67
METRO B, Můstek
CREDIT CARDS AE, DC, MC, V
HOURS Mon–Fri 2–7 P.M.
ENGLISH SPOKEN Yes

Owner Milli Várová spends her mornings and weekends combing Prague and the Czech countryside for vintage clothing and household kitsch from the twenties, thirties, and fifties. If this is your thing, the place is a gold mine.

Bazaars and Junk Shops

(4) RETRO BAZAR
Senovážná 2, Nové Město, Prague 1

TELEPHONE 24 22 43 43
METRO B, Náměstí Republiky
CREDIT CARDS AE, MC, V
HOURS Mon–Fri 9 A.M.–9 P.M.
ENGLISH SPOKEN Limited

If you are a garage-sale groupie or love prowling through secondhand stores, the bazaars in Prague are your kind of shopping experience. These glorified junk shops sell an array of paintings, jewelry, small furniture, dishes, glassware, and assorted stuff. They are well worth a browse because treasures do show up, and the prices are definitely in the Cheap Chic category. Retro Bazar is one of the best.

(5) P & J BAZAR
Anny Letenské 8, Vinohrady, Prague 2

TELEPHONE 24 23 53 75
METRO A, Náměstí Míru
CREDIT CARDS None
HOURS Mon–Fri 10 A.M.–1 P.M., 2–5 P.M.
ENGLISH SPOKEN Usually

This place is filled to overflowing with junk in various stages of repair and various levels of value. Some say it is their favorite Prague junk stop.

Beauty Shops and Hairdressers

(6) HANNY STUDIO
Národní třída 19, Nové Město, Prague 1

TELEPHONE 24 23 54 07
METRO B, Národní třída
CREDIT CARDS MC, V
HOURS Mon–Fri 9 A.M.–8 P.M., Sat 9 A.M.–2 P.M., Sun 2–8 P.M.
ENGLISH SPOKEN Depends on the operator, but usually

Hanny is well located in the center of Prague on the busy Národní třída, and it's easy to get to by public transportation. At this full-service salon, in addition to getting your hair done, you can have a manicure, facial, massage, or any one of their other beauty treatments. The best part is the cost, which is about one-third of what you would pay at home.

Bookstores

(7) BIG BEN BOOKSHOP
Malá Štupartská 5, Josefov, Prague 1

TELEPHONE 23 28 021
FAX 23 19 848
EMAIL books@bigbenbookshop.com
METRO B, Náměstí Republiky
CREDIT CARDS AE, DC, MC, V
HOURS Mon–Fri 9 A.M.–6 P.M., Sat–Sun 10 A.M.–5 P.M.
ENGLISH SPOKEN Yes

It may be small, but it has a good selection of books and maps on Prague as well as nonfiction English-language books. There is a second location at the British Council, Národní 10, Prague 1. There is no telephone at this location. Hours are Monday to Thursday 10 A.M. to 6 P.M., and Friday 10 A.M. to 4 P.M., closed weekends.

(8) GLOBE BOOKSTORE & COFFEEHOUSE
Janovského 14, Holešovice, Prague 7

TELEPHONE AND FAX 66 71 26 10
EMAIL globe@login.cz
INTERNET www.ini.cz/glo
METRO C, Vltavská; or Tram Nos. 5 or 12 and get off at Stossmajerovo náměstí
CREDIT CARDS AE, V
HOURS Daily 10 A.M.–midnight
ENGLISH SPOKEN Yes

The Globe Bookstore is owned and run by American expats. With an inventory of ten thousand new and used English books, current periodicals, and daily newspapers, it has become a drawing card for every young American drifting through Prague. There is a popular café connected to the shop (see *Cheap Eats in Prague, Vienna, and Budapest*).

(9) KIWI
Jugmannova 23, Nové Město, Prague 1

TELEPHONE 24 23 47 56
FAX 96 24 55 55
METRO B, Národní třída
CREDIT CARDS None
HOURS Mon–Fri 9 A.M.–6 P.M., Sat 9 A.M.–2 P.M.
ENGLISH SPOKEN Yes

Come here for their great selection of maps, not for the travel agency that takes up most of the space. They also stock the only pedometers I found in Prague.

(10) U KNIHOMOLA
Mánesova 79, Vinohrady, Prague 2

TELEPHONE 62 77 767
FAX 27 26 84
METRO A, Jiřího z Podébrad
CREDIT CARDS AE, MC, V
HOURS Mon–Thur 10 A.M.–11 P.M., Fri–Sat 10 A.M.–midnight, Sun 11 A.M.–8 P.M.
ENGLISH SPOKEN Yes

U Knihomola carries the largest and best collection of English-language books in Prague—covering art and literature, travel, reference, and children's titles—and they have books in Czech, French, German, and Spanish as well as magazines and newspapers. They will also special order and ship. The café in the basement is a comfortable place to thumb through your purchases while enjoying a light meal or a glass of wine (see *Cheap Eats in Prague, Vienna, and Budapest*).

Clothing and Shoes

(11) BAT'A SHOES
Václavské náměstí 6, Nové Město, Prague 1

TELEPHONE 24 21 81 33
METRO A or B, Můstek
CREDIT CARDS AE, MC, V
HOURS Mon–Fri 9 A.M.–7 P.M., Sat 10 A.M.–6 P.M., Sun 11 A.M.–5 P.M.
ENGLISH SPOKEN Yes

Bat'a is the famous Czech footwear company that left the country after the Nazi takeover and did not return until 1989. The six-story store occupies an important place on Wenceslas Square and carries the full line of Bat'a shoes and accessories, plus clothing for men and women.

(12) IVANA FOLLOVÁ
Maislova 21, Josefov, Prague 1

TELEPHONE AND FAX 23 19 529
METRO A, Staroměstská
CREDIT CARDS AE, DC, MC, V
HOURS Daily 10 A.M.–7 P.M. from Mar–Dec; closed Sun from Jan–Feb
ENGLISH SPOKEN Yes

Ivana Follová draws her inspiration from the kimono. Her creative, flowing designs are almost works of art in themselves, and they appeal to imaginative women who are not afraid to make a beautiful fashion statement with unique clothing. She also displays works of art and fashion by other Czech fashion designers.

Collectibles

(13) ART DÉCORATIF
U Obecního domu, Nové Město, Prague 1

    TELEPHONE 22 0023 50, 22 00 23 51
    METRO B, Náměstí Republiky
    CREDIT CARDS AE, MC, V
    HOURS Daily 10 A.M.–8 P.M.
    ENGLISH SPOKEN Yes

If you appreciate Art Nouveau, this is a must-stop on your shopping rounds. The prices are high, but it costs nothing to admire the merchandise, and the staff is used to this and very tolerant. This is one of the shops around the corner from the magnificent Obecni Dům, a masterpiece of Art Nouveau splendor that serves as Prague's Municipal House.

Crafts

(14) BOEMA
Nerudova 49, Malá Strana, Prague 1

    TELEPHONE 53 49 24
    METRO A, Malostranská
    CREDIT CARDS AE, DC, MC, V
    HOURS Daily 10 A.M.–6 P.M. in summer, and until 5 P.M. in winter
    ENGLISH SPOKEN Yes

Boema specializes in fine arts and crafts by top Czech artisans. In addition to museum copies and hand-painted folk glass, there is jewelry designed by Alphonse Mucha's daughter, stained-glass hangings by Milos Forman's wife, and works by fourth-generation family glassmakers. The quality is excellent and the prices fair.

(15) ČESKÁ LIDOVÁ ŘEMESLA
Mostecká 17, Malá Strana, Prague 1

    TELEPHONE Main office, 24 24 87 92, 24 21 08 59
    FAX 24 24 87 90
    EMAIL cnp@ms.anet.cz
    METRO A, Malostranská
    CREDIT CARDS AE, DC, MC, V
    HOURS Mon–Thur, Sun 10 A.M.–6 P.M., Fri–Sat until 7 P.M.
    ENGLISH SPOKEN Yes

For traditional Czech handcrafts, these shops are the best. There are branches all over town, so you will never be too far away from one of their stores. Here are the branch addresses: in Staré Město, Melantrichova 17, Jilská 7 and 22, and Karlova 12; in Malá Strana, Mostecká 17 and Nerudova 23 and 31; and near Prague Castle, Zlatá ulička 16.

(16) CZECH KERAMICS
Havelská 21, Staré Město, Prague 1

TELEPHONE 68 41 600
METRO A or B, Můstek
CREDIT CARDS AE, MC, V
HOURS Daily 10 A.M.–6 P.M.
ENGLISH SPOKEN Yes

This is the only shop in Prague selling individually hand-painted southern Moravian pottery. The production of pottery in Tupsy, southern Moravia, goes back to the arrival of Swiss protestants, who fled their country in the first half of the sixteenth century. Because of their attitude toward secular authority, they were persecuted, their communities fell apart, and many were finally driven away as far as the Black Sea. For those who remained in Tupsy, their tradition of high-quality pottery craftsmanship survived and is now recognized as the Tupsy school of pottery. Each piece in the shop is a handmade original and charming. Shipping is available.

(17) SLOVENSKÁ IZBA (SLOVAK COTTAGE)
Purkyňova 4, Nové Město, Prague 1

TELEPHONE 24 91 07 92
METRO B, Národná Třída
CREDIT CARDS AE, DC, MC, V
HOURS Mon–Fri 10 A.M.–1 P.M., 2–6 P.M., Sat–Sun 10 A.M.–5 P.M. in summer; closed Sun in winter
ENGLISH SPOKEN Yes

The Slovak Cottage sells a wide assortment of handmade decorative and household objects made from natural Slovakian materials, such as wood, clay, metal, leather, wicker, straw, horn, and various textiles, including embroideries, lace, cotton, and wools. You will also find glass paintings, decorated Easter eggs, wonderful corn husk dolls, and authentic national costumes from all the regions of Slovakia. It is a great shop—don't miss it.

NOTE: The popular restaurant that operated in conjunction with the shop has closed, but they were planning to reopen it soon.

(18) U DVOU LUCEREN
U Lužického semináře, Malá Strana, Prague 1

TELEPHONE 57 31 16 78-9
FAX 53 66 23
METRO A, Malostranská
CREDIT CARDS MC, V
HOURS Daily 11 A.M.–6 P.M. (sometimes later) in summer; Wed–Sun 11 A.M.–6 P.M., closed Mon–Tues in winter
ENGLISH SPOKEN Yes

The "Two Lanterns" is two side-by-side shops—even though none of the four signs above them say "U Dvou Luceren." You can recognize the shop by the two telltale lanterns hanging on either side of the string of deceptive signs. The shop sells an above-average selection of Prague miniature houses, Art Nouveau silver-plated glass and jewelery, large glass flowers, and paperweights.

(19) VYBOR DOBRÉ VŮLE (OLGA HAVEL FOUNDATION)
Shop: Zlatá ulička (behind the Prague Castle), Hradčany, Prague 1
Foundation: Box 240, 111 24 Prague 1, Czech Republic

TELEPHONE Foundation office, 24 21 73 31
FAX 24 21 70 82
METRO A, Malostranská
CREDIT CARDS None
HOURS Daily 10 A.M.–6 P.M.
ENGLISH SPOKEN Yes

The Vybor Dobré Vůle—Committee of Goodwill—was formed in 1991 by Olga Havel, the ex-wife of Václav Havel. The foundation sponsors projects relating to health, education, and social welfare. It distributes medicines and other necessities to children's homes, hospitals, and mental institutions. One of its main purposes is to support projects that promote opportunities for education and independent living for people with disabilities of all kinds. The foundation also sponsors trips in the Czech Republic and abroad for chronically sick children and for those with no family of their own, and it arranges for internships for Czech and Slovak doctors in North American hospitals. Olga Havel states: "It is our wish that all members of society have the right to a dignified life, no matter if they have a disability or illness, are old or alone, have a different colored skin or alternative lifestyle. It is in this spirit that we call upon people of good will to help others. We extend our gratitude to all those who respond to this call." You can respond to this worthy cause by patronizing the Olga Havel Foundation Shop on Zlatá ulička, otherwise known as the famous Golden Lane behind the Prague Castle. The shop sells artwork and handcrafts made by children and adults with disabilities. As well as providing the artists with a source of income, the proceeds of sales support projects sponsored by the foundation.

Crystal and Glass

A word or two about crystal and glass, which you will see everywhere—concentrated in shops and boutiques around Old Town Square, in department stores, in hotel lobbies, and sometimes hawked by street vendors. How do you tell crystal from just plain glass? It is all in the ping. To know which is which, lightly tap the inside lip of the glass with a pen or pencil. If it's glass, you will hear a thud. Crystal resounds with a high ping.

(20) CELETNÁ CRYSTAL
Celetná 15, Staré Město, Prague 1

TELEPHONE Not available

METRO B, Náměstí Republiky

CREDIT CARDS AE, DC, MC, V

HOURS Daily 10 A.M.–6 P.M., later in summer

ENGLISH SPOKEN Yes

This is one of the best—and most expensive—stores to shop for crystal, amber, and china. You may pay more, but you will get quality merchandise, either to take home with you or have sent.

(21) CRYSTALEX
Malé náměstí 6, Staré Město, Prague 1

TELEPHONE 24 22 84 59

TELEPHONE AND FAX 24 22 92 21

METRO A, Staromestská

CREDIT CARDS AE, MC, V

HOURS Daily 10 A.M.–6 P.M., later in summer

ENGLISH SPOKEN Usually

This is a factory-direct store with a wide variety of everything fragile and breakable in crystal and glass. Prices are very good, and they will ship.

(22) DEKORGLAS
Křižovnická 3, Staré Město, Prague 1

TELEPHONE 90 00 36 29

METRO A, Staroměstská

CREDIT CARDS AE, DC, MC, V

HOURS Daily 9:30 A.M.–6 P.M.

ENGLISH SPOKEN Yes

Dekorglas specializes in crystal and glass from Novy Bor. The prices are good, and they will ship.

(23) GALERIE SKLO PETR
U Lužického semináre 7, Malá Strana, Prague 1

TELEPHONE Not available

METRO A, Malostranská

CREDIT CARDS AE, MC, V

HOURS Daily 11 A.M.–6 P.M., later in summer

ENGLISH SPOKEN Yes

After a while, all these crystal and glass stores begin to look alike. At Galerie Sklo Petr, the selection of smaller glass flowers and glass Christmas ornaments is good.

Second location: Zlatá ulička, behind Prague Castle; tel and fax: 69 23 759.

(24) MOSER
Na Příkopé 12, Nové Město, Prague 1

TELEPHONE 24 21 12 93-4

FAX 24 22 86 86

METRO A or C, Můstek

CREDIT CARDS AE, DC, MC, V

OPEN Mon–Fri 9 A.M.–7 P.M., Sat–Sun until 4 P.M.

ENGLISH SPOKEN Yes

There is no question: Moser is the Rolls Royce of Czech crystal. You can't buy finer. Moser crystal has been made in Karlovy Vary since 1857 and is rightfully known as the "King of Glass" and the "Glass of Kings." Naturally the prices reflect this, but please do not let this deter you from visiting either of their exquisite shops in Prague—and perhaps buying one small item. The store on Na příkope is the original; it's where the family sold their beautiful crystal until the Nazis forced them to flee during World War II. After the war, the company was nationalized, but the standards remained high, and now it is back in the family. The second location on Malé náměstí by Old Town Square is in an eight-hundred-year-old building that was in ruins before Moser reconstructed it in 1990. Moser will ship your purchase or deliver it to any hotel in Prague.

Second branch: Malé náměstí 11, Prague 1; tel: 21 61 15 20; fax: 21 61 15 27.

Department Stores

(25) BÍLÁ LABUT'
Na poříčí 23, Nové Město, Prague 1

TELEPHONE 24 81 13 64, 24 21 14 73

FAX 23 27 905

METRO A or C, Můstek

CREDIT CARDS AE, MC, V

HOURS Mon–Fri 8 A.M.–7 P.M., Sat until 6 P.M.

ENGLISH SPOKEN Usually

Bílá Labut' stocks mostly Czech-made items, and it is useful only if you are curious about what was available before 1989 and how far the other stores have come since then. However, the basement grocery isn't bad at all. There is a branch at Václavské náměstí 59, which is slightly more upmarket.

(26) KOTVA
Náměstí Republiky 8, Nové Město, Prague 1

TELEPHONE 24 80 11 11

FAX 24 80 12 30

METRO B, Náměstí Republiky

CREDIT CARDS AE, DC, MC, V

HOURS Department store, Mon–Fri 9 A.M.–8 P.M., Sat–Sun until 4 P.M.; grocery, Mon–Fri 7 A.M.–8 P.M., Sat 8 A.M.–4 P.M., Sun 10 A.M.–4 P.M.

ENGLISH SPOKEN Usually

As an expat living in Prague in the early 1980s, I regarded Kotva as the only game in town if I was desperate enough to have to buy some item of clothing or housewares. Gone are the depressing displays of hopelessly out-of-date fashions and home furnishings and the rude sales staff who waited only for sunset and payday. Now it has been transformed into a four-level shopping experience selling every imaginable consumer item, from auto parts to zippers. The cosmetics department looks like any you would see in New York, and in addition to all the familiar names, it carries my favorite French cosmetic brand, Bourjois, the prototype for Chanel that sells for a fraction of the price. Yves St. Laurent and Guy Laroche both have boutiques here; the other ready-to-wear clothes are fashionable and affordable; the electronics department has at least a half-dozen brand-name choices for every appliance; and the glass and porcelain section on the third floor has great prices. Other store services include a snack bar, travel agency, bureau de change, shoe and watch repairs, supermarket with an excellent bakery, and an underground car park.

(27) KRONE
Václavské náměstí 21, Nové Město, Prague 1

TELEPHONE 24 23 04 77
METRO A or B, Můstek
CREDIT CARDS AE, MC, V
HOURS Mon–Fri 8 A.M.–8 P.M., Sat 8 A.M.–7 P.M., Sun 9 A.M.–6 P.M.
ENGLISH SPOKEN Yes

Krone is definitely a middle-of-the-road shopping option, with the exception of the Julius Meinl supermarket in the basement, the Bourjois cosmetic line, and the fast-food steam-table buffet, an either stand-up or sit-down affair with styrofoam plates and plastic utensils.

(28) TESCO
Národní třída 26, Nové Město, Prague 1

TELEPHONE 24 22 79 71-9
FAX 24 22 98 10
METRO B, Národní třída
CREDIT CARDS MC, V
HOURS Department store, Mon–Fri 8 A.M.–8 P.M., Sat 9 A.M.–6 P.M., Sun 10 A.M.–6 P.M.; grocery, Mon–Fri 7 A.M.–8 P.M., Sat 8 A.M.–6 P.M., Sun 9 A.M.–6 P.M.
ENGLISH SPOKEN Usually

If it is new in town, Tesco has it first. In the old days it was known as Maj, and it sold the usual ugly Communist-inspired goods. Soon after the Velvet Revolution it was bought by K-Mart, which sank plenty of hard currency into it to bring it into the modern age. In 1996, K-Mart sold to Tesco, a British company. The department store now sells midrange fashions, but the grocery store in the basement is something else. It is always packed, with lines waiting to get in to strip the shelves clean of all the major international brand names. There is a decent wine selection, a better-than-average produce and meat section, a bakery, and a huge frozen food selection. If you forgot your Skippy extra chunky peanut butter, yearn for an Oreo, or crave a taste of Tex-Mex, Tesco is the place to go.

Food and Grocery Stores

See the "Department Stores" section (page 188) for a listing of the major department stores in Prague that sell food. When shopping for food, you will be expected to bag your own order in your own bag, or you must pay a few crowns for a bag (*tašků*) from the store.

(29) DŮM LAHŮDEK
Malé námestí 3, Staré Město, Prague 1

TELEPHONE 24 23 80 24
FAX 26 71 30
METRO A, Staroměstská
CREDIT CARDS AE, MC, V
HOURS Mon–Sat 9:30 A.M.–7 P.M., Sun noon–7 P.M.
ENGLISH SPOKEN Yes

Similar to Fauchon in Paris, Dům Lahůdek is *the* place for fancy grocery shopping in Prague. There are four floors of every type of food you can think of, a great wine section (with a wine bar open daily from 2 P.M. to midnight), smoked fish, meat, cheese, deli and sandwich counters, a bakery, plus coffee by the cup or bag and a restaurant. For more about the eat-in food sections, see *Cheap Eats in Prague, Vienna, and Budapest.*

(30) FRUITS DE FRANCE
Jindřišská 9, Nové Město, Prague 1

TELEPHONE 24 22 03 04
FAX 24 21 68 82
METRO A or B, Můstek
CREDIT CARDS None
HOURS Mon–Fri 9:30 A.M.–6:30 P.M., Sat 9:30 A.M.–1 P.M.
ENGLISH SPOKEN Yes, and French

Fruits de France looks, smells, and acts like a Parisian market, and why not? It is owned by a clever Frenchwoman, who opened it in 1991 when Prague was still a virtual food desert with nothing but limp and listless choices that sat on the shelves for weeks. From day one, Fruits de France has been a huge success. Weekly deliveries of French produce, fine cheese and butter, eggs from Brittany, wines, and even Poilâne bread are scooped up by locals who know and appreciate good food. None of it comes cheaply, but judging from the crowds eager to buy everything in sight, price does not seem to matter.

(31) STARÉ MĚSTO MARKET
Havleská, Staré Město, Prague 1

TELEPHONE None
METRO A or B, Můstek
CREDIT CARDS Depends on stall
HOURS Mon–Fri 8 A.M.–6 P.M., Sat–Sun 8 A.M.–1 P.M.
ENGLISH SPOKEN Depends on stall

This market sells the cheapest produce, and the prices are relatively standard, but you do need to comparison shop for quality. Plan to do your food shopping during the week, since on the weekend the produce takes a back seat to the tourist trinkets.

(32) VACEK BIO-MARKET
Mosteká 3, Malá Strana, Prague 1

TELEPHONE Not available
METRO A, Malostranská, or Tram Nos. 12 or 22 to Malostranská náměstí
CREDIT CARDS None
HOURS Mon–Fri 6 A.M.–10 P.M., Sat from 6:30 A.M., and Sun from 10 A.M.
ENGLISH SPOKEN Limited

There is not much to recommend Vacek Bio-Market except its hours. The mentality of the help is still frozen in the pre-Velvet Revolution days, and so are the jammed shelves. It reminds me of a 7-11 with attitude. However, if you are staying in Malá Strana, it is a handy place to know about, since it is the only food shop in the vicinity.

Jewelry

(33) GRANÁT TURNOV
Dlouhá 30, Josefov, Prague 1

TELEPHONE 23 15 612
METRO B, Náměstí Republiky
CREDIT CARDS AE, MC, V
HOURS Mon–Fri 10 A.M.–6 P.M., Sat until 1 P.M.
ENGLISH SPOKEN Yes

If garnets are on your shopping list, start here, as there are loads of fakes and imitations out there. Granát Turnov is a factory-direct shop selling the best quality garnets at the best prices. The garnets are set in gold and silver or gold plate. The selection is varied and the service is good.

Museum Shops

(34) PRAŽSKY HRAD (PRAGUE CASTLE MUSEUM SHOP)
Jiršká 6, Hradčany, Prague 1

TELEPHONE 33 37 32 64
FAX 33 37 32 55
METRO A, Malostranská, then Tram No. 22
CREDIT CARDS AE, MC, V
HOURS Daily 10 A.M.–6 P.M.
ENGLISH SPOKEN Yes

The choices are wonderful and the quality superb. Here is the place to shop for original souvenirs related to the treasures found in Prague's museums. Look for posters, cards, beautiful art books in all languages, jewelery, silk ties and scarves, porcelain, glass, and quality fine art reproductions of works in Prague Castle, Strahov Monastery, the National Gallery, the National Museum, and the Jewish Museum, to name only a few.

Puppets

(35) MANHARTSKY DŮM
Celetná 17, Staré Město, Prague 1

TELEPHONE 24 80 91 56
METRO B, Náměstí Republiky
CREDIT CARDS None
HOURS Mon–Fri 10 A.M.–5 P.M., Sat until 1 P.M.
ENGLISH SPOKEN Yes

Handcrafted wooden puppets are among the best buys in Prague, and this is one of the better places to buy them. The quality of their handmade marionettes is better than others sold on the street and in tourist shops, and they are priced accordingly. The shop operates in conjuction with a puppet theater, the Divadelní Ústav, and you can book tickets for the performances here.

(36) OBCHOD LOUTKAMI
Nerudova 47, Malá Strana, Prague 1

TELEPHONE 53 00 65
METRO A, Malostranská
CREDIT CARDS AE, MC, V
HOURS Daily 9:30 A.M.–6 P.M., later in summer
ENGLISH SPOKEN Yes

Half of the two-room shop is packed with leering trolls and wicked witches sold on strings, sticks, or for your fingers. The selection is enormous and the quality above average.

Toys

(37) IVRE—RENÁTA LÖFELMANNOVÁ
Husova 12, Staré Město, Prague 1

TELEPHONE None
METRO A, Staroměstská
CREDIT CARDS AE, DC, MC, V
HOURS Mon–Sat 10 A.M.–7 P.M., Sun until 6 P.M.
ENGLISH SPOKEN Usually

There is bound to be something here the children on your list will love. The handmade soft toys are adorable and easily packable in your luggage. The shop is not well marked, but look for the smiling sunflower sign outside and that's it.

(38) VLAKY DĚTSKYCH SNŮ
Tynská 8, Staré Město, Prague 1

TELEPHONE 23 26 938
METRO A or B, Můstek, or A, Staroměstská
CREDIT CARDS AE, DC, MC, V
HOURS Mon–Fri 10 A.M.–6 P.M., Sat 10 A.M.–4 P.M.
ENGLISH SPOKEN Yes

If you or anyone you know loves model trains, this shop, aptly named "Trains of Childhood Dreams," is an absolute *must*. Everything is made here, and the selection is excellent.

Cheap Chic in Vienna

Vienna is a window-shopping paradise, but actually purchasing things can get expensive, since prices for consumer goods and clothing are higher in the Austrian capital than in most other major European cities. Best buys continue to be the beautiful handcrafts, known worldwide for their quality of workmanship. In addition to well-made, long-lasting Alpine clothing, look for enamel jewelry, hand-painted ceramics, and petit point. If you are lucky enough to be in Vienna from the last part of November through Christmas, you will be able to experience the fairy tale world of the outdoor Advent and Christmas Markets, where you can shop for original treasures, fill up on fat sausages, and drink *Glühwein* (mulled wine) to ward off the cold.

Shopping Hours

Shopping hours are strictly government controlled. Stores are open Monday to Friday from 9 A.M. to 6 P.M. and on Saturday at least until 1 P.M. Recently, Saturday hours were deregulated and stores are now allowed to remain open until 6 P.M., but not all do. At press time it was not known what new Saturday hours all the different stores would adopt. It is probably safe to assume that shops in the first district will stay open beyond 1 P.M., but to be safe, the Saturday hours listed in Cheap Chic reflect the traditional 1 P.M. closing.

Only kiosks in the railway stations can remain open on Sunday; everything else is closed tightly on Sunday until right before Christmas, when shops have extended hours and are open at least the Sunday before December 25. This, too, may be changing. Stores in the suburban multiplex malls have been opening on Sunday, and this has led to renewed debate about the liberalization of store opening hours. Studies have shown that Saturday shopping is seen by many Viennese as an alternative to other entertainment, which has thus created additional revenue for retailers and led to the deregulation of Saturday shopping hours. The Austrian Economic Chamber is now calling for a complete deregulation of hours on Sunday for all stores, no matter what the size. The unions will have none of this, and have been joined in the protest by the Catholic Church, which argues that allowing stores to be open on Sunday would weaken family life and undermine society as a whole. It is a huge debate and who knows how it will all end.

Shopping Areas and Streets

The majority of shops are concentrated in the first district and are within easy walking distance of each other. Start by walking along the pedestrian-zoned Kärntner Strasse, then move on to Graben, Herrengasse, and Kohlmarkt and the streets radiating from them, which have fashion and folk-art boutiques side by side with stores selling exquisite jewelry, furniture, and antiques. Along the way, take time to stop for a welcome break at one of the coffeehouses and treat yourself to some fabulous Viennese pastries. Another area that is well known for unique shops, art galleries, and one of the best outdoor Advent-Christmas markets is Spittelberg in the seventh district. Mariahilferstrasse, which runs from the Kunsthistorisches Museum to the Westbahnhof, is lined with modern shops, and it is where most locals do their shopping as well as those Eastern European visitors who come to Vienna for a day or two to literally shop until they drop.

Tax Refund

If you spend more than 1,000AS per day per shop, you are entitled to a 13 percent rebate. This rebate can be claimed in cash at the airport or at the border when you leave Austria. Here is what to do. Ask the shop to fill out a Tax-free Check for you, being sure to include your name and address on the form, and have them give it to you along with the Tax-free envelope, which has a listing of every location where you can claim your refund. Be sure to attatch the original receipts to the Tax-free Check. When you leave the country, be prepared to show your purchases to the customs official, who will stamp your Tax-free Check. *Without this customs stamp, you cannot claim your refund.* Either claim your Tax-free rebate immediately at the Tax-free Rebate Cash Payment desk at the airport or border; or you can claim your rebate by mail by mailing your Tax-free Check, enclosed in the Tax-free envelope. For further information, contact 798 44 00-0.

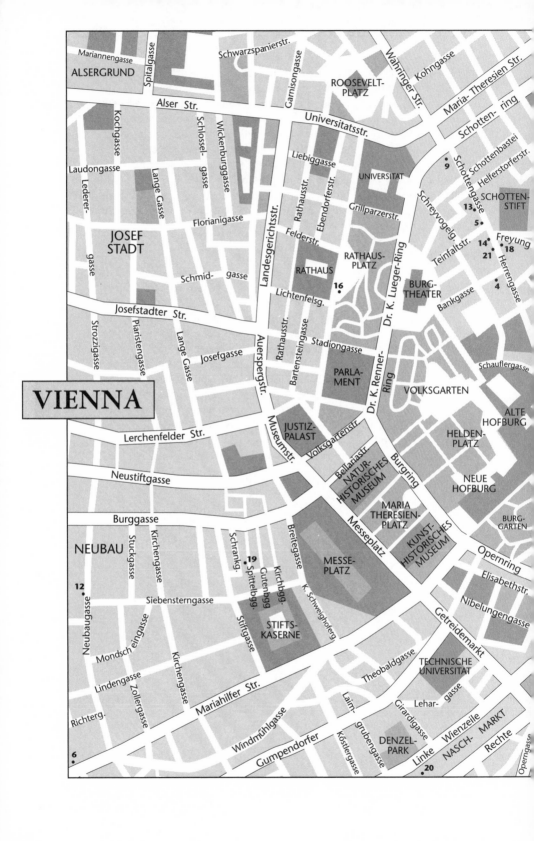

VIENNA

ALSERGRUND

JOSEFSTADT

NEUBAU

Mariannengasse
Schwarzspanierstr.
ROOSEVELT-PLATZ
Wahringer Str.
Kohngasse
Maria- Theresien Str.
Schotten- ring
Spitalgasse
Garnisongasse
Alser Str.
Universitatsstr.
Schottenbastei
Schottenbastei
Helferstorferstr.
• 9
Kochgasse
Schlossel- gasse
Wickenburggasse
Liebiggasse
UNIVERSITAT
Schottengasse
SCHOTTEN-STIFT
Laudongasse
Lange Gasse
Rathausstr.
Ebendorferstr.
Grillparzerstr.
13 •
Schreyvogelg.
Lederer-
Florianigasse
Felderstr.
5 •
Freyung
gasse
Schmid- gasse
RATHAUS-PLATZ
14 •
• 18
Teinfaltstr.
Landesgerichtsstr.
RATHAUS
16 •
Dr. K. Lueger-Ring
BURG-THEATER
21 •
Herrengasse
Josefstadter Str.
Lichtenfelsg.
Bankgasse
• 4
Strozzigasse
Piaristengasse
Josefgasse
Rathausstr.
Stadiongasse
Schauflergasse
Lange Gasse
Auerspergstr.
Bartensteingasse
PARLA-MENT
Dr. K. Renner-Ring
VOLKSGARTEN
Lerchenfelder Str.
Museumstr.
JUSTIZ-PALAST
Volksgartenstr.
ALTE HOFBURG
HELDEN-PLATZ
Neustiftgasse
Bellariastr.
NATUR-HISTORISCHES MUSEUM
Burgring
NEUE HOFBURG
Burggasse
Breitegasse
MARIA THERESIEN-PLATZ
Messeplatz
BURG-GARTEN
NEUBAU
Stuckgasse
Kirchengasse
Schrankg.
19 •
Gutenbgg.
Spittelbgg.
Kirchbg.
K. Schweighoferg.
MESSE-PLATZ
KUNST-HISTORISCHES MUSEUM
Opernring
12 •
Neubaugasse
Siebensterngasse
Stiftgasse
STIFTS-KASERNE
Elisabethstr.
Mondscheingasse
Nibelungengasse
Lindengasse
Kirchengasse
Zollergasse
Getreidemarkt
Theobaldgasse
TECHNISCHE UNIVERSITAT
Lehar- gasse
Richterg.
Mariahilfer Str.
Windmühlgasse
Gumpendorfer
Girardigasse
Laim-grubengasse
Köstlergasse
DENZEL-PARK
Linke Wienzeile
Rechte
NASCH- MARKT
Opemgasse
6 •
20 •

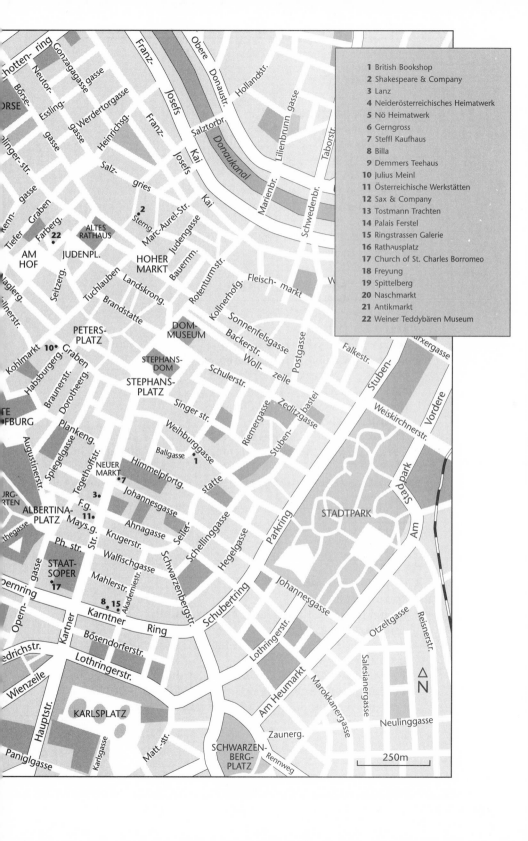

1 British Bookshop
2 Shakespeare & Company
3 Lanz
4 Neiderösterreichisches Heimatwerk
5 Nö Heimatwerk
6 Gerngross
7 Steffl Kaufhaus
8 Billa
9 Demmers Teehaus
10 Julius Meinl
11 Österreichische Werkstätten
12 Sax & Company
13 Tostmann Trachten
14 Palais Ferstel
15 Ringstrassen Galerie
16 Rathausplatz
17 Church of St. Charles Borromeo
18 Freyung
19 Spittelberg
20 Naschmarkt
21 Antikmarkt
22 Weiner Teddybären Museum

Schotten-ring
Gonzagagasse
Neutor-
Essling-
Werdertorgasse
gasse
Heinrichsg.
Franz-
Josefs
Börse
-linger-str.
BÖRSE
gasse
Renn-
Tiefer Graben
Farberg.
Salz-
gries
Franz-
Josefs
Kai
Salztorbr.
Obere Donaustr.
Hollandstr.
Donaukanal
Lilienbrunn gasse
Taborstr.
Marienbr.
Schwedenbr.
Schwedenbr.
22 ALTES RATHAUS
AM HOF
JUDENPL.
Seitzerg.
Nglerg.
-llnerstr.
2
Sterng.
Marc-Aurel-Str.
Judengasse
HOHER MARKT
Bauernm.
Tuchlauben
Landskrong.
Brandstatte
Rotenturmstr.
Kollnerhofg.
Fleisch- markt
Sonnenfelsgasse
Backerstr.
Postgasse
Falkestr.
-xergasse
PETERS-PLATZ
DOM-MUSEUM
Woll- zeile
Stuben-
Vordere
Kohlmarkt
10
Graben
Habsburgerg.
Braunerstr.
Dorotheerg.
STEPHANS-DOM
Schulerstr.
Riemergasse
Zeditzgasse
Zedlitzbastei
Weiskirchnerstr.
TE FBURG
STEPHANS-PLATZ
Singer str.
Plankeng.
Spiegelgasse
Tegethoffstr.
Weihburggasse
Stuben-
Augustinerstr.
NEUER MARKT
7
Himmelpfortg.
Ballgasse
1
statte
Stadpark
JRG-TEN
F.g.
Johannesgasse
Schellinggasse
STADTPARK
Am
ALBERTINA-PLATZ
Mays.g.
11
Ahnagasse
Seiler-
Hegelgasse
Pakring
-thegasse
Ph. str.
Krugerstr.
Walfischgasse
Schwarzenbergstr.
Johannesgasse
STAAT-SOPER
17
Mahlerstr.
Akademiestr.
Otzeltgasse
Reisnerstr.
Opern-ring
Karntner
8 15
Karntner Ring
Schubertring
Lothringerstr.
Salesianergasse
-edrichstr.
Bösendorferstr.
Lothringerstr.
Am Heumarkt
Marokkanergasse
Neulinggasse
Wienzeile
Hauptstr.
KARLSPLATZ
Karlsgasse
Matt.-str.
SCHWARZEN-BERG-PLATZ
Zaunerg.
Rennweg
N
Paniglgasse

250m

Bookstores

(1) BRITISH BOOKSHOP
A-1010, Weihburggasse 24-26

> TELEPHONE 512 1945
> U-BAHN 1, 3, Stephansplatz
> CREDIT CARDS AE, DC, MC, V
> HOURS Mon–Fri 9 A.M.–6:30 P.M., Sat 10 A.M.–5 P.M.
> ENGLISH SPOKEN Yes

The British Bookshop has a good selection of travel guides, books about Vienna and Austria, best-sellers, videos, a children's section, and board games such as Pictionary, Scrabble, and Monopoly.

(2) SHAKESPEARE & COMPANY
A-1010, Sterngasse 2

> TELEPHONE 535 50 53
> FAX 535 50 53 16
> EMAIL booksellers@shakespeare.co.at
> INTERNET www.ping.at/members/shbook
> U-BAHN 1, 4, Schwedenplatz
> CREDIT CARDS AE, DC, MC, V
> HOURS Mon–Fri 9 A.M.–7 P.M., Sat until 5 P.M.
> ENGLISH SPOKEN Yes

The name is the same as the famous bookstore in Paris, but the connection between the two ends there. The shop is comfortably jumbled and browsers are welcome. No one seems to be in a hurry to sell books. The travel and children's sections are good, and so is their selection of art and architecture books.

Clothing

(3) LANZ
A-1010, Kärntner Strasse 10

> TELEPHONE 512 2456
> U-BAHN 1, 2, 4, Karlsplatz, or 1, 3, Stephansplatz
> CREDIT CARDS AE, MC, V
> HOURS Mon–Fri 9 A.M.–6 P.M., Sat until 1 P.M.
> ENGLISH SPOKEN Yes

Everyone has heard of Lanz clothes, and this well-known Austrian brand name is sold exclusively here. The selection is geared for women and children, and the prices are for those with no budget concerns.

(4) NEIDERÖSTERREICHISCHES HEIMATWERK
A-1010, Herrengasse 6

TELEPHONE 533 3495

U-BAHN 3, Herrengasse

CREDIT CARDS AE, MC, V

HOURS Mon–Fri 9:30 A.M.–6 P.M., Sat until 1 P.M.; closed Aug 1–15

ENGLISH SPOKEN Yes

For a wide selection of traditional Austrian clothing for every member of the family, shop at this three-level emporium. Handmade gifts also are available.

(5) NÖ HEIMATWERK
A-1010, Herrengasse 6-8

Please see description under "Handcrafts," page 201.

Department Stores

(6) GERNGROSS
A-1070, Mariahilferstrasse 38-48, at the corner of Kirchengasse

TELEPHONE None

U-BAHN 3, Neubaugasse

CREDIT CARDS MC, V

HOURS Mon–Fri 9:30 A.M.–7 P.M., Sat 9 A.M.–5 P.M.

ENGLISH SPOKEN Sometimes

This sensible department store has a great bedding department that carries duvets in all sizes, barbells in the sporting goods section, clothes for all the family, a photo department, and lockers to stash your loot while you keep shopping. Don't miss the basement grocery (see page 200).

(7) STEFFL KAUFHAUS
A-1010, Kärntner Strasse 19

TELEPHONE 514 310

U-BAHN 1, 2, 4, Karlsplatz, or 1, 3, Stephansplatz

CREDIT CARDS AE, MC, V

HOURS Mon–Fri 9 A.M.–6:30 P.M., Sat until 1 P.M.

ENGLISH SPOKEN Yes

This is considered one of the best-stocked department stores in Vienna, and it's the only one in the Inner City. There are five floors of everything, from souvenirs and accessories on the ground level to books on the top.

Food and Grocery Stores

Vienna is full of neighborhood grocery stores, but selection is limited. For the freshest and cheapest food shopping, go to the Naschmarkt (see Outdoor Markets, page 204).

(8) BILLA
A-1010, Ringstrassen Galerie, basement level, Kärntner Ring 5-7

TELEPHONE Not available

U-BAHN 1, 2, 4, Karlsplatz

CREDIT CARDS MC, V

HOURS Mon–Sat 10 A.M.–6 P.M.

ENGLISH SPOKEN Depends

Billa food stores are all over Vienna, but none are better than this glossy market in the basement of the beautiful Ringstrassen Galerie shopping mall. It is a great place to pick up the ingredients for a room picnic or a few snacks for between-meal munching.

(9) DEMMERS TEEHAUS
A-1010, Mölkerbastei 5

TELEPHONE 533 5995

U-BAHN 3, Herrengasse

CREDIT CARDS MC, V

HOURS Mon–Fri 9 A.M.–6 P.M., Sat 9:30 A.M.–noon

ENGLISH SPOKEN Yes

Demmers is a tea-lover's mecca, with over two hundred varieties available, plus small gift items and a tearoom upstairs.

(6) GERNGROSS
A-1070, Mariahilferstrasse 38-48, at Kirchengasse

TELEPHONE 521 800

U-BAHN 3, Neubaugasse

CREDIT CARDS MC, V

HOURS Mon–Fri 9:30 A.M.–7 P.M., Sat 9 A.M.–5 P.M.

ENGLISH SPOKEN Some

The department store has good prices and so does the huge supermarket in the basement (see page 199 for description of the department store).

(10) JULIUS MEINL
A-1010, Graben 19

TELEPHONE 710 1100

U-BAHN 1, 3, Stephansplatz

CREDIT CARDS MC, V

HOURS Mon–Fri 8:30 A.M.–7 P.M., Sat until 5 P.M.

ENGLISH SPOKEN Sometimes

This is the main outlet of the German deli and supermarket chain. Some of the branches are small and seedy, but this one is gourmet all the way with separate deli, cheese, meat, wine, and produce departments in addition to every canned, bottled, and packaged item imaginable. They also sell their own vodka and an impressive range of flavored coffees. The place is perennially packed, but the service is sketchy at best.

Gifts

(11) ÖSTERREICHISCHE WERKSTÄTTEN
A-1010, Kärntner Strasse 6

TELEPHONE 512 2418
U-BAHN 1, 2, 4, Karlsplatz
CREDIT CARDS AE, MC, V
HOURS Mon–Fri 9 A.M.–6 P.M., Sat until 1 P.M.
ENGLISH SPOKEN Yes

This outstanding artist's cooperative, housed in a three-level shop, sells unusual one-of-a-kind items, handmade handcrafts, gifts, quality souvenirs, modern jewelry, textiles, and ceramics.

(12) SAX & COMPANY
A-1070, Neubaugasse 34

TELEPHONE 523 6103
FAX 523 61 034
U-BAHN 3, Neubaugasse
CREDIT CARDS None
HOURS Mon–Fri 9 A.M.–6 P.M., Sat until 1 P.M.
ENGLISH SPOKEN Yes

Not far from the busy Mariahilferstrasse is this gem of a shop selling beautiful cards, wrapping paper, small gift items, and great little presents for children. It is especially nice right before Christmas when the choice of colorful decorations is endless.

Handcrafts

(5) NÖ HEIMATWERK
A-1010, Herrengasse 6-8

TELEPHONE 533 3495
FAX 533 6840-16
U-BAHN 3, Herrengasse
CREDIT CARDS AE, MC, V (5% discount for cash)
HOURS Mon–Fri 9:30 A.M.–6 P.M., Sat 9:30 A.M.–5:30 P.M.
ENGLISH SPOKEN Yes

The philosophy of the shop is to encourage Austrian art and culture by showcasing exclusive work by a variety of artists. The first level is devoted to gift items and the basement to traditional Austrian clothing. There is a tailor on duty to do the necessary nips and tucks to get the perfect fit for your dirndl, loden coat, or lederhosen (leather shorts). Prices are competitive and the help friendly. Ask for Louise.

(13) TOSTMANN TRACHTEN
A-1010, Schottengasse 3a

TELEPHONE 533 5331, 533 6864

FAX 533 5331-32

U-BAHN 3, Herrengasse, or 2, Schottentor

CREDIT CARDS MC, V (3% discount for cash)

HOURS Mon–Fri 10 A.M.–6:30 P.M., Sat 10 A.M.–5 P.M.

ENGLISH SPOKEN Yes

All I can say is don't miss this shop if you are interested in Austrian handcrafts. The displays are artistically arranged in the nooks and crannies of a rabbit warren of rooms, which extend to a second shop across the courtyard. At Christmastime it is a virtual fairyland . . . but anytime is wonderful.

Malls and Arcades

(14) PALAIS FERSTEL
A-1010, Freyung 4

TELEPHONE Not available

U-BAHN 3, Herrengasse

CREDIT CARDS Depends on store

HOURS Mon–Fri 10 A.M.–6 P.M., Sat until 1 P.M.

ENGLISH SPOKEN Usually

The Palais Ferstel is a magnificent palace with marble stairways, glass domes, and a beautiful fountain. Lining the carved arcade are upscale shops, a hair salon, art galleries, a café, and a restaurant.

(15) RINGSTRASSEN GALERIE
A-1010, Kärntner Ring 5-7

TELEPHONE Not available

U-BAHN 1, 2, 4, Karlsplatz

CREDIT CARDS Depends on store

HOURS Mon–Sat 10 A.M.–6 P.M.

ENGLISH SPOKEN Usually

This is Vienna's showcase indoor shopping mall across from the Opera on Kärntner Strasse. Glitz and glamour abound. For refueling, there are coffee and juice bars and a large Mövenpic on the basement level (see *Cheap Eats in Prague, Vienna, and Budapest*), as well as Billa, a full-service supermarket.

Outdoor Markets

ADVENT AND CHRISTMAS MARKETS

Every year the outdoor Advent and Christmas markets spring up around Vienna like wrapped presents under the tree. Some of them, like the one on Rathausplatz in front of Vienna's City Hall, seem to be more like ongoing carnivals, catering to kitsch-seeking tourists and *Glühwein*-thirsty Viennese, who go elsewhere to do their real shopping. However, at the Rathausplatz Advent market, the enormous 25.5-meter lighted Christmas tree and the life-size Nativity scene surrounding it are beautiful sights. For children, there is an old-fashioned merry-go-round, miniature railway, and pony rides; for everyone, there are over 140 stalls selling food and drinks, decorations, and toys. Continually wafting over it all are traditional Christmas carols played on loudspeakers. Friday through Sunday, choirs from around the world serenade with carols and folk songs in the Rathaus's Festival Halls. Admission is free, and you can come and go as you please. Hidden down many alleys and smaller streets throughout Vienna are other Advent and Christmas markets filled with original treasures. Along the weaving side streets artists have their craft shops and stalls, chefs grill wurst and flip potato pancakes, and the famous *Glühwein* huts are filled to capacity—this hot, delicious drink is the perfect way to warm up a thirsty shopper's frozen feet and fingers. In addition to the Rathausplatz, which is the biggest, the Advent and Christmas markets mentioned below are particularly delightful. They are open from the last ten days in November until Christmas Eve.

(16) RATHAUSPLATZ
In front of the Rathaus

U-BAHN 2, Rathaus
CREDIT CARDS Depends on stall
HOURS Daily 9 A.M.–9 P.M. from around Nov 15–Dec 24
ENGLISH SPOKEN Depends on stall

(17) CRAFTS MARKET
In front of the Church of St. Charles Borromeo on Karlsplatz

U-BAHN 1, 2, 4, Karlsplatz

(18) VIENNESE CHRISTMAS MARKET
At Freyung, in the heart of the city

U-BAHN 3, Herrengasse
HOURS Daily 9:30 A.M.–7:30 P.M.
It's smaller, with many traditional holiday crafts.

ART AND CHRISTMAS MARKET
In front of Schönbrunn Palace, the Hapsburg's summer palace on the outskirts of Vienna

HOURS Mon–Fri noon–8 P.M., Sat–Sun from 10 A.M.

(19) CHRISTMAS MARKET
In Spittelberg, in central Vienna

U-BAHN 2, 3, Volkstheater
HOURS Mon–Fri 2–8 P.M., Sat–Sun 10 A.M.–8 P.M.
This market is one of the best.

FLEA MARKETS

(20) NASCHMARKT
Linke and Rechte Wienzeile, starting at Getreidemarkt

U-BAHN 1, 2, 4, Karlsplatz, exit at Session
CREDIT CARDS Depends on seller
HOURS Sat 7 A.M.–1 P.M., rain or shine
ENGLISH SPOKEN Depends on seller

Vienna's popular food market extends on Saturday to include rows of sellers hawking everything from cheap cosmetics and clothing to some serious antiques. Die-hard bargainers show up early to sniff out the best finds.

FOOD MARKETS

BRUNNENMARKT
Brunnengasse

U-BAHN 6, Thalaistrasse
CREDIT CARDS None
OPEN Mon–Sat
ENGLISH SPOKEN Depends on stall
Two kilometers of all kinds of food and produce.

(20) NASCHMARKT
Linke and Rechte Wienzeile, starting at Getreidemarkt

U-BAHN 1, 2, 4, Karlsplatz, exit at Session
CREDIT CARDS None
HOURS Mon–Fri 7 A.M.–5 P.M., Sat until noon
ENGLISH SPOKEN Depends on stall

No trip to Vienna would be complete without an hour or two spent at the Naschmarkt, Vienna's biggest and most colorful market. It has every kind of foodstuff known to the civilized world. The best day is Saturday when farmers fill the back section, and the flea market is in full form. Snack bars selling schnitzels, pancakes, Indian food, Chinese stir-frys, and tempting pastries are hard to resist anytime.

MISCELLANEOUS OTHER MARKETS

(21) ANTIKMARKT
Herrengasse

U-BAHN 3, Herrengasse
CREDIT CARDS Depends on stall
HOURS Fri–Sat 11 A.M.–5 P.M. from Mar–Dec 24
ENGLISH SPOKEN Depends on stall

This is a small, expensive antique market open on Friday and Saturday from March until Christmas. It is worthwhile to browse here and get an idea of prices, and then to be able to know when a bargain pops up elsewhere.

(19) SPITTELBERG
Spittelberggasse

U-BAHN 2, 3, Volkstheater
CREDIT CARDS Depends on stall
ENGLISH SPOKEN Depends on stall

In addition to the Christmas market (see "Christmas Markets" above), you can find arts and crafts sold along the streets of this quaint part of Vienna every third weekend from April to June and September to October. In August and in December the market is open daily.

Toys

(22) WIENER TEDDYBÄREN MUSEUM
A-1010, Drahtgasse 3

TELEPHONE AND FAX 533 4755
INTERNET www.teddybear.org
U-BAHN 3, Herrengasse
CREDIT CARDS AE, MC, V
HOURS Daily 10 A.M.–6 P.M.
ENGLISH SPOKEN Yes

Who doesn't like teddy bears, or remember his or her own with fondness? The Wiener Teddybären Museum is a loving testimony to the special place we all have in our hearts for teddy bears . . . both past and present. The museum displays a collection of historic bears—in old picture books and photographs and on clocks, fine china, and postcards. Some are in pristine condition, others have obviously been well-loved. In the museum shop there are traditional bears, hand-painted teddy bear portraits, and teddy bear related accessories. The museum is about a five-minute walk from Stephansplatz, between Am Hof and Judenplatz. It is a sentimental journey for most of us.

Cheap Chic in Budapest

Even before the collapse of Communism in 1989, shopping in Budapest was enjoyable. In the past decade, the shopping possibilities have mushroomed, and so have the supplies of Western goods. Some older stores still specialize in selling one thing, making one wonder how this old-fashioned concept could generate enough business to stay open. For instance, there is one store in Pest dealing exclusively in women's buttons. Nothing here for a man, mind you. Another sells only shoelaces. Best buys are still the folk arts and crafts, and their famed porcelain, chiefly Herend, Zsolnay, and Hollóháza. While the porcelain prices don't fall into the bargain category, prices are still much less than they would be in the West. There are still some buys to be had in antiques, especially if you haunt the state-owned BÁV shops, check out the shops that line Falk Miksa in Pest, or comb the flea markets. Who could return from a trip to Budapest without a package or two of paprika, a salami from Pick Salami (a brand made in the eastern city of Szeged), or a bottle of Tokay wine? As for ready-to-wear clothes . . . better forget it. There is not much that a visitor would find appealing. As for the service, it can be similar to that still found in Prague: the staff make you feel they are doing you a favor by letting you shop there, and they smoke and eat on the job, carry on lengthy personal telephone calls, and generally ignore you. Don't expect them to do two things at once, such as wait on one customer and answer a question from another. People are waited on and served one at a time, and you will be left to stand there and feel you are taking root until it is your turn.

Shopping Hours

Shops are open Monday to Friday from 10 A.M. to 6 P.M., and until 1 P.M. Saturday. The exceptions are some of the shops along Váci utca and in the Castle District, which may stay open later in the summer, all day Saturday, and for a few hours on Sunday. Right before Christmas, all stores are open on Sunday, but between Christmas and New Year's, many of the smaller ones don't open at all.

Shopping Streets and Areas

Most of Budapest's shops are concentrated in Pest, where the central shopping district is the mile-long, pedestrian-zoned Váci utca and the streets and courtyards around it. All are fertile ground for souvenir shopping, boutique buying, and people-watching. However, not every shop is visible from the street. Many of the shops along Váci utca are underground, and their goods appeal to mall rats and fashion victims. The area is also popular with pickpockets, scam artists, and hookers, who come out after the sun sets. Be aware of this, and be on your guard. All

Budapest visitors go to the Castle District on the Buda side of the Danube. Shopping here is tourist targeted, and it consists of one Hungarian folk and handcraft store after another, as well as art galleries.

The natives do not do their shopping in either of these two areas. You will find them in Pest cruising through the shops on Kossuth Lajos utca and its continuation, Rákóczi út, and in Buda around Móricz Zsigmond körtér near the Buda Skála department store and along Margit körút.

Shipping It All Home

Very few shops will ship your purchases for you. I always recommend taking an extra suitcase and some bubble wrap to pack fragile items so you can carry your treasures home with you. True, the airline might charge you an excess baggage fee, but believe me, it will be cheap at twice the price if you have ever tried to work your way through the red-tape maze created by the Magyar Posta. If you don't want to pack and carry yourself, the following two companies can and will also handle customs.

AmExS Transport can provide packing materials and customs clearances for air freight. Goods are delivered to the airport closest to your home. Prices start around $3 per kilogram, minimum 45 kilograms (1 kilogram = 2.2 pounds). They speak English and are open daily 8 A.M. to 6 P.M. They are at XIII. Szent István körút 20 I/1; tel: 269-2725, 269-2467; fax: 269-2466; metro: M3, Nyugati pályaudvar; no credit cards.

TNT Express is cheaper than AmExS Transport. Ten kilograms sent to the United States runs about 20,000Ft ($92). They speak English and are open Monday to Friday 8 A.M. to 6 P.M. They are located at VII. Nagy Diófa utca 7; tel: 269-6464; metro: M2, Blaha Lujza tér; no credit cards.

Value-Added Tax (VAT)

Purchases made in Hungary have a 25-percent value-added tax (VAT). If you spend more than 25,000Ft (about $120) at one store at one time, you are entitled to a refund on any amount that *exceeds* the 25,000Ft. The VAT refund applies to everything but antiques or works of art. The refund process is rather convoluted, but it's worth the effort, especially if you spend big. First you must show the items to customs when you are leaving the country and get a Customs Certification form. No more than 90 days must pass from the time of purchase until you leave the country, and no more than 183 days from the time you leave Hungary until you submit the claim for a refund. Save all receipts, including those from your credit card, and attach them along with the original invoice of sale and the Customs Certification to the refund claim form and send them to: Foreigners' Refund Office, APEH Budapest Directorate, V. Sas utca 2, 1051 Budapest. For questions, further information, or to get a refund claim form before your departure, go to their office directly or call 318-1910. Another source of VAT refunding information is Inteltrade, I. Csalogány u. 6-10; tel: 356-9800; fax: 375-0616.

BUDAPEST

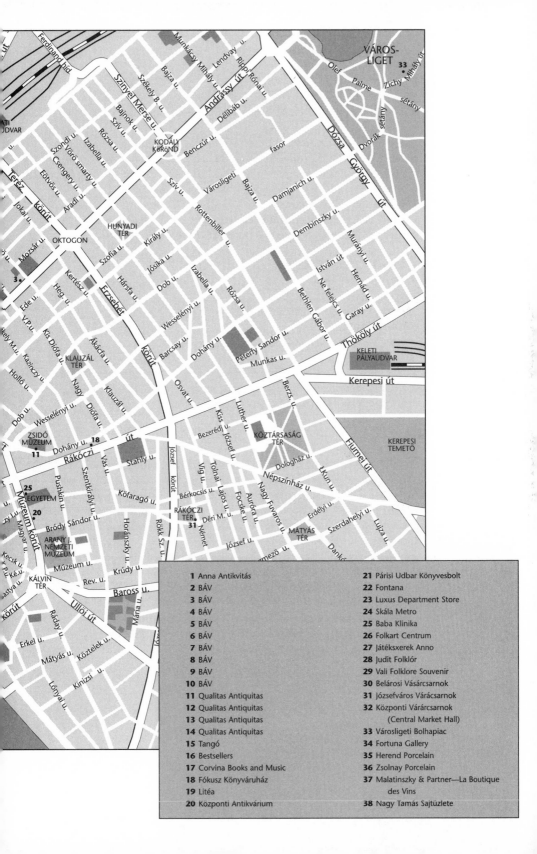

VÁROS-LIGET

Városligeti Bolhapiac **33**

1 Anna Antikvitás
2 BÁV
3 BÁV
4 BÁV
5 BÁV
6 BÁV
7 BÁV
8 BÁV
9 BÁV
10 BÁV
11 Qualitas Antiquitas
12 Qualitas Antiquitas
13 Qualitas Antiquitas
14 Qualitas Antiquitas
15 Tangó
16 Bestsellers
17 Corvina Books and Music
18 Fókusz Könyváruház
19 Litéa
20 Központi Antikvárium

21 Párisi Udbar Könyvesbolt
22 Fontana
23 Luxus Department Store
24 Skála Metro
25 Baba Klinika
26 Folkart Centrum
27 Játéksxerek Anno
28 Judit Folklór
29 Vali Folklore Souvenir
30 Belárosi Vásárcsarnok
31 Józsefváros Várácsarnok
32 Központi Várárcsarnok
   (Central Market Hall)
33 Városligeti Bolhapiac
34 Fortuna Gallery
35 Herend Porcelain
36 Zsolnay Porcelain
37 Malatinszky & Partner—La Boutique
   des Vins
38 Nagy Tamás Sajtüzlete

Antiques

If you want to concentrate your antiques shopping, one of the best places to do it is along Falk Miksa utca off Szent István körút in Pest. The street is lined for several blocks with shops carrying everything from massive Art Deco furniture to little baubles you can stick in your pocket. Most are open Monday to Friday from 10 A.M. to 6 P.M., and on Saturday until 1 P.M. Some close on one other day, but there doesn't seem to be a rhyme or reason to these closings. Whatever you do buy, be aware that any object over seventy years old requires registration with the Ministry of Culture and a special customs stamp before it can legally be taken out of Hungary. The dealers have the information you will need.

(1) ANNA ANTIKVITÁS
V. Falk Miksa u. 18-30

TELEPHONE 302-5461
METRO M3, Nyugati pályaudvar
CREDIT CARDS MC, V
HOURS Mon–Fri 10 A.M.–6 P.M., Sat until 1 P.M.
ENGLISH SPOKEN Yes

Anna Antikvitás has one of the nicest collections of old lace, beaded bags, boxes, and old Herend porcelain on Falk Miksa utca. English is spoken, and service is informative and gracious.

BÁV

Some of the best antique finds are at the BÁV shops. These are a string of state-owned consignment/pawn shops you can recognize by the Venus de Milo logo on all their signs. Each shop has a specialty—along with many other items—and prices are lower than at regular antiques shops. Shopping at a BÁV shop does not mean you are slumming. On the contrary, the well-displayed goods are in excellent condition and your fellow shoppers will be well-dressed locals and a few other tourists in the know. Auctions are held several times a year. For information about dates and times, call 217-6072, extension 287. The auctions are held at IX. Lónyay utca 30-32; metro: M3, Kálvin tér.

Below are addresses for only a few of the many BÁV shops. For a more complete list, ask at any location. All branches are open Monday to Friday 10 A.M. to 6 P.M., Saturday until 1 P.M.; they accept all credit cards and usually have someone who speaks enough English.

(2) VI. Andrássy út 27

TELEPHONE 342-5525
METRO M1, Opera
SPECIALTY Art objects

(3) VI. Andrássy út 43

TELEPHONE 342-9143
METRO M1, Opera
SPECIALTY Jewelry and gold

(4) V. Bécsi u. 1-3

TELEPHONE 317-254
METRO All lines, Deák Ferenc tér
SPECIALTY Jewelry, silver, furniture, chandeliers

(5) I. Hess András tér 1 & 3 in the Castle District

TELEPHONE 375-0392
METRO M2, Moszkva tér, then Várbusz to the Castle Hill
SPECIALTY Porcelain and silver

(6) V. Falk Miksa u. 21

TELEPHONE 331-0513
METRO M3, Nyugati pályaudvar
SPECIALTY Art objects

(7) V. Ferenciek tere 5

TELEPHONE 318-3773
METRO M3, Ferenciek tere
SPECIALTY Carpets

(8) V. Ferenciek tere 12

TELEPHONE 318-3381
METRO M3, Ferenciek tere
SPECIALTY Porcelain and bronze

(9) V. Kossuth Lajos u. 1-3

TELEPHONE 317-3718
METRO M2, Kossuth tér
SPECIALTY Porcelain, furniture

(10) V. Szent István körút 3

TELEPHONE 131-4534
METRO M3, Nyugati pályaudvar
SPECIALTY Furniture, porcelain, art

QUALITAS ANTIQUITAS

This is a privately owned group of four shops, each one specializing in different antiques. The prices are higher than those at BÁV shops, but still not as high as most other dealers. They are open Monday to Friday 10 A.M. to 6 P.M., and they accept MC and V credit cards and have someone who can speak some English. Auctions are held on Thursday at 5 P.M. at V. Váci utca 36; tel: 267-3539.

(11) VII. Dohany u.1, in front of the Synagogue
TELEPHONE 341-5585
METRO M2, Astoria
SPECIALTY Paintings, icons, carpets, Jewish religious articles, silver, glass, and china

(12) V. Falk Miksa u. 32
TELEPHONE 111-8471
METRO M3, Nyugati pályaudvar
SPECIALTY Herend and Zsolnay china

(13) V. Kígyó u. 5
TELEPHONE 318-3246
METRO M3, Ferenciek tere
SPECIALTY Silver, china, glass, painting, and sculpture

(14) I. Krisztina körút 73, in back of the Castle District
TELEPHONE 375-0658
METRO M2, Moszkva tér, then Várbusz to Castle Hill
SPECIALTY Art and small furniture

(15) TANGÓ
V. Váci utca 8
TELEPHONE 318-9741
METRO M1, Vörösmarty tér
CREDIT CARDS AE, DC, MC, V
HOURS Mon-Fri 10 A.M.-6 P.M., Sat until 1 P.M.
ENGLISH SPOKEN Yes
Tangó has a wonderful collection of antique and handmade linens.

Bookstores

(16) BESTSELLERS
V. Október 6. u. 11
TELEPHONE 312-1295
FAX 302-3026
EMAIL bookshop@ceu.hu
METRO M3, Arany János utca
CREDIT CARDS MC, V
HOURS Mon–Sat 9 A.M.–6 P.M.
ENGLISH SPOKEN Yes

Bestsellers is one of the top English-language bookstores in the city. In addition to a good selection of Eastern European travel books, you will find contemporary fiction, books on history and politics, and a large selection of paperbacks, newspapers, and magazines, all in English.

(17) CORVINA BOOKS AND MUSIC
V. Kossuth Lajos u. 4

TELEPHONE 318-3603
METRO M3, Ferenciek tere
CREDIT CARDS AE, DC, MC, V
HOURS Mon–Fri 10 A.M.–6 P.M., Sat until 2 P.M.
ENGLISH SPOKEN Yes

Corvina is one of the most important foreign-language book publishers in Hungary. They stock guidebooks and Hungarian authors translated into English.

(18) FÓKUSZ KÖNYVÁRUHÁZ
VII. Rákóczi út 14

TELEPHONE 268-1103/4, 267-9205
FAX 267-9769
METRO M2, Astoria
CREDIT CARDS AE, MC, V
HOURS Mon–Fri 10 A.M.–7 P.M., Sat 9 A.M.–5 P.M., Sun 10 A.M.–6 P.M.
ENGLISH SPOKEN Yes

You will need to go upstairs to find English-language books. Shopping baskets are provided for your collection of children's books, novels, coffeetable travel books, cookbooks, tapes, and videos.

(19) LITÉA
I. Hess András tér 4, in the Castle District

TELEPHONE 375-6987
METRO M2, Moszkva tér, then Várbusz to Castle Hill
CREDIT CARDS AE, DC, MC, V
HOURS Daily 10 A.M.–6 P.M.
ENGLISH SPOKEN Yes

This delightful bookshop has a small café and terrace where coffee, tea, and light refreshments are served and lingering is encouraged. It is in the Fortuna Passage across from the Hilton Hotel on the Castle Hill. They stock a large selection of travel guides, books on Hungary, maps, and cards.

(20) KÖZPONTI ANTIKVÁRIUM
V. Múzeum körút 15

TELEPHONE 315-3514
METRO M2, Astoria
CREDIT CARDS AE, MC, V

HOURS Mon–Fri 10 A.M.–6 P.M., Sat until 1 P.M.

ENGLISH SPOKEN Yes

This is a friendly shop across from the Hungarian National Museum, and it's known for its collection of rare books and its wide selection of used English-language books. They also carry old posters, cards, and maps.

(21) PÁRISI UDBAR KÖNYVESBOLT
V. Petőfi Sándor u. 2

TELEPHONE AND FAX 318-3136

METRO M3, Ferenciek tere

CREDIT CARDS AE, DC, MC, V

HOURS Mon–Fri 9 A.M.–7 P.M., Sat until 1 P.M.

ENGLISH SPOKEN Yes

Who could not be enthusiastic about a bookstore in Budapest that stocks titles in the *Cheap Eats/Cheap Sleeps* series! This hidden shop is in the turn-of-the-century Párisi Udvar (Paris Arcades), just off Váci utca. The bookshop is family owned and run and devoted exclusively to foreign-language books, many of which are about travel. They have a second location at VIII. Rákózy út 27B, which stocks only Hungarian books.

Department Stores/Malls

DUNA PLAZA
Váci út 178, at the Gyöngyösi metro station

TELEPHONE 465-1220

INTERNET www.plazaclub.com

METRO M3, Gyöngyösi utca, or Bus No. 4 from Deák ter

CREDIT CARDS Depends on store

HOURS Mall, Mon–Thur, Sun 10 A.M.–1 A.M., Fri–Sat 10 A.M.–4 A.M.; Stores, Mon–Fri 10 A.M.–9 P.M., Sat–Sun until 7 P.M.

ENGLISH SPOKEN Depends on store

Duna Plaza looks just like any mall in the United States: it has the familiar food courts, multiplex theaters, an ice skating rink, child-care center, and 150 shops and chain stores filled with all the same Western goods you can get at Walmart or Target. If you come to this American-style mall on the edge of Budapest, the bus from the city center drops you at the door. Arriving via metro, shoppers board the escalator going directly from the platform to the ground floor of the mall.

(22) FONTANA
V. Váci u. 16

TELEPHONE 338-2004, 318-9166

METRO M1, Vörösmarty tér

CREDIT CARDS AE, MC, V

HOURS Mon–Fri 10 A.M.–6 P.M., Sat until 1 P.M.

ENGLISH SPOKEN Usually

This store has trendy fashions for men, women, and children—as well as a decent toilet on the top floor.

(23) LUXUS DEPARTMENT STORE
V. Vörösmarty tér 3

TELEPHONE 318-2277, 318-3550

FAX 318-3555

METRO M1, Vörosmarty tér

CREDIT CARDS AE, MC, V

HOURS Mon–Fri 9 A.M.–9 P.M., Sat until 2 P.M.

ENGLISH SPOKEN Yes

Luxus specializes in luxury goods and luxurious prices on three floors displaying Europe's best names in fashion for men and women. Their restrooms definitely fall short of their reputed image: they lack both soap and any sort of paper.

(24) SKÁLA METRO
Nyugati tér (can access from metro station)

TELEPHONE Not available

METRO M3, Nyugati pálydovar

CREDIT CARDS MC, V

HOURS Mall, daily 10 A.M.–10 P.M.; stores, hours vary, but generally Mon–Fri 10 A.M.–6 P.M., Sat until 1 P.M., closed Sun

ENGLISH SPOKEN Depends on store

There isn't much I would actually want to buy here, but it makes for an interesting hour or two just looking at what the normal blue-collar worker in Budapest has available, and then wondering how they can afford it. There is a large grocery in the basement.

Second location: Buda Skála on Október 23 utca, near Móricz Zsigmond körtér in Buda.

Handcrafts

Hungary is well known for its traditional folk art and handcrafts. In shops along Váci utca and lining the streets near the Castle, you will see enough weaving, embroidered table linens, costume dolls, ceramics, and woodwork to last a lifetime. The range of quality is broad, and you should distinguish between machine-made goods and handmade items; the shops listed in Cheap Chic all sell handmade crafts. Some of the most authentic folk art, and certainly the least expensive, is sold by Transylvanian peasant women who sell their wares around Moszkva tér and on corners near Parliament.

(25) BABA KLINIKA
V. Múzeum körút 5

> **TELEPHONE** 267-2445
> **METRO** M2, Astoria
> **CREDIT CARDS** None
> **HOURS** Mon–Fri 9:30 A.M.–5:30 P.M., Sat until noon
> **ENGLISH SPOKEN** Yes

If you love dolls, or know a collector, this shop is a required stop. The address houses two separate shops under one roof, a money-saving device many individual shopkeepers still cling to. On the left are some very ugly purses and sweaters. You are not here for this stuff. You are here for the doll clinic on the right, run for decades by Mrs. Berényi (who is in her nineties), her daughter, and her granddaughter. The shelves are stacked with dolls in despair, which these dedicated ladies lovingly repair. They also make dolls and doll clothes.

(26) FOLKART CENTRUM
V. Váci u. 14

> **TELEPHONE** 318-5840
> **METRO** M1, Vörösmarty tér
> **CREDIT CARDS** AE, DC, MC, V
> **HOURS** Daily 9:30 A.M.–6:30 P.M.
> **ENGLISH SPOKEN** Yes

Folkart Centrum is the main store of the state-owned Folkart Háziipar, a distributor of Hungarian folk art. You can shop here with confidence because all items on sale have been approved by a folk art jury and labeled with an approval sticker, which displays a circle and a bird in the center and the words Folkart/Népművészeti Hungary. Not everything is hand-made, but if it is, then the number 900 will follow the third digit of the serial number on the sticker. There are other Folkart Centrum stores in Budapest, but this is the main one and has the longest hours. Consult this store for a listing of their other locations.

(27) JÁTÉKSXEREK ANNO
VI. Teréz körút 54

> **TELEPHONE** 446-553, 302-6234
> **METRO** M1, Oktogon
> **CREDIT CARDS** None
> **HOURS** Mon–Fri 10 A.M.–6 P.M., Sat 9 A.M.–1 P.M.
> **ENGLISH SPOKEN** Limited

Here you will find beautiful metal wind-up toys in limited editions plus metal soldiers, soft animals, and other toy collectibles to delight the child in us all. There is something for everyone and within all budgets. Be sure to ask for your purchase to be gift wrapped. The boxes and ribbons are wonderful.

(28) JUDIT FOLKLÓR
I. Szentháromság u. 5

TELEPHONE 356-3997

METRO M2, Moszkva tér, then Várbusz to Castle Hill

CREDIT CARDS AE, MC, V (5,000Ft minimum)

HOURS Daily 9 A.M.–6:30 P.M.

ENGLISH SPOKEN Yes

These four privately owned folk art shops in the Castle District sell only handmade items, from the smallest thimble to elaborate, expensive costumes. They specialize in dolls with silk and porcelain heads, dressed in traditional dresses that represent all parts of Hungary. They also stock elaborate tablecloths and hand embroidery made by peasant women in the countryside.

Other locations on Castle Hill: Országház utca 12, and Tárnok utca 1 and 8.

(29) VALI FOLKLORE SOUVENIR
V. Váci u. 23, in the courtyard

TELEPHONE 318-6495, 337-6303

METRO M1, Vörösmarty tér

CREDIT CARDS AE, DC, MC, V

HOURS Mon–Sat 10 A.M.–6 P.M., Sun noon–5 P.M.

ENGLISH SPOKEN Some

Look here for Hungarian and Transylvanian costumes and other true folk items collected from countryside villages by the shop owner.

Markets

Open-air and indoor market halls are the best places to get a colorful look at everyday life in Budapest. They open early Monday through Saturday, are closed on Sunday, and no one speaks much English or accepts plastic. Every district has an open-air market, but not all are equally interesting. These three provide the best local color: XI. Fehérvári út; metro: M3, Kálvin tér, then bus or tram to Móricz Zsigmond körtér. The market is a block away, in front of Buda Skála department store. Also try XIII. Lehel tér; metro: M3, Lehel tér; and XIV. Bosnyák tér; bus No. 7 to Bosnyak tér.

MARKET HALLS

(30) BELÁROSI VÁSÁRCSARNOK
V. Hold u.

METRO M3, Arany János utca

CREDIT CARDS None

HOURS Mon 6:30 A.M.–5 P.M., Tues–Fri until 6 P.M., Sat until 2 P.M.

ENGLISH SPOKEN Not much

The ground floor has stalls selling produce, meat and poultry, cheese, bakery goods, wine, and deli items. There is a bar lined with red-faced locals tossing back libations and a mezzanine dotted with retail shops and a few fast-food joints.

(31) JÓZSEFVÁROS VÁSÁRCSARNOK
VIII. Rákóczi tér

METRO M2, Blaha Lujza tér

CREDIT CARDS None

HOURS Mon–Sat 6:30 A.M.–6 P.M., Sun until noon

ENGLISH SPOKEN Not much

Come here for an interesting look at life near the Jewish Quarter. There are food stalls plus some retail vendors selling what look like garage-sale rejects, but you never know. Prices in these stalls are dirt cheap.

(32) KÖZPONTI VÁSÁRCSARNOK (CENTRAL MARKET HALL)
IX. Vámház kőrút

METRO M3, Kálvin tér

CREDIT CARDS None

HOURS Mon–Fri 6 A.M.–6 P.M., Sat until 2 P.M.

ENGLISH SPOKEN Depends on stall

If you have time to do only one market, let it be this one. Not only is it one of the best, but the location at the end of the Váci utca pedestrian zone makes it the easiest one for a visitor to get to. Beautifully restored in 1995, the three-level market has countless food sellers, several snack bars, a top-floor devoted to crafts from Hungary and Russia, enough embroidered linens and laces to keep you ironing for weeks, and the usual cheap clothing stalls hawking T-shirts and tacky outfits.

FLEA MARKETS

ECSERI FLEA MARKET
XIX. Nagykőrösi út 156

METRO Bus No. 52 from Boráros tér

CREDIT CARDS None

HOURS Mon–Fri 8 A.M.–3 P.M., Sat until 2 P.M.

ENGLISH SPOKEN Depends on seller

The area is huge, the selection overwhelming, and it's packed on the weekends—in other words, great fun if you are a flea market buff. The antiques sellers know the value of their wares, so even though you are not expected to pay the first price, don't expect many stunning bargains. Wear a hidden money belt—pickpockets love the place.

(33) VÁROSLIGETI BOLHAPIAC
XIV. Zichy Mihály út

TELEPHONE 251-2485

METRO M1, Széchenyi Fürdő

CREDIT CARDS None

HOURS Sat–Sun 7 A.M.–2 P.M.

ENGLISH SPOKEN Depends on seller

This one is easier to get to than the Ecseri flea market, it is smaller, and the junk is above average.

Porcelain and Ceramics

Hungarian porcelain and ceramics are considered to be some of the best buys in the country. Prices are not at the give-away level, but you will pay much less here than you would for the same items at home. If you are considering any ceramics from Korond or black ceramics from Hódmezővásárhely, plan to use them for display only . . . they are both loaded with lead.

(34) FORTUNA GALLERY
I. Fortuna u. 11 (50 meters from the Hilton Hotel)

TELEPHONE 201-8984

FAX 201-7594

METRO M2, Moszkva tér, then Várbusz to Castle Hill

CREDIT CARDS AE, MC, V

HOURS Daily 10 A.M.–6 P.M.

ENGLISH SPOKEN Yes

The best part about this shop, which sells hand-painted, dishwasher- and microwave-safe Herend Village pottery, is that they will ship. The brightly colored pottery, with simple primitive designs, costs less than the Herend porcelain and is much more casual.

(35) HEREND PORCELAIN
V. József Nádor tér 11

TELEPHONE 317-2622

FAX 317-4818

METRO All lines, Deák Ferenc tér, or M1, Vórósmarty tér

CREDIT CARDS AE, DC, MC, V

HOURS Mon–Fri 10 A.M.–6 P.M., Sat 9 A.M.–1 P.M.

ENGLISH SPOKEN Yes

Hand-painted Herend porcelain is known and appreciated worldwide. While in Budapest, you will also see the delicately beautiful porcelain for sale in many shops in the city. This factory-direct shop has the most extensive selection, which is sold by icy, abrupt saleswomen who will bubble wrap your purchases, take your money, and inform you that the store does not ship.

There are is another shop on Castle Hill, where the sales ladies seem to have more heart, at I. Szentháromság út, 5; tel: 375-5857; metro: M2, Moszkva tér. A third location is at V. Kígyó utca 5; tel: 318-3439; metro: M3, Ferenciek tere.

(36) ZSOLNAY PORCELAIN
V. Kigyó u. 4

TELEPHONE 318-3712

METRO M3, Ferenciek tere

CREDIT CARDS AE, DC, MC, V

HOURS Mon–Fri 9 A.M.–6 P.M., Sat until 1 P.M.

ENGLISH SPOKEN Limited

The Zsolnay Porcelain is made in Pécs and is known for its brightly colored dinnerware. Again, no shipping.

Wine and Cheese

WINE

(37) MALATINSZKY & PARTNER—LA BOUTIQUE DES VINS
V. Jozsef Attila u. 12

TELEPHONE AND FAX 317-5919

METRO All lines, Deák Ferenc tér

CREDIT CARDS AE

HOURS Mon–Fri 10 A.M.–6 P.M., Sat until 3 P.M.

ENGLISH SPOKEN Yes

If you appreciate wine, you will definitely enjoy a visit to this smart wine shop, where the English-speaking owner is knowledgeable and informative about his stock. The emphasis is on Hungarian wines, with a few French, Spanish, and Italian vintages carried to please the locals. Stick to the Hungarian varieties. Prices are amazing. It would be hard to spend more than $10 or $12 for a very good bottle, and you can spend less and still be satisfied.

CHEESE

(38) NAGY TAMÁS SAJTÜZLETE
V. Gerlóczy u. 3

TELEPHONE 317-4268, 337-7014

METRO All lines, Deak Ferenc tér

CREDIT CARDS None

HOURS Mon–Fri 9 A.M.–6 P.M., Sat until 1 P.M.

ENGLISH SPOKEN Some

After you've purchased your wine at La Boutique des Vins, come here and select some cheese to go with it from the over one hundred varieties offered from Hungary and Europe.

Index

BUDAPEST

Accommodations in Budapest